PENGUIN BOOKS

SYDNEY

Anglo-Welsh by birth, Welsh by loyalty, Jan Morris divides her time between her library-house in North Wales, her dacha in the Black Mountains of South Wales and travel abroad. She is an Honorary D.Litt. of the University of Wales and a Fellow of the Royal Society of Literature.

Her books include the *Pax Britannica* trilogy (*Heaven's Command*, *Pax Britannica* and *Farewell the Trumpets*); *Spectacle of Empire*, about the aesthetics of British imperialism; *The Venetian Empire*; *Stones of Empire*, a book on Indian architecture; and *Fisher's Face*, a fanciful study of Admiral Lord Fisher. She has also written works on Wales, Oxford, Venice, Manhattan, Spain, Canada, Hong Kong and Sydney, six volumes of collected travel essays, two autobiographical volumes, and the novel *Last Letters from Hav*, which was shortlisted for the Booker Prize in 1985. She has edited the *Oxford Book of Oxford* and the travel writings of Virginia Woolf. Many of her books are published by Penguin.

Sydney Harbour from 16,000 feet, 1966. Photograph by David Moore

JAN MORRIS

———

SYDNEY

PENGUIN BOOKS

PENGUIN BOOKS

Published by the Penguin Group
Penguin Books Ltd, 27 Wrights Lane, London W8 5TZ, England
Penguin Books USA Inc., 375 Hudson Street, New York, New York 10014, USA
Penguin Books Australia Ltd, Ringwood, Victoria, Australia
Penguin Books Canada Ltd, 10 Alcorn Avenue, Toronto, Ontario, Canada M4V 3B2
Penguin Books (NZ) Ltd, 182–190 Wairau Road, Auckland 10, New Zealand

Penguin Books Ltd, Registered Offices: Harmondsworth, Middlesex, England

First published by Viking 1992
Published in Penguin Books 1993
3 5 7 9 10 8 6 4 2

Maps drawn by Reginald and Marjorie Piggott

The author and publisher are grateful to the following for permission to quote
extracts: Mrs Nicolete Gray and The Society of Authors on behalf of the
Laurence Binyon Estate for an extract from 'For the Fallen' from *Collected Poems
of Laurence Binyon: Lyrical Poems 1943*; Hamish Hamilton for an extract from
A. D. Hope's *Collected Poems 1930-1965*; Collins/Angus & Robertson and
Paul Slessor for an extract from Kenneth Slessor's poem 'Five Bells'
from his *One Hundred Poems* (1944). Charles Causley and David Higham
Associates for an extract from 'HMS Glory at Sydney', taken
from the *Collected Poems 1930-75*, published by Macmillan.

Printed in England by Clays Ltd, St Ives plc

For
Sam Provstgård Morys
born 1988

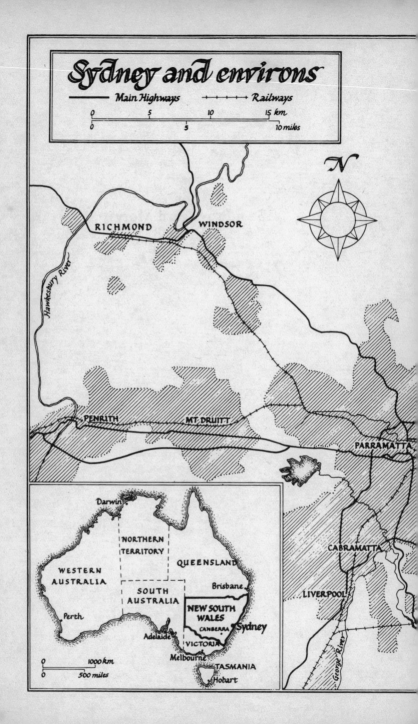

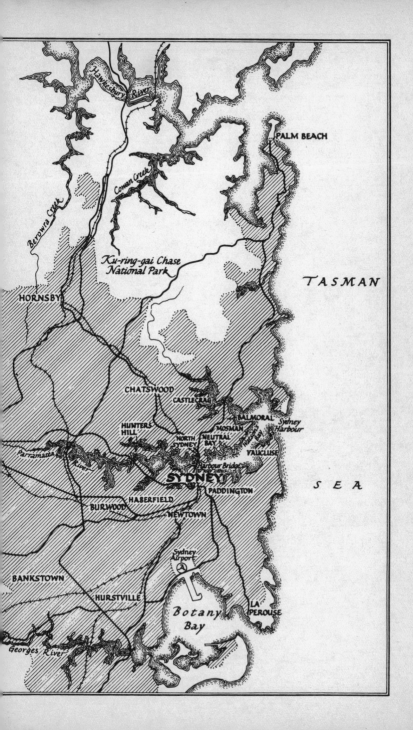

CONTENTS

VIEWPOINT

ON A SUNDAY AFTERNOON IN LATE SUMMER TWO ELDERLY people in white linen hats, husband and wife without a doubt, and amiably married for thirty or forty years, stand at the parkland tip of Bradley's Head on the northern shore of Sydney Harbour in Australia – a promontory whose eponym, Rear-Admiral William Bradley, RN, was sentenced to death in 1814 for defrauding the Royal mails. She wears a flowery cotton dress, he is in white shorts, though not of the very abbreviated kind known to Australians as stubbies. They are leaning on a rail below a white steel mast, the preserved fighting-top of His Majesty's Australian Ship *Sydney*, which sank the German sea-raider *Emden* in 1914. In front of them a Doric column, protruding from the water, marks the beginning of a measured nautical mile; it used to form part of the portico of the Sydney General Post Office. Across the water the buildings of the south shore glitter from Woolloomooloo to Watson's Bay. Both husband and wife have binoculars slung around their necks, both have sheets of white paper in their hands – lists of bird species, perhaps? – and even as we watch them, with a sudden excitement they raise their binoculars as one, and look eagerly out across the water.

At such a time – Sunday arvo in the Australian vernacular – Sydney Harbour is prodigiously crowded. It is a kind of boat-jam out there. Hundreds upon hundreds of yachts skim, loiter, tack and race each other in the sunshine, yachts slithery and majestic, yachts traditional and experimental, solitary or in bright flotillas. Stolid ferryboats plod their way through the confusion. The Manly hydrofoil sweeps by. An occasional freighter passes on its way to the Pyrmont piers. A warship makes for the ocean. Distantly amplified guide-book voices sound from excursion cruisers, or there may be a boom of heavy rock from a party boat somewhere. And presently into our line of sight there burst the 18-footers of the Sydney Flying Squadron, which is what our dedicated pensioners have really been waiting for – not bower-birds or whistle-ducks, but furiously fast racing yachts.

They are hardly yachts in any ordinary sense. Their hulls are light rafts of high technology with immensely long bowsprits, and they carry overwhelming, almost impossible masses of sail. Their crews, laced into bright-coloured wet suits, faces smeared with white and yellow zinc, lean dizzily backwards from trapezes. Their sails are emblazoned with the names of sponsors, the Bank of New Zealand, Xerox, Prudential, and they come into our vision like thunderbolts. Dear God, how those boats move! It makes the heart leap to see them. Foaming at the prow, spinnakers bulging, purposefully, apparently inexorably they beat a way through the meandering traffic, sending more dilettante pleasure-craft hastily scattering and even obliging the big ferry-boats to alter course. They look perfectly prepared to sink anything that gets in their way, and so like predators from some other ocean they scud past the *Sydney*'s mast and the pillar from the GPO, sweep beyond Bradley's Head and disappear from view.

Romantics like to think that the 18-footers have developed from the hell-for-leather cutters of rum-smugglers, and in evolving forms they have certainly been a beloved and familiar facet of this city's life for more than a century. Behind them, in the harbour *mélange*, we may be able to identify a smallish ferry-boat pursuing them up the harbour:

this is a beloved and familiar facet too, for unless it has lately been raided by plainclothes policemen, its passengers include a complement of punters, elderly people many of them, who go out each Sunday to place their illegal bets on the flying yachts before them – and some of whom, we need not doubt, were once themselves those sweating young toughs, brown as nuts, agile as cats, driving so tremendously before the harbour wind.

I choose to start a book about Sydney with this scene because I think it includes many of the elements which have created this city, and which sustain its character still. The glory of the harbour, the showy hedonism of its Sunday afternoon, the brutal force of the 18-footers, the mayhem aboard the gamblers' ferry-boat, the white-hatted old lovers – the mixture of the homely, the illicit, the beautiful, the nostalgic, the ostentatious, the formidable and the quaint, all bathed in sunshine and somehow impregnated with a fragile sense of passing generations, passing time, presents to my mind a proper introduction to the feel of the place.

Books about Sydney are innumerable, but they are mostly guide-books, works of civic history or social analyses, and they have nearly all been written by Australians. No foreigner has tried to write a full-scale study or evocation, and this is not surprising; it is only in the last years of the twentieth century that Sydney has joined the company of the great metropoles. To inhabit a 'world-class' city was always an aspiration of Sydney people, but it took them two centuries to achieve it.

Of course everyone had long had an idea of the city – if the world thought of Australia at all it generally thought of Sydney. Its harbour was popularly ranked for beauty with those of San Francisco, Rio de Janeiro, Hong Kong, Naples, Vancouver and Istanbul. Its sad origins as an eighteenth-century penal colony exerted an unhealthy fascination, and fostered many a gibe about criminal tendencies. Its accent was a gift to humorists. Its harbour bridge had been one of the world's best-known structures since 1932, and since 1966 its Opera

House had provided one of the most familiar of all architectural shapes. Bondi beach was an archetypal pleasure beach, the quarter called King's Cross was an international synonym for Rest and Recreation of the racier kind, and the interminable suburbs of Sydney, so vast that in built-up area this city is twice as large as Beijing and six times as large as Rome, had long figured in travellers' tales as an epitome of urban error. As for the people of Sydney, they had impressed themselves upon the universal fancy as an esoteric sub-species of Briton – sunburnt, healthy, loud, generous, misogynist, beery, lazy, capable, racist and entertaining, strutting along beaches in bathing-caps carrying banners, exchanging badinage or war memoirs in raw colonial slang, barracking unfortunate Englishmen at cricket matches they nearly always won.

It was a vivid image, but it was essentially provincial. Sydney was thought of, by and large, as second-rate – far from the centres of power, art or civil manners, of uncouth beginnings and ungentlemanly presence. Throughout the twentieth century visiting writers, mostly British, had been variously condescending and abusive about the city. At the turn of the century Beatrice Webb the radical thought it chiefly notable for its bad taste: its people were aggressive in manner and blatant in dress, while its Mayor and Aldermen were one and all 'heavy common persons'. In 1923 D. H. Lawrence, who spent two days in the city, declared it no more than a substitute London, made in five minutes – 'as margarine is a substitute for butter'. Robert Morley the actor, in 1949, thought the city misnamed – 'why didn't they call it Bert?' Neville Cardus the music critic, in 1952, said it was just like Manchester, except that the harbour was at the bottom of Market Street instead of the River Irwell. Denis Brogan the political philosopher, in 1958, thought the old-fashioned ladies' underwear on display in the big stores revealed 'all too plainly the acceptance of a non-competitive mediocrity'. 'By God, what a site!' cried Clough Williams-Ellis the architect in the 1950s. 'By man, what a mess!' And nobody was ruder than I was, when I first went to Sydney in the early 1960s. It was, I wrote then, no more than a harbour surrounded by suburbs – its origins unsavoury, its temper coarse, its organization slipshod, the expressions of its society ladies 'steely, scornful, accusatory and plebeian, as though they are expecting you (which Heaven forbid) to pinch their tight-corsetted behinds'. It was five full years before the last letter of complaint reached me from down under.

The world turns; societies, like authors, age and mature; today Sydney really is, by general consent, one of the great cities of the world. Its population, though still predominantly British and Irish in stock, has been alleviated by vast influxes of immigrants from the rest of Europe and from Asia. Modern communications and the shifts of historical consequence mean that it is no longer on the distant perimeter of affairs, but strategically placed upon the frontier of twentieth-century change, the Pacific Rim. Its prickly old parochialism has been softened by a perceptible ability to laugh at itself, and a flood of Sydney talent has been unleashed upon us all, greatly changing perceptions of the city. When in 1988 the bicentennial of European settlement in Australia was spectacularly celebrated around the harbour, with fireworks and operas and tall ships, a new vision of Sydney, resplendent, festive and powerful, was once and for all stamped upon the general imagination.

I have often visited and written about the city since that reckless foray of 1962, and I return now primarily as an *aficionado* of British imperial history. Having commemorated in a series of books the rise and decline of the Victorian Empire, having written its elegy in a study of the last great colony, Hong Kong, I wanted to conclude my imperial commitment with a book about something grand, famous and preferably glittering left on the shores of history by Empire's receding tide. Pre-eminent among such flotsam, it seems to me, is the city of Sydney – not I think the best of the cities the British Empire created, not the most beautiful either, but the most hyperbolic, the youngest in heart, the *shiniest*. I do not entirely retract my judgements of thirty years ago, but like the rest of us I have come to view Sydney in a different light, and I think now that of all the strangers who have written about the city, since it first emerged from the origins I was fool enough to emphasize then, perhaps the poet Charles Causley got the municipal flavour most nearly right in his *HMS* Glory *at Sydney*,

1951, which celebrates all the mixed offerings of a shore leave in this city, barmaids and tram rides, theatres and hangovers, besides the beauty of a sea-entrance:

> O! I shall never forget you on that crystal morning!
> Your immense harbour, your smother of deep green trees,
> The skyscrapers, waterfront shacks, parks and radio towers,
> And the tiny pilot-boat, the *Captain Cook*,
> Steaming to meet us . . .

Back to Bradley's Head; and as we watch the 18-footers storm out of view, that crystal light and smother of trees is all around us, and the skyscrapers look back at us from over the water (though alas the elegant *Captain Cook* long ago sailed its last). And to add to the authenticity of the scene, now it turns out that our friends in the white hats have a little money on the boats too. 'Betting?' they say with poker faces. 'We don't know the meaning of the word.' But those papers in their hands are race cards, not bird-spotting charts, and when Xerox and Prudential disappear behind the trees they cheerfully hasten down the woodland track around the point, the better to follow their fancies. The contest lasts for another couple of hours, and sends the boats twice scudding up and down the harbour along courses dictated by the weather; thus making sure that whether it is the dry west wind that is blowing that day, or the maverick they call a Southerly Buster, or a humid nor'-easter out of the Tasman Sea, in one direction or another the Flying Squadron is sure to go pounding through, as our old enthusiasts might say, like a Bondi tram.

GENESIS

A GAP BETWEEN ROCKY SCRUB-COVERED HEADLANDS, ABOUT a mile wide, is the entrance to Sydney's harbour and thus the sea-gate to the city itself and all its history. It stands at longitude 151°112′ East, latitude 33°52′ South, and the welcome it offers voyagers is allegorically benevolent. Outside, the Tasman Sea stretches away towards South America, New Zealand, South Africa and the Antarctic; inside, the landlocked haven promises every kind of comfort, navigational, climatic, sensual and domestic. Sydney Harbour is really a twisted valley, flooded by the sea a few millennia ago. It has two principal arms and a myriad smaller bays, and it disperses in the west into two channels which, though they are really more sea-inlets than fresh-water streams, are called the Parramatta and the Lane Cove Rivers. The harbour is 16 miles long, covers an area of 21 square miles, reaches a depth of 160 feet and, despite the presence of the great city that lies around its shores, remains organically antipodean. Inland the low line of the Blue Mountains, for years the frontier of white settlement, still seems to speak of a wilderness beyond, especially when a golden-grey haze, like the suggestion of a desert, masks the suburbs at its feet, or when a bushfire smokes and flickers on the horizon; and even within the easy limits of the harbour itself, to a stranger from the north matters can feel sufficiently esoteric.

Over Sydney Harbour the moon wanes and waxes topsy-turvy, and on its shores, as everyone knows, water goes the wrong way down the plug-hole. The climate is benign in reputation and enviable in statistic (mean averages range from 22.3° in February to 12.3° in July), but in practice rather queer. It is said most closely to approximate that of Montevideo, in Uruguay, and can be disconcertingly capricious – hot one moment, cold the next, wet in one part when it is dry in another, with abrupt rainstorms and terrific winds which suddenly blow every-thing banging and askew, or instantly make the temperature plummet. It never snows in Sydney, but on average there is rain 140 days each year, and while the winter can be superbly bracing the summer often drags on week after week in muggy debilitation. Allergies and asthmas are common; in earlier times, before the European metabolism was acclimatized perhaps, Sydney people often complained of chronic sleepiness – 'born tired', they used to say.

Then the green which is still the predominant colour of the harbour shores is a peculiarly Australian olive-green, overlaid sometimes with a pinkish veil which is said to come from the vaporous essence of gum trees, and interspersed with a drab primordial grey of rocks. Many of the trees look to a foreign eye somehow inside-out, with a ghostly glint of silver to them, and an indolent drooping of leaves: eucalyptus trees of many kinds, cabbage palms, blackboys, iron-barks, turp-entines, mangroves, trees whose barks look as though they have been scribbled all over, trees bearing huge squashy figs, mighty pines of the South Pacific, strangely mixed with old familiars like limes and chest-nuts and often encouched in ferns, orchids and casuarinas, or attended by plants with strange and lovely names – milkmaids, parrot-peas, lilly-pillys. Botanists still find surprises here: the scraggy pseudo-oak *Allacasuarina portuensis* was first identified in 1989, and only ten speci-mens have yet been discovered.

Swathes and patches of evergreen foliage are everywhere around the harbour. Wild ravines survive below busy streets, tangles of scrub lap commuters' houses. There are fine windy headlands above the ocean cliffs, and the Great North Walk, a 160-mile bush track, starts in the heart of the suburbs. Heaven knows what fauna you will encounter, if you explore these glades, gulleys and inlets. Possums will certainly be about, and wallabies perhaps, and multitudes of cackling, shouting and coughing birds – manas, cockatoos, kookaburras, lyre-birds, egrets, languorous pelicans, sea-eagles, the Red-Whiskered Bulbul, the Black-faced Cuckoo-Shrike, or most maddeningly a kind of cuckoo called the Koel, which emits for hours on end a tuneless cry like a small boy's early attempts at whistling. There may be koalas, or bandicoots, or possibly even duck-billed platypuses. The cicadas will be shrilling in the various timbres attributed to their kinds – the Black Princes in one key, the Yellow Mondays allegedly in another. Crayfish skulk on the beds of streams. At night squirrel-like marsupials called sugar-gliders saunter from tree to tree. Even the Sydney gulls seem to me particular to the place: in grassy spots I have sometimes seen them staring fixedly between their legs for minutes at a time, yawning a great deal and settling themselves amply in the green like hens.

Some of these creatures sound alarming. Watch out for the Tiger Snake, which has enough toxin in it to kill 6,000 mice.[1] Beware the nephila spider, whose web can be strong enough to snare a small bird, or worse still the Sydney funnel-web spider, which lives only in these parts, and is one of the most venomous arachnids on earth. An awful fish, the goblinfish, swims the Sydney waters, carrying poison in its spines. And the terrible star of all Sydney creatures is undoubtedly the shark, which is surrounded by legend, fear and wry humour. Frequently pieces of human limbs have been discovered in the bellies of sharks, or regurgitated from them, and more than one murder case has been linked to a shark's digestion. A Maginot Line of permanent nets, stretched across twenty-three beaches, protects Sydney from this

[1] Or in the case of the most prolific recorded specimen, milked of its venom in 1934, enough to kill 40,000.

monster, but still the most persuasive of Sydney injunctions is the one
in many languages, accompanied by a grisly picture, warning people
that there may be sharks about.

For the most part, though, it is a kindly enough strangeness that
informs the Sydney setting. Very few people are really vomited by
sharks. You are extremely unlikely to be stung by the goblinfish, or to
feel in yourself the twitching of muscles, the profuse flow of sweat,
tears and saliva that shows the funnel-web has got you. Sydney Harbour's allegory is just: it really is a haven, for people as for ships.

We are told that natives of Australia have been living in the region of
the harbour for 20,000 years, but no literate person is known to have
set eyes on the Sydney Heads, the sea-entrance, until 1770. In that
year Lieutenant James Cook, Royal Navy, accompanied by the scientist Joseph Banks and Daniel Solander the Swedish botanist,
brought HMS *Endeavour* to this coast, made the acquaintance of its
native tribespeople, and called it New South Wales.[1] He spent a
week ashore at a large inlet some ten miles south of Sydney Harbour, and that he called Botany Bay.[2] When he sailed on to the
north he passed the Heads and, noting that there appeared to be a
safe anchorage within, named it Port Jackson.[3] However he was
doubtless in a hurry to get home after many months at sea, and did
not enter the haven.

It was accordingly Botany Bay, rather than Sydney Harbour, that
the British Government had in mind when, seventeen years later, it
dispatched a fleet to colonize New South Wales in the name of the

[1] Mysteriously, it may be thought – there is no record of his having seen South Wales,
the coast is very different, and there was a New South Wales already, on Hudson's
Bay in Canada – but the name was apparently chosen as a favour for Thomas
Pennant, the Welsh patriot and botanist, who was a great friend of Banks, and
perhaps really means the New Wales of the South.
[2] More obviously, since on its shores Banks and Solander collected scores of plants
hitherto unknown to science.
[3] After George Jackson, a Secretary of the Admiralty, who presently spurned this gift
of immortality by changing his name to Duckett.

Crown. No European had been there in the meantime, and Cook was dead by then; but it had been decided that this arcane far corner of the world would be a suitable site for a penal settlement. The American colonies having lately been lost, the West African colonies being generally more lethal than even villains deserved, a new dumping-ground was needed for Britain's felons. The prison hulks of the Thames and Medway were hideously over-crowded, and there were thousands of miscellaneously convicted criminals, rebels, layabouts and ne'er-do-wells that the British Establishment wished only to be rid of. Botany Bay was far away, relatively temperate and might one day prove strategically or commercially useful; that it was already occupied by its native people was no handicap, in the political morality of the time; for a start 775 luckless misfits, 582 males, 193 females, average age twenty-seven, were packed into six chartered transports and sent to the Antipodes.[1]

Many of them were habitual offenders, though their crimes were mostly trivial. Their sentences were for seven years, fourteen years, or life, but good behaviour might earn them tickets-of-leave before the expiry of their sentences, giving them limited freedom within the settlement, and the right to a grant of land. They might indeed be pardoned altogether at Government's discretion, but for the vast majority transportation to Botany Bay meant perpetual exile – very few would ever accumulate enough cash to buy a passage home. The convicts were accompanied by a couple of hundred marines, with twenty-seven wives and twenty-five children, and by miscellaneous livestock.[2] With the transports sailed two small warships and three ships carrying supplies.[3] The route took the First Fleet of Australian history via Rio de Janeiro and the Cape of Good Hope – 13,950 miles in all – and never before had so many people travelled so far together.

[1] I take these figures, which are uncertain, from Mollie Gillen's *The Founders of Australia*, Sydney 1989.
[2] Including the chaplain's cats.
[3] Including, for instance, 40 wheelbarrows, 747,000 nails and 250 women's handkerchiefs.

For most of the convicts, never having heard of Captain Cook, let alone read his reports (for they were almost all illiterate), it must have been like sailing to the moon. It is hard to imagine a more violent contrast, between departure-point and destination. In England Jane Austen was at work, the Marylebone Cricket Club had lately codified the rules of cricket and the House of Commons was considering a motion for the abolition of slavery. In New South Wales the cicadas chafed, the parrots squawked and Aborigines speaking unknown tongues hunted inconceivable marsupials. Cowering in their creaking ships, often in chains, the prisoners of the First Fleet went all unknowing from one to the other.

Thus it was that on 21 January 1788 the first Europeans passed through the Sydney Heads. The First Fleet's commander, Captain Arthur Phillip, RN, was also to be Governor of the colony, and he had very soon decided that Botany Bay was not after all the right place for a settlement, being wan of vegetation and short of fresh water. Instead he took a party of three boats northwards along the coast to investigate Port Jackson, and spent two days exploring its waters.

We have a contemporary description of him in a boat – 'his face shrivelled, and his aquiline nose under a large cocked hat, gathered up in a heap, his chin between his knees' – and so perhaps we may imagine him as his boat-crews of sailors and Marines rowed up the harbour towards a historic landfall. I suppose that after all those months at sea any coast looked pleasant, and Port Jackson was certainly more welcoming than Botany Bay. Even so, with its low and featureless shores covered all over with dense green, its rocks, as somebody said at the time, like bones that have had the fur rubbed off them, it must have looked desolate and monotonous enough. Here and there a park-like effect gladdened the English eye – the tribespeople regularly burnt brushwood, to make hunting easier – but for the most part the bush was thick and forbidding. A few naked black people stared impassively as they passed, standing with fishing-spears on rocks, or hunched over cooking-fires in flimsy bark canoes. There were flashes of strange birds, no doubt, and perhaps glimpses of grey wallabies. Otherwise, only the rocks, the water and the changeless bush: to one of my own temperament Sydney Harbour in 1788 would have offered a discouraging spectacle.[1]

Not, however, to the naval eye. As he was later to report, Phillip realized this to be 'one of the finest harbours in the world, in which a thousand sail of the line might ride in perfect security'. Persevering well past Bradley's Head, almost to the mouth of the Parramatta River at the western end of the harbour, presently the boat-crews found a place where fresh water ran into an anchorage down a gentle declivity in the bush – 'a small snug cove on the southern side', is how Captain Watkin Tench of the Marines described it. They called this V-shaped inlet Sydney cove, after the Home Secretary, Thomas Townshend, first Baron Sydney of Chislehurst;[2] and on its banks on 26 January 1788, they ran up the Union Flag and founded a city. They intended to call it Albion, but somehow or other it became known as Sydney too.

No great city, not even Rome which was founded by wolf's sucklings, has had more unlikely beginnings, and the first years of Sydney were predictably tough and lonely. The merchantmen of the fleet soon sailed away, three to China to pick up tea, five to England in ballast, leaving only one storeship and the two little naval vessels. The convicts were set to work building – houses for the officers, huts for themselves – but there were few skilled craftsmen among them, and at first mud, reeds, wattles and unseasoned wood were their only materials, together

[1] As it certainly did twenty years later to the littérateur Barron Field, who came to Sydney as a Supreme Court Judge, thought evergreen trees inimical to the poetic urge, and said he could 'hold no fellowship with Australian foliage'. When Field left Australia in 1824, the British *Dictionary of National Biography* delicately tells us, 'the complimentary address of the lawyers did not represent every shade of public opinion'.

[2] And last, the title dying with him. Why he called himself Sydney the *Dictionary of National Biography* does not say, and it suggests that were it not for the Australian city named after him he would probably be best-remembered by a line of Oliver Goldsmith's about Edmund Burke: 'Though fraught with all learning, yet straining his throat/To persuade Tommy Townshend to give him his vote.' However citizens of Sydney, Nova Scotia, founded 1785, might disagree.

with lime made from crushed mussel shells. The soil was poor. The
fauna was unnerving. The natives, belonging to a tribe called the
Iora, proved largely incomprehensible. A second fleet-load of convicts,
arriving in 1790, discharged a horrifying complement of dead and
dying, and for a time it seemed that everybody might starve – a
convict was given 1,000 lashes for stealing three pounds of potatoes, and
dinner guests at the Governor's table had to bring their own victuals.
The whole colony was in a state of dejection, and there were moments
when even the most sanguine of Phillip's officers thought it might be
better to give up. It was the poorest country in the world, wrote
Lieutenant Ralph Clark of the Marines. Nature there was nearly
worn out, wrote Major Robert Ross. There was hardly anything to
see but rocks, reported the Reverend Richard Johnson, chaplain to
the colony, and hardly anything to eat but rats. The first suicide soon
occurred: an aged perjurer named Dorothy Handland, said to be the
oldest person in the colony, hanged herself from a gum tree.

Yet Phillip himself was convinced that one day this miserable settlement might outgrow its origins to become a free British nation on the
other side of the earth. Bolstered by this conviction he held things
together until he went home in 1792, and by the turn of the century the
worst was over. The place was still generally known in England as
Botany Bay, as the penal colony always would be, but in fact the city of
Sydney had taken root. It was no longer the only Australian settlement
– it had founded its own subsidiary penal colony on Norfolk Island, a
thousand miles out in the Pacific. Nor was it now utterly isolated in the
world at large, because trading ships had begun to find their way there
in the wake of the transports. A third convict fleet from England had
raised the population to rather more than 7,000, including some 500
free citizens, and around the cove a proper town had arisen, built by
now largely of brick and the local reddish-brown sandstone. The rivulet
that had first attracted Phillip to the site had been channelled into small
reservoirs and named the Tank Stream, and a stone bridge had been
built across it; this formed a rough boundary between more disreputable
quarters on the west side of the cove, more respectable on the east – a
social demarcation which was to linger for a century and more.

A bumpy sandstone outcrop formed the western arm of the cove. Along its edge ran a track called Sergeant-Major's Row, and in lines above stood the huts the prisoners had built for themselves, single-room houses put together of mud, wood and thatch in the old English way, with small gardens and lines of washing. There were a few more sizeable houses up there too, and a hospital of single-storey buildings, one of them brought out in prefabricated parts from England. Not far away were the gallows, and the stocks, and the barracks of the New South Wales Corps, which had by now replaced the Marines as a garrison and police force. On the promontory at the end stood a signal tower, a simple observatory and a gun embrasure. At night a beacon fire burnt for the guidance of ships.

On the other side of the cove, the bourgeois side, lived the Establishment. There were no quays then, ships anchoring offshore, but to the east of the Tank Stream a jetty protruded, announcing the portals of Sydney officialdom. On the slope immediately behind it the Governor occupied a two-storeyed white house with a veranda, looking over a garden to the water and picturesquely supplied with tame wallabies; nearby were substantial houses for his chief officials. The Superintendent of Convicts lived there *ex officio*, and the Garrison Commander, and the Chaplain, and the Surveyor General, and to the east, over a low ridge, gamely struggled a Government Farm, where the first attempts had been made to grow European vegetables in an uncongenial soil.

Beside the bridge a guardhouse protected one half of the town from the other. Near it was the Government Lumber Yard, where convicts worked at saws and forges, and beyond it the settlement straggled away to the south, meandered through by mud roads. A pair of windmills crowned the higher ground behind the waterfront, together with the tower of Sydney's only church: it was named St Phillip's, with two Ls, in honour of the first Governor.[1] On the northern side of the harbour there were a few houses, too, and from them tracks went

[1] A common imperial practice: St Stephen's at Ootacamund, for example, is named not for the proto-martyr, but for Stephen Lushington Esquire, Indian Civil Service.

off to the infant farming settlements already established on the Hawkesbury River, twenty miles to the north. To the west the first proper road in Australia, shaded by thick foliage, led to the ancillary village of Parramatta, where the Government had a second experimental farm, and the Governor a second Government House. By now there were about a thousand head of cattle in the settlement, together with 6,000 sheep and 4,000 pigs, and several thousand acres had been sown with wheat, corn and barley.

Pictures of the time make Sydney look quite elegant and well-ordered, with ships on the stocks at the Government shipyard on the cove, neat rows of cottages, boats scurrying here and there, the hospital spanking and Government House gracious above its gardens. Decorous natives generally appeared in these scenes, and sometimes well-dressed stockmen drove cattle down pretty lanes. However all this was largely artistic convention, and was often heightened when, far away from the discomforts of Sydney Cove, on-the-spot sketches were turned into engravings. In reality those buildings were rickety, amateurish, riddled by white ants and spongy with wet rot. Government House was horribly damp, besides being plagued by vile and unexplained smells from its foundations, while the hospital on the ridge, which looks so commendable in the pictures, was appallingly filthy and overcrowded. Sydney was a prison, but a kind of open prison; the only gaol was a primitive lock-up, and the convicts were still left to house themselves as best they could. Their home-made cottages were generally no more than hovels, often simultaneously serving as *ad hoc* taverns and brothels; many of the more feckless transportees lived in caves among the rocks, in seashore crannies or even in holes in trees. The bush around was still like a sombre green cage. Convicts who ran away into it generally returned disoriented, and no European had ever crossed the Blue Mountains, only thirty miles to the west.

Besides, we must add to our mind's picture the truly extraordinary features of everyday life in Sydney, *c.* 1800, which seldom show in the watercolours: tatterdemalion gangs of male convicts clanking about in irons, incorrigible female prisoners screeching ribaldry and obscenities, soldiers everywhere with high hats and enormous fixed bayonets, petty offenders sitting in the stocks, sex-starved sailors raunching around the grog-shops and Aborigines wandering stark naked or in cast-off English finery. Wallabies and chickens strayed here and there, caged cockatoos screeched, and in the public cemetery pigs and goats scavenged among the graves, the pigs sometimes interrupting themselves to eat the goats. Hundreds of ragged homeless children mooched through the streets; on the island called Pinchgut, off the cove, swung the skeletonic remains of a hanged Irishman, as a *memento mori* for the rest.[1]

The convicts formed an extremely rough and ready proletariat. Many of them had no idea where they were, and some thought that China lay just beyond the Blue Mountains. Governor John Hunter, in the 1790s, said of them that 'a more wicked, abandoned and irreligious set of people had never been brought together in any part of the world', and they were kept under control largely by the use of the cat-o'-nine-tails, with which a quarter of a million strokes were administered in an average year. If they remained intractable they could be sent off to still worse punishment on Norfolk Island, the end of the road. The soldiery, their guards, were hardly more reassuring than the felons. The rankers were brutal riff-raff, the officers, scoured one assumes from regiments not anxious to retain their services, soon congealed into a rapacious clique of opportunists, and grabbed a near-monopoly of the colony's commerce. The local Aborigines were already being debased with alcohol, mockery, abuse and condescension, besides being decimated by smallpox and other diseases. There were virtually no machines, and few draft animals; almost every labour had to be done by hand, with the help of the flogger's whip.

It is easy to conjure up the look of early Sydney. Probably no city has ever been so meticulously pictured from the day of its foundation, by naval and military officers professionally trained to sketch and map, and by variously gifted amateurs. The atmosphere, though, is

[1] Pinchgut is said to have got its original name either because of the poor convicts deposited there in punishment, and fed only bread and water, or (more probably) because the harbour narrowed around it. It is now officially called Fort Denison.

quite another thing, and perhaps we can never quite conceive what it was like to live in such a place, where the gentry were gaolers, where the people were prisoners, where the natives were like creatures out of another age, and where the terrible sound of the scourge was heard so often above the cries of the birds, the parade-ground shouts and the wind through the gum trees all around.[1]

All changed in the Victorian century, as further British colonies were founded one by one elsewhere in Australia, and Phillip's dream was fulfilled. There was a slight *coup d'état* in 1808 – the so-called Rum Rebellion, when Governor William Bligh of *Bounty* fame was deposed in a military putsch. Order however was soon restored and Sydney became a thrusting enclave of capitalism in the south. A civilian establishment took over from the military. A thriving sea-trade developed. The merino sheep, imported from Spain, gave the colony a profitable commodity. A Governor of artistic leanings, Lachlan Macquarie, gave it some sense of style. Penal transportation to New South Wales was ended in 1840; by then about 83,000 convicts had been shipped in, but they were almost balanced by some 70,000 free Britons given Government-subsidized passages in the cause of imperial development. Soon both categories would be outnumbered by native-born Europeans. The illimitable bush still hemmed in the town – when his parishioners left church after evensong, the vicar of St Thomas, North Sydney, once remarked, their hurricane lamps disappeared into the empty valleys 'like stars into infinity' – but there was a road across the Blue Mountains now, and the town had a well-populated hinterland. No longer were these alien people fumbling their way through the strangeness of climate, fauna and flora; a generation had grown up that felt at home with the land, and knew the tricks of survival.

In 1856 Sydney became the capital of the self-governing Colony of New South Wales. Its economy was distinctly of the boom-and-bust

---

[1] We shall return to the penal environment; for a complete evocation of convict Australia Robert Hughes' *The Fatal Shore* (1986) has no rival.

variety, and in size and wealth it was rivalled by Melbourne to the south, but still, as the imperial century proceeded towards its apogee, and Victoria the Queen–Empress towards her Golden Jubilee, the former penal settlement matured into a proper imperial outpost, peer to Toronto and Singapore, Durban and Madras. The poor indigenes had all but disappeared; the British had made a city in their own image. In the second half of the century Sydney's population increased by about 100,000 in every decade. By the 1880s, the centenary decade, it was approaching 400,000, and the city Government moved into a new Town Hall proper to its responsibilities, a mile or so to the south of the cove. This was almost excessively municipal, extravagantly towered and housing a terrific organ, and beside it stood a hardly less diocesan Anglican Cathedral, with three towers and much stained glass. Here was the nexus, functional and symbolical, of High Victorian Sydney.

As a very simulacrum of Britishness in the age of free trade and imperial expansion, the Sydney of the 1880s was intensely self-conscious. Among the professional people, the civil servants, the landowners who maintained their town houses in the city, life seems to have been almost suffocatingly genteel. All the paraphernalia of Victorian decorum flourished. Etiquette was severe, morality ostentatious, social behaviour was derived directly from the example of what was still generally thought of as Home, or the Mother Country. Families competed in splendour of transportation and fashionableness of costume, and we read of incessant visiting among the ladies, of busy club life, political activity and sporting enthusiasm among the gentlemen, the whole revolving around the Governor in his new and far grander Government House in the green Domain above the harbour. People from Melbourne thought it all absurd, and called Sydney Sleepy Hollow; visitors from England thought it rather charming.

The central city looked very British, too. 'The houses,' Charles Dilke had written sourly in the 1860s, 'are of the commonplace English ugliness, worst of all possible forms of architectural imbecility.' Sydney's chief park was called Hyde Park, its lovely botanical gardens looked consciously towards Kew, its university was a transplanted fragment of Oxbridge and its best shops were modelled on the London style – W. H. Soul the pharmacists, for instance, blue-and-white and heraldically crested, or David Jones the draper, which prided itself upon its silky service.[1] A mighty Post Office, with a Renaissance tower and elaborate decoration, stood in the heart of the business district. Overlooking Sydney Cove was a solid Customs House with a bust of Queen Victoria above the door, and behind it sundry great Government buildings had arisen, portentous in golden sandstone and rich in symbolisms. The Treasury Building had a portico with Ionian columns, just like something in Whitehall. The brand-new Lands Department building had an onion-domed tower and was equipped with forty-eight niches for statues of famous citizens. The Colonial Secretary's Office was guarded by images of Wisdom, Justice and Mercy. The Legislative Assembly and the Mint were housed in some of Governor Macquarie's ambitious Georgian buildings, and Macquarie Street upon which they stood was lined with handsome town houses, some of them very opulent, looking out across a green expanse of parkland in genuinely English style.

Utterly English too were the villas which now speckled the outskirts of town, and were implanted on suitable promontories throughout the harbour – white-gardened mansions in classical style, with ornamental gates, leafy drives and lodges. The Chief Secretary lived in one such pleasant house, the Bishop of New South Wales in another, and sometimes there were cottages appended for servants, for all the world like an English estate. In less advantageous parts of town the middle classes occupied pleasant terraced houses, and the better-off artisans lived in rows of cottages that were often charming, and were decorated ornately with iron filigree.

All the symptoms of British imperial system were apparent. Big warehouses dominated the harbour front, and around Sydney Cove had been built a modern landing-place, the Semi-Circular Quay – later, though if anything squared up rather by then, renamed the

[1] And which was founded, like several of the great London stores, by a 'Cardi' – a Welshman from Cardiganshire.

Circular Quay. There were steam trams in the streets, and steam ferries across the harbour, and trains to Parramatta. There were up-to-date hospitals and water supplies, and the Tank Stream had been diverted into underground channels. A brand-new sewerage system discharged its effluent not into the harbour, but into the open sea. There was an *Illustrated Sydney News*, and a Sydney *Punch*.

But of course, here as in Victorian Britain itself, behind these complacent scenes there teemed an underclass, some of it extremely raw. Slums festered, for all the civic propriety. Public health was terrible despite the sewage system. Society was still full of mayhem and corruption – political shenanigans, drug abuse, prostitution – and most vices were legal. As a contemporary said even of the Imperial Temperance Hotel in King Street, 'there is no knowing what you can do, if you only know how to work the ropes'. And if you could sin at the Imperial Temperance in King Street, just think what you could do at the sailors' taverns at the Rocks, that sandstone outcrop above the Cove where the convicts had built their huts! Down the years the Rocks had developed into one of the Pacific's most notorious sailor-towns, where some of the toughest people in the world lodged hugger-mugger among the courts and narrow alleys, drinking furiously, banding together in ferocious street gangs, living by thievery and prostitution and frequently given new blood by deserting seamen and peripatetic rascals from all the oceans.

The Bishop and the Chief Secretary lived handsomely enough in their villas; the poor of Sydney lived miserably enough down below, despite the sunshine, the space and the freedom. 'Drifting past, drifting past, To the beat of weary feet', is how Henry Lawson the poet thought of them, 'In the filthy lane and alley, and the cruel heartless street'. Perhaps, after all, the city had not quite transcended its beginnings; sometimes, as we read about its aldermanic pride and prosperity, the grand celebrations with which it greeted its own centennial and Victoria's fifty years upon the throne, we can just see poor old Dorothy Handland still swinging from her eucalyptus.

Not for much longer. The Rocks were largely demolished when in
1900 a bubonic plague fell upon Sydney. The worst of the slums
disappeared then, most of the vices were made illegal, and in a
generation or two the physique of Sydney working people almost
miraculously improved. In the new century, as the various Australian
colonies banded themselves together into a Federal Commonwealth,
Sydney became an epitome of the Workers' Paradise – as democratic
a city as any on earth, with powerful trade unions to fight the poor
man's cause and a burning sense of social equality. Its standards of
living were said to be higher than those of any British or American
city, and its people had developed, said a local writer in 1907, 'a sort
of clever hecticness, an almost unnatural sharpening of the wits in the
furious race for wealth, and a constant and all but unappeasable
itching for excitement and amusement and change for its own sake'.
When the city's young men went to war, in 1914, they went with
terrific brio. In Victorian times they had been described as 'wanting
in power and weight'; now John Masefield, the English poet, could
compare them to 'kings in old poems'.

Australia became a nation, people still like to say, upon the battle-
fields of Gallipoli, and the Sydney that emerged from the Great
War was a different Sydney too. Conscious of itself as an Australian
city, no longer just a transplanted city of the English provinces, Sydney
had acquired an urban character of its own. Although its people were
still 98 per cent British in origin, by now they looked, sounded and
dressed differently. Let us visit them finally at the start of the 1930s,
when the Great Depression was falling upon Sydney as it was falling
upon every city of the capitalist west. All the miseries of the slump
were visible here then, the shanty towns and the soup kitchens, the
unemployed thousands sleeping in parks, at railway stations, on ramshackle houseboats, the mothers with their children scavenging among
the seashore flotsam. Communism was strong. Organized crime was
rampant. Mutilated survivors of the Great War haunted the city
streets, reproachfully begging. Amidst this unhappiness the personality
of the community, now more than a million strong, had reached some
kind of climax.

The economy had been more or less stagnant throughout the century, but the city now extended in immense swathes of suburbia far out from the Town Hall: beyond Parramatta towards the Blue Mountains in the west, down to Botany Bay in the south, joining up with the old Hawkesbury River settlements to the north. At the same time the beach culture was developing fast – the Sydney preoccupation with sun, sand and surf, exemplified in bright ocean-front suburbs, and in the competitive pageantry of the life-savers. The city felt more southern, more Pacific than it had seemed in the 1880s, as though it were consciously changing direction. Even the architecture, so slavishly British fifty years before, had acquired extra sub-tropical mannerisms – eaves, overhangs, arcades, verandas, and the canopies over sidewalks, supported by iron wires to keep the sun at bay, which had become characteristic of the Australian urban style.

After generations of sunshine and general plenty, the people themselves had been mutated, too. The women were tall and robust, the men had acquired that somewhat louche, shambling, easygoing but powerful gait that for a time was to be their hallmark. This was the real heyday of the dinkum Aussie – the Aussie of the slouch hat, the long-short trousers and the knee-length socks, with his Sheila who stuck with the rest of the girls at the far end of the room, and his well-known place at the bar. It was a macho, philistine, cocky Sydney, or as Kenneth Slessor the poet preferred, 'gaslight, straw hat, bunch-of-bananas, tram-ride Sydney'.[1] 'In things of the mind,' declared the Sydney cartoonist Will Dyson in 1929, 'we show about as much spirit as a suburban old maid.'

It was Sydney at its most truly provincial. Inevitably the place half thought of itself still as an imperial metropolis, and figured in works of imperial self-gratification as the Second City of the Empire. But it was really neither one thing nor another. Though it was still a State capital, now it was only one of six in a self-governing Australia whose federal capital was at Canberra, 180 miles away. Its governing classes remained, by and large, almost ridiculously royalist and conventional,

[1] From his text for the picture-book *Portrait of Sydney*, 1950.

but many of its working people were generally indifferent to the British link, often republican of tradition, often Communist of sympathy, militantly organized and Irishly inclined.

It was not really much of a place, by international standards. Its Victorian landmarks and Georgian relics had been swallowed up in run-of-the-mill commercial development, of no particular style. Its suburbs, often cruelly deprived of trees, were mostly unlovely. Since the Great War hardly a public building had gone up which was worth a second look, or would seem in future decades worth preserving. The cockiness was probably largely chip-on-shoulder, and I would think it fair to say that the early 1930s were Sydney's nadir. The city looked back still with bitterness to its squalid start; it was torn between a sickly imperial loyalty and a raucous independence; one would hardly guess, surveying its philistine parochialism and sense of resentment, that within another fifty years it would have burst into the buoyant post-imperial prodigy that this book is going to describe.

Yet only two years later, in a gesture of anomalous exhilaration, at the worst time of the depression Sydney opened its Harbour Bridge, one of the talismanic structures of the earth, and then by far the most striking thing ever built in Australia. At that moment, I think, contemporary Sydney began – perhaps definitive Sydney. Another World War, a few more booms and slumps, confirmed Sydney's economic status. The decline of the British Empire shifted its attitudes to the world. A tremendous migration of continental Europeans and Asians drastically altered its manner. We have arrived at our Sunday arvo of the 1990s, with the 18-footers storming past Bradley's Head, and the skyscrapers gleaming on the foreshore.

Sydney people often say their city lacks a sense of history, but I do not find it so. I find the past more easily retrievable in Sydney than in most cities, so familiar to us are the people who founded this place, whether we know them by name or simply as generic figures, and so

easy is it to imagine the scenes of earlier times. Many a monument of
the Victorian age stands grandly Victorian still. David Jones now
claims to be 'The Most Beautiful Store in the World', and W. H. Soul
the Pitt Street pharmacy offers a SOULCOLOR fast film service. The
Treasury's cortile now shelters the coffee shop of the Intercontinental
Hotel. The Land Department Building still has vacant niches for
twenty-five heroes. When George Street (né Sergeant-Major's Row)
swerves near its northern end, it is avoiding the vanished boundary of
the original Government shipyard; when it veers to the east and back
again by the Town Hall it is shying away from the ghosts of the first
city graveyard, where the pigs molested the goats. The unpredictable
street-pattern of downtown Sydney relates still to the site of Phillip's
malodorous little mansion. The Tank Stream, sometimes fierce with
storm-water, still empties itself into Sydney Cove beside Pier 6 at
Circular Quay. Graffiti remain from the days of the First Fleet. Often
in the evening, around the harbour, I see solitary meditative figures
sitting on rocks just as the Aborigines sat long ago; and after dark,
when the riding light of some small fishing-craft swims across the
water, I find it easy to expect one of those elementary canoes to come
paddling out of the night, with a naked black woman in the stern,
and a cooking-fire burning amidships.

And the bush survives. We will end this skim through the Sydney
past with a glimpse of the wild present – more than mere *rus in urbe*,
more nature indestructible. We stand on a road bridge in one of the
northern suburbs, looking down upon one of those tangled gulleys of
bush far below the sidewalk. It is dusk. A full moon is rising, and little
groups of people, in twos and threes, are fitfully assembling on the
bridge. The traffic is light, the evening is sultry, there is not much sign
of life in the houses which are scattered among the trees. Below us the
river glints through huge ferns. A youth with tattooed forearms throws
a cigarette end over the bridge, and it floats into the gulley in a
scatter of sparks. A couple of small children race each other up and
down the sidewalk. We are waiting for the Sydney fruit bats, the big
flying-foxes, which nest somewhere down there in their hundreds of

thousands, allegedly emitting a frightful vespertilian smell.[1] Each evening they leave their perches in the wood to go foraging through the city, all over the northern suburbs and far across the harbour, where they are often to be felt, rather than exactly seen, fuzzily passing apartment windows. They are among the southernmost fruit bats, the largest community in Sydney, and they have survived everything that history has been able to do to them. Today they have many admirers, and I went once to a protection-society meeting, up the road in the well-heeled suburb of Gordon, whose enthusiasm the bats themselves would have been astonished to discover – bat friends of all ages were there, wearing bat badges and bat-ornamented T-shirts, listening to zealous bat lectures, examining a bat skeleton in a glass case and distributing bat pamphlets with missionary zeal.

Night begins to fall. The little audience crowds to the parapet. Out of the murky bush there emerges a solitary *Pteropus poliocephalus*, flapping over our heads and wheeling southwards towards the harbour. After a minute or two another follows, and then a couple more. It seems a desultory progress, and the children begin to lose interest, and start racing up and down the pavement again. 'Is that all?' says a girl to her young man. 'Fucking hell,' says the youth with the tattoos. But after a few minutes the pace theatrically quickens, the bats appear in threes and fours, and then in batches, and then in squadrons, and then in fleets, until the whole darkening sky is full of them, and they pour out of the bush in an apparently endless stream, hundred upon hundred, thousand upon thousand, like a furious reassertion of old supremacies.

After a while their interminable passage into the night becomes a bit of a bore, and long before the last bat has flown over that bridge the children have seen enough of them, and are clamouring to go home.

---

[1] Transmitted, I am told unnervingly by one who has tried, into the sweat of those who eat them.

APPEARANCES

1. Urbs

FOR MOST PEOPLE IN THE WORLD THE LOOK OF SYDNEY IS the grand-slam look, the whole hog, flag-and-fireworks look. This can certainly be magnificent. Little in contemporary travel beats flying down the coast from Newcastle on a fine spring day, following the line of the northern ocean beaches and abruptly turning westward at the Sydney Heads to make the home run down the harbour. It makes you feel majestic even in an elderly shuddering seaplane. It gives you a triumphant feel, as though there ought to be incidental music in the air, preferably *Waltzing Matilda*.

The Heads fall away below you, bashed by their Pacific waves, the Middle Harbour runs off to the north, and then there are wide red-roofed suburbs below, splodged with green wooded protrusions, with the gleam of innumerable swimming-pools, and glorious splashes of flame trees and jacarandas. A couple of small islands slide beneath your wings. The harbour is streaked with the wakes of ships, freighters

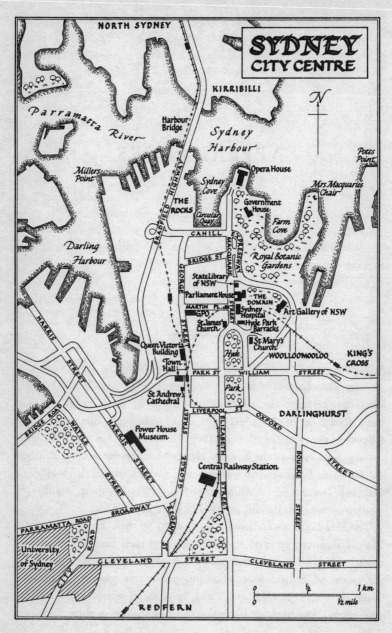

SYDNEY CITY CENTRE

off to sea, hydrofoils rushing to and from the city, and here and there
stand fine white villas on desirable sites. There goes Bradley's Head,
with the *Sydney*'s fighting-top, and there is the little island citadel of
Pinchgut, and then – *tara! tara!* – the heart of Sydney splendidly
greets us, the great old arch of the bridge, the splayed shells of the
Opera House, the stunning green of the Domain, the skyscrapers of
the city centre all flash and swank. Beyond it, as in diminuendo, the
suburbs fade away dingy around the maundering Parramatta River,
and beyond them again is the grey-blue ridge of the mountains, that
ne plus ultra to the early settlers. Few cities on earth can offer so
operatic an approach.

On the ground the purlieus of Sydney offer some histrionic vistas,
too. Sometimes you can see nothing of the distant city but the
arch of the Harbour Bridge, mysteriously protruding above thick
woods. Sometimes you can so arrange your line of sight that the
downtown structures are framed in green ridges, like a city among
country hills. There are places on the harbour's north shore where
the size and power of Sydney, ranged along its waterfront, is hal-
lucinatorily exaggerated by sunshine and reflection, and on a very
hot day from far to the south, from the brackish beaches of
Botany Bay, the skyscrapers on the horizon shimmer like a towering mirage. Although the colours of Sydney are seldom gaudy, in
the tropical kind, but more often hazed and muted, this is a city
born for show, with a façade of brilliance, and a gift for exhibitionism.

Somebody once lent me five video cassettes of the bicentennial
celebrations in 1988, which were the most spectacular of all the city's
spectacular occasions. I played them at high speed, fast forward, and
never was there such an exhilarating succession of images: yachts and
symphony orchestras and flags and dancing Aborigines – airships,
firefloats spouting, princes arriving, bands playing – vast cheering
crowds, curtseys, soldiers saluting, gabbled speeches – now a wide
shining shot of the harbour, now the Opera House from the air – gun
salutes I think, helicopters certainly, flowers, children singing, and as
the day rapidly changed to night before my eyes, a violent eruption of

rockets into the sky, and a pyrotechnical waterfall over the lip of the bridge.

Speeding it up in this way seemed perfectly proper to me – aesthetically Sydney is made for the instant exciting impact, not five full cassettes of contemplation – but I slowed the tape down in the end when, as the city broke into a last tremendous blaze of rejoicing light, they really did play *Waltzing Matilda*.

The original city, on the south shore of the harbour, was built upon shallow hills and outcrops – the gentle bumps and slopes that surrounded Phillip's Tank Stream. This gave it pictorial advantages, but it also meant a certain meanness of scale, and time and again efforts were made to give the place a more formal dignity. Phillip himself apparently envisaged a Sydney of inspirational quality, like Raffles' Singapore – 'built in characters of light'. He decreed that its principal streets should be 200 feet wide, and he imagined a waterfront square with the chief buildings of State grouped around it, and Government House above. Perhaps he was thinking of Greenwich on the Thames, or the foreshore arrangements at Rio, which he must have known well. It never happened, anyway. When the Italian navigator Alessandro Malaspina arrived at Sydney in 1793 with two Spanish corvettes, he was assured that there *was* a city plan, but could not make out how it operated: today the only relic of it is Lang Street in the heart of the downtown city, the remains of a projected Grand Parade which runs at an unexpected angle towards the spectral plaza by the water.

Governor Macquarie, who arrived in 1810, also had visionary plans for the city, in which he was abetted by a convict architect, Francis Greenway of Bristol, transported for fourteen years for forgery but pardoned after six. Like Phillip, Macquarie wanted to minimize the convict taint, visually at least, and he fancied a city centred not upon the waterfront, but around a cathedral square a mile or so inland; upon this piazza all the city streets, named after members either of the British royal family or of the Macquarie clan, would geometrically

converge, providing both splendour and the easy control of riots.
Macquarie's inspiration was probably Edinburgh, with a touch of
British Calcutta thrown in. At the same time his protégé Greenway
dreamed of building a castle on the Rocks, and a monumental colon-
nade around the cove to be Sydney's ceremonial gateway. Once
again the greater designs came to nothing, but before accusations of
extravagance stifled them Macquarie and Greenway did manage to
get some agreeable building done – a church or two, civilized-looking
convict barracks, a beguiling fort on the water's edge, a nice lighthouse, a turreted toll-house like a Gothic folly, a market with a street
to its own wharf and a gubernatorial stable block which, if it was not
in fact the castle of Greenway's dreams, looked remarkably like one.

Ever since then there have been sporadic proposals for the monu-
mentalization of Sydney, usually based upon some variation of Phil-
lips and Greenway – majestic harbour-front developments, that is,
together with broad boulevards into town. Sir Robert Garran,
Solicitor-General of the Commonwealth of Australia, mused in the
1930s that a Great Fire might be a good idea; they could give the
rebuilt city 'impressive exits and entrances, open up a scenic drive
along the harbour foreshore, and provide a fair allowance of stately
boulevards'. In the 1950s a redevelopment scheme for William Street,
one of the chief east–west thoroughfares, imagined it transformed into
a café-lined, tree-shaded, eight-laned ceremonial highway, elegant
with plazas, malls and colonnades and with a stream running down
the middle – 'at least the equal', as the plan's chief progenitor foresaw,
'of the Champs Elysées of Paris'.[1] More recently the Sydney Planning
Committee (ever hopeful as planners must be, or they would lose
heart) has envisaged a downtown divided into twelve zones each of
'unique character' – a zone for cinemas, for instance, an educational
zone, a 'business area with heritage flavour', a Chinatown zone and a
ceremonial civic zone.

There was a time when the Victorians did manage to give this city,

---

[1] William Street in 1991 is chiefly notable for car salerooms in the daytime, prostitution
at night, and is bounded at its eastern end by an enormous Coca-Cola sign.

as they gave to so many others throughout the British Empire, a discernible unity of style and purpose. The Town Hall complex had definite authority, and pictures of Circular Quay in the late nineteenth century show it, too, handsomely balanced, the Customs House centrally presiding, sandstone offices of State on the slopes behind, Gothic Government House stately in its gardens above. The Government's private Domain had become a superb park, stretching in uninterrupted green down the eastern flank of the city centre, and lively sandstone devices of Baroque and Rococo gave the downtown streets exuberance. For a few years, too, in the early 1880s, the scene was majestically crowned by the domed Garden Palace of Sydney's first International Exhibition, looking rather like a basilica from Central Europe; but this was only made of wood, and burned down in a matter of hours in 1882.[1]

With the turn of the twentieth century the balance was lost, and by the time I first reached this city, at the start of the 1960s, its centre was uncompelling indeed. Its principal streets were dowdy, its older quarters were run down and its skyline, limited until 1957 to a height of 150 feet, lacked either panache or romance. Sydney Cove, far from being grandly colonnaded, had been crassly masked by the Cahill Expressway, an overhead ring road which hideously blocked the city's central vista, and went on to cut the lovely Domain in two.[2] On the point where the Opera House now stands there was a tram station thinly disguised as a fort, and the tallest structure in town was a radio mast on top of an office block, forlornly pretending to be the Eiffel Tower.

Things are not half so dull today. The Victorian balance has never been restored, and architecturally Sydney's is certainly not one of the most distinguished of the New World's city centres. Nevertheless the explosion of steel, glass and concrete in the past twenty years has

[1] 'In a great lustrous sea', the *Sydney Morning Herald* reported with relish at the time, 'of red-hot metal and burning woodwork'. The Palace gates are still there, on Macquarie Street.

[2] Passing, by an act of rare justice, within a few feet of the dining-room windows of the Royal Automobile Club.

given it a cohesive excitement, and the central clump of high rise is nothing if not energetic. It is capped by the burnished gold steeple of the Sydney Tower, the tallest structure in the southern hemisphere, and though the caprices of post-Modernism have hardly affected it yet, it does present a lively variety of shapes, levels and angles. The radio tower has long been submerged in the mass, but many of the Victorian monuments still manage to assert themselves, if only in daintily preserved façades, and here and there graceful survivors of Macquarie's day stand assiduously preserved amidst the frenzy.

Downtown Sydney, the square mile or so south of Circular Quay, remains somewhat warren-like. A kind of grid system has been imposed upon its streets, but only just, and visitors are surprised to discover that it is really rather picturesque – in character not unlike lower downtown Manhattan, and far more crannied and quirky than most of the other great modern cities of the world. This is partly because of its irregular terrain, which has required steep streets, unexpected staircases and interesting variations of level, but partly because of its *ad hoc* origins.

The early planners having failed in their designs, the city was to retain for ever a touch of the ramshackle, and even now it is possible to discern in corners of inner Sydney glimpses of ancient social styles – styles Dickensian or Hogarthian, or older still, inherited from England. Deep-worn steps in waterside lanes, unexpected squares, the occasional unimproved pub, back alleys littered with leaves and blown blossoms, smells of rot and damp wood in about-to-be-gentrified cottages – all these easily evoke for me times and manners long gone.

Anthony Trollope thought the same, when he came to Sydney in 1873. He was baffled by Sydney's sense of antiquity, since it was then less than a century old, but charmed by its intricacy. It had few of the straight lines and obvious vistas of most modern cities – it was not, he remarked approvingly, parallelogrammic. Ten years later Richard Twopenny, also direct from England, thought its tangled streets 'like old friends', and the artist Lloyd Rees, entering the city centre for the first time in 1917, was delighted by its sense of enclosure – 'one cannot see *through* Sydney'.

Flower, fruit and food stalls add to this feeling of organic age, together with the crowded arcades, full of small shops like medieval markets, that burrow between the streets. The Rocks have long been prettied up for the tourists, but still cherish a few nooks of suggestive shadow, lanes where the whores once lurked, steps where you might once have had your throat cut for your cash, taverns where unscrupulous landlords might have dropped you through a trap-door and Shanghai'ed you off to sea. Sometimes there are glints of the harbour, between the office blocks, as one used to see snatches of the Thames down waterside staircases of Wapping or Limehouse. Sometimes the enormous girders of the Harbour Bridge loom high above a row of terrace houses, cast their shadow over a park or close the prospect of a busy street: and this always suggests to me the presence of a mighty cathedral, in whose lee for a thousand years some far more antique town has flourished and suffered.

Within the general jumble there are several enclaves or patches of distinction. There is Macquarie Street for a start, a fashionable residential street when we visited it in the 1880s, now a street of politicians, doctors, lawyers and institutions. Parliament is here, and the State Library of New South Wales, and the modern Supreme Court, and the rambling Sydney Hospital, and the whole street looks out over the Domain, part park, part the purlieus of Government House, still all a prodigy of light and colour running down to the water's edge through the flowers, trees, lawns and greenhouses of the Royal Botanic Gardens.[1]

---

[1] It was Melbourne's Botanic Gardens, not Sydney's, that the Prime Minister Sir John Gorton eulogized in a famous speech in 1970, but I cannot resist quoting his words anyway: 'If this collection here in these gardens is not thoroughly matchless and I think it probably is, but if it's not, and if it's not unique of its kind, then I have no doubt that under the guidance of Mr Shoobridge it very shortly will be, if it isn't already.'

This quarter of Sydney has the air of a true capital, and Government House within the Domain is the nearest thing Sydney has to a palace – as the home of the Governor of New South Wales it is indeed the proxy palace of the British monarchy far away. People sometimes confuse it with its nearest neighbour, the battlemented pile which Greenway built as the gubernatorial stables, but which now houses the Conservatorium of Music. Government House is battlemented too, but was built a quarter of a century later by Edward Blore, designer of Sir Walter Scott's mock-feudal home at Abbotsford in Scotland, and is a jolly caprice of Ivanhoe Gothic, described by John Hood, when it went up in 1843, as being 'somewhat in the Elizabethan style, but not exactly'. The buildings of upper Macquarie Street look towards it across the green rather as the apartment blocks of Manhattan look over Central Park, and all in all there is something very invigorating about this thoroughfare, especially when you reach it up the gentle hill from the cramped financial district, to be greeted by its wide sunny space and its air of consequence, its palm trees, its flags, its flowers and its general impression of statuary.

Just up the road is Hyde Park, and this green oblong, frequented by lovers, tramps and chess-players, is properly metropolitan too. The ornate Great Synagogue overlooks it from the western side, on the east is the heavily pilastered Australian Museum, and among the trees stands the Anzac Memorial, for my tastes one of the noblest things in the city. Hyde Park's most admired monuments, however, stand to the north, around the site Governor Macquarie envisaged as the ceremonial centre of the city. They include two of Francis Greenway's best buildings – his graceful St James's Church, which would be unremarkable perhaps in London or in Boston, but which looks exceptionally urbane here, and his Hyde Park Barracks across the way. This he designed for Macquarie in 1819 to provide, for the first time, a place of confinement for male convicts; for nearly thirty years its initials, HPB, were stamped on their clothing. As an ex-con himself Greenway was presumably reluctant to design anything too gloomy (though there was a triangle in the yard for floggings) and he created a building that has remained an ornament to the city ever since. A big rectangular block with a pitched roof, a cupola and a fine old clock, it stands in a wide courtyard behind grand gates, and always suggests to me some mellow institutional building, an examination hall or a proctor's office, within the precincts of academe.[1]

Hyde Park's other dominant building is St Mary's Catholic Cathedral, at the north-west corner. This is huge. It is not quite as long as Lincoln Cathedral, its model, but it is probably the largest Christian church anywhere in the overseas British Empire, and I suspect that when it was completed in 1882 it may have been the largest building of any kind erected by the British in their imperial territories – astonishing to contemplate, when one remembers how small was the city it was built to serve. It is a kind of standard Gothic cathedral, such as you might order from an ecclesiastical catalogue, with high pointed arches, dim transepts, a crypt and three towers;[2] two heroic statues outside the south door are not of saints nor martyrs, but of recent Archbishops.

The area around the Town Hall, the pride of the 1880s, still has some swagger. St Andrew's Anglican Cathedral, it is true, is infinitely less grandiose than its Roman rival, and is indeed curiously unobtrusive nowadays; its main entrance used to open to the west, but when in the late nineteenth century new streets and buildings hemmed it in the arrangements were turned back to front, so that the entrance is now where the high altar ought to be, giving the structure a slightly shamefaced air. The Town Hall itself, on the other hand, is as cocksure as ever, and could well serve as a manual of architectural styles. Eleven architects are said to have had a hand in its design at one time or another, and the result is a defiantly eclectic mix of intentions, crowned with a five-layered, arched, columned, windowed,

---

[1] Although wandering around it one day when it was being converted into a museum, and wondering at its gentlemanly proportions (far more civilized than many a barracks I have myself been obliged to occupy) I was chilled to see faintly legible on a wall a relic from some intermediate stage in its career, announcing the Master in Lunacy's Office, Top Floor.

[2] All three originally intended to have been surmounted by steeples, which are optimistically shown in all their glory in one of the best-known Victorian engravings of Sydney.

porticoed, architraved, buttressed, domed, urned and flag-staffed clock-tower.

Even better is the adjacent Queen Victoria Building. This was built in 1898 as a market, and after housing a library, a wine store and various bureaucratic offices, has now been gloriously done up by Malaysian entrepreneurs to be one of the most sumptuous shopping centres on earth. Not only is its exterior wonderfully entertaining, with a galaxy of domes, domelets and roof pavilions, but its complex galleried interior suggests to me a happier Piranesi at work; there is also a glorious hanging clock which, every hour on the hour, displays a series of mechanically moving tableaux of British kings and queens, heralded by loud automaton trumpeters and ending with the very slow beheading of Charles I. [1]

Not far away is the city's newest architectural set-piece, Darling Harbour. Called by the early settlers Cockle Cove, this is the next harbour inlet west of Sydney Cove, and until a few years ago was one of the city's chief dock areas. Now it is a tourist and convention centre of a certain slapdash splendour. It straggles around the old wharfs in a sequence of white and glass buildings like so many winter gardens, linked over the inlet by the Pyrmont Bridge, the oldest working electrical bridge in the world, and crossed by the concrete viaduct of a motorway. There is a fun-fair and an aquarium, a Chinese garden, a huge convention centre, multitudinous shops and two museums: strewn as it all is around the water, and backed by some fairly drab old industrial buildings, it has a frisky fancy to it, and is linked to the city centre by a mono-rail train which sweeps over the water, circles around those spiky white buildings, like a portly red-and-cream worm. On a sunny Saturday Darling Harbour is a cauldron of activity, and on one such day I came across a group of stilt-dancers, painted and feathered, prancing in weird silence beneath the motorway bridge; oddly enough their tall gliding motions, with the spinning of the fun-fair mechanisms, the comings-and-goings of the boats, the wavering of

[1] 'Well worth waiting for,' as a bystander with a pronounced Irish accent once remarked to me.

fugitive toy balloons and the easygoing crowds sauntering here and there, gave Darling Harbour that afternoon an unexpected air of power.

Sydney's substitute for a truly ceremonial centre is Martin Place, three blocks back from the waterfront in the heart of the business district. This has been developed in fits and starts from one of the old crosstown streets; widened, cleared of traffic and planted with trees, it now extends from George Street, the city's original main thoroughfare, to Macquarie Street on the edge of the Domain. It is the pulse of downtown Sydney, especially at lunchtime on a working day, and an index to the city's style and sensibility. The Cenotaph is there, guarded by sculpted servicemen with bowed heads. An unfortunate essay in modern imagery, like a tower of aluminium kites, commemorates the Sydney artist William Dobell and is nicknamed the Silver Shish-Kebab. There is a small sunken arena with a stage, and a big splashy fountain at the western end.

All is dominated by the General Post Office, which after nearly 120 years still has a claim to be Sydney's central and archetypal building. It holds its own bravely against the mass of the surrounding sky-scrapers, and its Italianate colonnades greatly add to the dignity of the street. Its series of noble Letter-Boxes (officially called Apertures and certainly worthy of capital letters) are set in magnificent brass surrounds.[1] There are brass railings inside, too, and flags, and a picture of the Queen, and big ball lights, while on the Pitt Street façade there are some cheerful sculptures illustrating the ever-willing public attitudes of the postal service. These were thought to be down-right indecent when they were first unveiled; the worst I can see in them, however hard I try, is a possibly slightly lascivious smirk on the face of a postman delivering the morning mail to a perhaps too invitingly smiling housewife in the righthand panel.

[1] Maintained in varying degrees of polish: when I asked one of the cleaners why OVERSEAS, SPECIAL POSTINGS AND INTERSTATE were so much more shiny than SUBURBAN, COUNTRY, A.C.T. AND SYDNEY CITY, he just said 'Ah, well, SUBURBAN AND COUNTRY's the other shift.'

Martin Place is lined with big banks and insurance houses, and crossed by four busy streets which unfortunately reduce the plaza effect. Nevertheless at its best it can be delightful. Flower stalls and newsstands give it colour. The Coolibah Hut offers Satay and Asian Food. There are always people doing nothing in particular on the big semi-circular benches beneath the trees. Sometimes street musicians strike up, guitarists, Irish harmonica players, and when there is a concert in the arena, as there generally is at noon, hundreds of young people give the scene a cheerful animation, unwrapping their sandwiches on the rim of the fountain, doing frantic things on skateboards (penalty A$200), queuing for cut-price theatre tickets at the Halftix kiosk or dancing to disco music outside the Commonwealth Trading Bank. One Friday lunchtime I saw an elderly paralysed lady drawing a picture with a pencil attached to her head, watched by a large admiring audience.

Martin Place is Sydney's Trafalgar Square; Sydney Cove, where it all began, is its Piccadilly. There are pedestrian ways around it now, and it is dominated by the great pavilion of the Opera House, whose soaring and eccentric silhouette almost everyone knows. With its nine flying roofs of off-white tiling, its varying planes and mingled textures, Sydney Opera House is the hardest building I have ever tried to draw, and it has not been universally admired. Beverley Nichols the English journalist thought it was like something that had crawled out of the sea and was up to no good. The writer Blanche d'Alpuget likened it to 'an albino tropical plant rootbound from too small a pot'. I myself find it unattractive seen head-on from the harbour side, when its big teeth-like windows, framed by their hoods, have a distinctly rapacious look, likened by a Brisbane wit to that of Sydney's heroine Joan Sutherland in the mad scene from *Lucia di Lammermoor*.

It is an immensely suggestive building. When I walk down its wide shallow steps, with those soaring roofs above me, I feel remarkably like one of the minute stereotypical figures to be seen in architects' drawings of visionary cities – figures almost irrelevant to the scene,

and impelled only by the momentum of the future all around them.
But there is also something *unguent* about the Sydney Opera House,
something enveloping, so that when I have got over feeling like an
extra in an architect's scenario, I feel rather like an insect in an ice-
cream.

Yet in many ways the building is very sensible, and is far more than
an opera house in any conventional sense.[1] Sydney citizens use it
almost as a club, so accessible are its halls, cafés and restaurants, and
so handy its lesser buttresses for small boys to slide down. One rainy
Sunday afternoon I went there to hear the Sydney Youth Orchestra
playing in one of the foyers, and thought the place seemed positively
homely. The orchestra bravely played, and all around it people
wandered about, leant on rails, drank tea, pointed out their daughters
among the cello players or sat on the floor reading newspapers.
Through the windows I could see slanted umbrellas and hurrying
laughing women, Japanese taking each other's pictures in the wet,
gulls scudding around, yachts hastening home, ferries labouring
through the rain; snugly indoors the orchestra played Brahms, while
teacups tinkled, the crowd amiably chatted, and a little boy left
behind scuttled down the foyer stairs, two paces to a step, calling
'Daddy! Daddy!' through the music.

Sydney Cove is attended by some of the ugliest buildings in Sydney,
making for a meanness beneath the shine of it, but it is given character
by the remains of gabled old warehouses, like something from Bergen,
now serving as restaurants on the western side. There is a patch of
green above the Rocks, where the Observatory stands, and the Ocean
Terminal is properly hefty, and the skyscrapers rise behind, and to
complete the ensemble the Harbour Bridge lumbers immensely away
across the narrow harbour channel to the west. This is certainly not
the world's loveliest bridge, but it is one of the world's old friends by
now. It speaks of familiar loyalties, it does a good workaday job, and

[1] Far less, too, opera people say, since it is primarily a concert hall really, and its
operatic facilities are sadly inferior to those of the visually far less exciting Melbourne
Arts Centre. This has given rise to the quip that Australia has the best opera house in
the world – its exterior in one city, its interior in another.

is thus in every way a proper complement to the esoteric folly of the arts below.

Nothing can quite match the particular sensations of this scene. The cove foams with the passage of the ferry-boats. Cafés and bars are lively and sun-shaded. Perhaps there is a cruise ship moored at the terminal, towering above us with bunting and fresh paint. Cars rumble incessantly over the bridge, and sometimes the earth seems to shake when a train crosses it. Excursion boats circle around, their loudspeakers echoing; there is often a tinkle of zither, a thin strain of violins, a beat of drums from buskers on the quay. It always seems to me Australia idealized – so young, so energetic, so hopeful. The Opera House is like a very emblem of fresh starts, and the old bridge above, the jumble of the harbour front, the ceaseless turmoil of the water traffic, the sense of dazzle superimposed upon grubbiness, once more bring home to me Sydney's peculiar sensation of time truncated.

2. Suburbs

In a satellite photograph Sydney looks less like a city than a geological feature, and among its expanses of dark grey and red, between the sea and the mountains, the downtown quarter scarcely shows. The Central Business District – CBD as everyone calls it – has hardly grown in size since the last century. It is about as big as downtown Birmingham, England, or Dallas. Greater Sydney, though, that slab on the satellite picture, is as big as London. With a population of about $3\frac{1}{2}$ million it is one of the most sprawling of all the earth's cities, covering 670 square miles. It can take a couple of hours to drive out of Sydney, whichever way one goes, and there are said to be people in the remoter districts who have never set eyes on the Harbour Bridge. This is pre-eminently a city of suburbs – *the* city of suburbs, perhaps; a city which has whole books written about its suburbs, gazetteers and directories of its suburbs, architectural studies of its suburbs, social analyses of its suburbs, suburban Governments, suburban styles, suburban loyalties and intense suburban prides.

The city's epicentre is supposed to be somewhere around Parramatta, some fifteen miles inland from Circular Quay. This is proper, for Parramatta was the earliest of the out-settlements, and for a time at the end of the eighteenth century was bigger and busier than Sydney itself. Over the generations several such towns and villages have been absorbed into the metropolis, but the chief reason for Sydney's unnatural extent has been the inexorable outward growth of the city itself. Immigrants landing in Sydney were generally reluctant to go far into the interior, preferring to settle on the edge of town, and as long ago as 1900 the suburbs became more populous than the city proper. Since then they have expanded ever further, ever more coagulatively into the bush – it was in the 1950s that the last of Sydney's black swans, seeing the way things were going, flew away *en masse* from their lagoon in the suburb of Dee Why. Suburbia came naturally to Sydney. In 1836 Charles Darwin likened the entire city to a London suburb;[1] a century later D. H. Lawrence described it as 'crumbling out into formlessness and chaos'.[2]

The old inner-city suburbs are mostly of terraced houses in the European kind, economical of space. They line the streets convivially with small front gardens, verandas, assorted decorative addenda and a profusion of the fancy ironwork known as Sydney Lace – of which it is claimed that twenty different patterns can be seen in one row alone, Argyle Place above the Rocks. The outer suburbs are more absolutely Australian. They are mostly of bungalows, often built of a kind of cement known in Sydney as fibro, with red terracotta roofs, and their size has been dictated by one of Australia's most fervent and admirable beliefs, the conviction that a family should own its own house, with a garden all around it (in later years with a garage too, and nowadays preferably with space for a boat). Mile after mile the Sydney suburbs

[1] He thought it perfectly marvellous at first, but when he saw more of it 'perhaps my admiration fell a little'.

[2] In *Kangaroo* (1923), of which by the way an anonymous letter-writer in the Sydney *Bulletin* wrote: 'God save Australia from these cheap writers from semi-literate countries ... There are plenty of Australian writers of rubbish, and local rubbish should have the preference.'

illustrate this creed, with varying degrees of beguilement. The main roads that connect them must be among the least attractive city roads on earth, a dismal mixture of English provincial humdrum and tacky American display. The roads themselves are often narrow and twisty, being based upon the coach roads of long ago. The buildings that line them make the heart sink – not quite hideous enough to shock, but monotonous enough to make you feel, as you lurch from traffic-light to stop sign, through one unenticing shopping centre after another, as though they will never end. For myself I will do almost anything to avoid these gruesome arteries: but the suburbs themselves are another matter.

Robin Boyd the architect launched a famous attack on the more recent suburbs in his book *The Australian Ugliness*, 1960, using a fine vocabulary of invective – destructive . . . pretentious . . . stealthy crawl like dry rot . . . cold comfort conservatism. There is no denying that many Sydney suburbs are less than lovely, their plans tedious, their streets (as Lawrence thought) like children's drawings – 'little square bungalows dot-dot-dot . . .' I can see that socially progressive architects and planners must detest them. Nevertheless they represent, for several hundred thousand people of many national origins, true human fulfilment – the very antithesis of the crowded tenements from which so many of them or their forebears came. Besides, they often turn out to be more interesting than you expect, when at last you reach them along those interminable highways.

Some are historically interesting. Parramatta in particular illustrates the development of Sydney almost as well as the city centre. Its original plan was devised in 1790 by a naval officer of the First Fleet, Lieutenant William Dawes. He laid out a grid system of five wide streets, with one main highway running from Government House to the Parramatta River, and another terminating in a plaza with a Town Hall in it. Symmetrically around them were to be disposed the institutions of Church and State. Much of this plan, overlaid by urban sprawl, is apparent as in palimpsest still.

Grand as ever Government House stands in its park, with the lodge at its gates and the very tree where in 1847 Lady FitzRoy the Governor's wife was dashed from her carriage to her death. George Street runs away to the river's bank. St John's Cathedral with its twin towers stands in a rather Mediterranean way above its little gravel close. The cavalry barracks are elegant in their compound. The Town Hall still presides over its wide plaza, and nearby are the Centennial Clock-Tower of 1888 and the Bicentennial Fountain of 1988 (which portrays three ghoulish figures apparently about to be drowned in a waterfall, and was put up during the Town Clerkship of Mr R. G. Muddle). It may not be all as Dawes foresaw it, but the shape of Parramatta is recognizably his memorial.

Other interesting suburbs are simply rich. Not all rich suburbs are interesting, by any means, but Sydney's often are. All around the harbour, and intermittently along the ocean shore, houses of an infinite variety of styles are encouched in opulent green, their gardens dripping with bougainvillaea or frangipani, rich old trees shading their yards. Sometimes they stand defiantly on the edges of cliffs, or deep in bushland, or are built on hillside declivities so steep that cars and boats are parked on their roofs. Sometimes they have tree houses, gazebos or private external elevators ('inclinators' in the vernacular) connecting them with the harbour front. They have pools, they have awnings, they have sprinkled lawns, they have appropriated picturesque steps or urns from antique shops. They have two cars in the garage, and on their sidewalks, in good times at least, crates of empty champagne bottles habitually await the garbage men.

Some of these houses do strike me as arid and artificial, in the Hollywood manner. Many others seem all too enviably organic. I know of no city with so many houses that I would be extremely happy to acquire, and it is no surprise that the plutocratic old suburbs like Vaucluse, Point Piper or Clifton Gardens, sun-splashed on their headlands, like to call themselves generically The World's Best Address. Almost since the beginning of Sydney the rich have been building themselves homes in these parts, and many an old villa or cottage orné still basks among its flower-gardens as it has since some lucky official or wool factor commissioned it long ago; so that even in districts now glitzy with boutique and high rise, a sense of privileged continuity prevails.

Most of the suburbs have developed piecemeal, but some have been sociologically planned. The first was Woolloomooloo Hill, not far to the east of downtown and now more usually called Potts Point. In the 1820s Governor Ralph Darling earmarked this pleasant promontory as a place of residence for senior functionaries, well away from the penal quarters or the homes of vulgar emancipated convicts. Generous lots were granted to people like the High Sheriff or the Surveyor-General, and rigid planning restrictions were imposed – all buildings must face the town of Sydney, for instance, and no home was to be of less value than £1,000. Woolloomooloo Hill was fastidiously developed, with Gothic villas, well-wooded gardens of imported trees and shrubs, and stately nostalgic names – Craigend, Brougham Place, Telford Lodge. Few mansions remain, Woolloomooloo in general having long since been overwhelmed by urbanism, but the names of some have been inherited by the apartment blocks ('home units', they are called in Sydney) which now occupy their sites, and Potts Point remains, as Darling would have wished it, decidedly posh.

Several planned enclaves were built around the turn of the twentieth century, in the heyday of the Garden Suburb idea. The grandest was a very up-market development called Appian Way, completed in 1911 within the otherwise undistinguished suburb of Burwood. It was, and still is, like a very small slice of Newport, Rhode Island, and is now a popular location for film-makers. Its thirty-odd villas are set in wide gardens, surrounded by picket fences and shaded by magnificent brush box trees. In the middle is a small park, communally owned by the householders, in which one used to be able to play croquet, and can still play tennis, resorting for gossip and lemonade, I like to think, to a folly-like pavilion beside the green. At another social extreme was Daceyville, in the south. This was the first State-planned suburb, created in 1912 as an example of how it should be done. It was an extremely ambitious project, and architects' plans show it as an immense swathe of symmetry, ovals, squares and

residential oblongs interspersed with ample parks; but it rather petered
out when in 1924 an inquiry convicted the State Housing Board of
gross carelessness, incompetence and improper management, and all
one can see of it now is a kind of fizzled ghost of its pretensions,
festooned with telegraph wires, speckled lamely with ornamental
palms and made all too spacious by brownish grass medians.

Then in 1924 the American architect Walter Burley Griffin, fresh
from designing the new Australian capital at Canberra, arrived in
Sydney with his wife Marion, herself an architect (and supposed to be
of American-Indian blood). Appalled at the general standard of
Sydney suburbia, he set out to build an enclave in the Frank Lloyd
Wright manner, blending imperceptibly with nature and housing a
community of artistic or philosophic temperament. No tree was to be
unnecessarily felled, no inch of bush needlessly destroyed. There were
to be no fences, no boundaries and certainly no red terracotta roofs.
Griffin acquired 750 acres of land at Castlecrag, overlooking Middle
Harbour in the north, and laid out his streets around the contours of
a rock known locally as Edinburgh Castle. Half-buried in bush and
boulder, all different but united in conservational spirit, the houses
were built either of local sandstone or of a rough pre-cast concrete.
There were also a couple of shops, a golf club and a small amphitheatre in a gulley, where the Griffins put on ecologically compatible
plays. Many of the houses still stand, and the romantically rambling
streets of Castlecrag still bear their original castellan names – The
Bulwark, The Redoubt, The Citadel, The Parapet, The Rampart,
The Postern, The Bastion. 'We want to keep Castlecrag for ever part
of the bush,' declared the Griffins, and they have succeeded, for those
of their houses that have survived are half-obliterated by the foliage.[1]

The ultimate planned suburb, though, the Sydney suburb *in excelsis*, is
Haberfield, which survives only partly violated on the south side of
the Parramatta River, and is one of the most truly Sydneyesque places

---

[1] Griffin built six houses elsewhere in Sydney, besides a number of monumentally
styled and technically progressive incinerators.

in Sydney. Early in the present century a developer named Richard Stanton, together with his architect J. Spencer-Stanfield, set out to create the perfect urban living environment. It would be conveniently linked by rail and ferry to the city centre, and was to be everything Australians wanted, everything they deserved – unashamedly Australian in every way, and unashamedly profitable too. It would be, so the publicity said, a suburb 'Slum-less, Lane-less and Pub-less', where every house would have a bathroom, and every householder would be able to say, 'This is my own home – this is mine for life.' Some 1,500 houses were built, on a 200-acre site. They were all designed by Spencer-Stanfield, and most of them are still there.

The bungalow was the prime Sydney building form by then, and Haberfield is a town of them, sometimes extending into attics and even turrets, but for the most part compactly single-storeyed. They are built in the style called in Australia the Federation Style.[1] This is a blend of English, European and American influences, medieval to Victorian, suffused in specifically Australian allusions. It has a touch of Prairieism from the United States, and a hefty dose of Arts and Crafts from England, and grace notes of Art Nouveau. Its characteristics are, to my mind, hard to isolate. It is a Queen Anne-ish, Tudory, semi-countrified, sometimes whimsical sort of style, with eaves often, and fancy chimneys, and ornamental ridge cappings, and much woodwork. Stained-glass windows go well with the Federation Style, and tiled floors, and bargeboarding, and a veranda is almost essential. It is a style easy to mock or patronize, but on the whole it is humane, attractive, practical and fun, and it is a worthy instrument of the Australian Dream – to live in that house of one's own, with that garden all around it, in a respectable, healthy and thoroughly Australian neighbourhood. Such a neighbourhood was quintessentially Haberfield, and they call it still the Federation Suburb. It extends in unpretentious serenity, its streets lined with diverse trees, from the Parramatta Road to the edge of Iron Cove, an inlet of the Parramatta

[1] Because its emergence coincided with the federation, in 1901, of the six Australian colonies. It is the one truly Australian style, though the Central Sydney Heritage Inventory categorizes eighty-four, including Immigrants' Nostalgic and Post-war Stripped Medieval.

river, which has a tropical-looking island picturesquely wooded in the middle of it.

A good deal of shabby building has crept in since Stanton's day, much unadvised improvement has occurred, but part at least of Haberfield is protected as an urban conservation area, and it remains an endearing place. Although from its highest points you may see the skyscrapers in the distance, its streets are wonderfully quiet, its gardens are lush, people sit on porches reading newspapers and in the air, even now, one hears the cooing of pigeons, the humming of insects and the gossiping of neighbours over fences. Every single house in Haberfield is different. If one house has a hexagonal glass conservatory, the next has a conical turret. Here is a veranda decorated in fretted woodwork, here an elaborately tiled garden path. There are fancy roof-ridges. There are gables and wide eaves. There are stained-glass windows rich in kookaburras, watarahs, wattles or sinuous Art Nouveau abstractions. Stanton kept his promises. There are no back alleys, there are no slums, and to this day there is no pub.

But it is really only an apotheosis of your average Sydney suburb. Haberfield is occupied nowadays largely by Italian immigrants, but its aspirations have not changed. Wandering around it one day I happened to notice a crude sign tacked beside a modest house gate, and thought that while its lettering and style were perhaps not up to Spencer-Stanfield's standards, its message was purest Federation:

'STRICTLY'. RESIDENTS. CARS. ONLY. CAN. PASS. BEYOND. THIS POINT. THANK. YOU. ('OWNER')

There are many surprises in the suburbs – corners of survival, anomalies, sudden glimpses of eccentricity.

I am always surprised for instance to find the former Government House still in its park at Parramatta. A pleasant, middle-sized, easy-going English rectory sort of a house, it looks slightly surprised to find itself there, too, still extant in the suburban wasteland, and guarded by National Trust ladies so implacably didactic that they send me scuttling through its rooms like a rat. Hardly less incongruous are two nearby buildings which, set high and dry in milieux of ineffable modern ordinariness, both claim to be the oldest house in Australia, and are the prototypes of the sheep-station house that appears in every self-respecting Australian movie. Elizabeth Farm and Experiment Farm Cottage are surrounded now by bungalows, in plain bourgeois streets, but they have wide pillared eaves, stone-flagged floors, verandas for the supervision of estates, whitewashed outbuildings for the stacking of mealies or the slaughtering of pigs, and dark cellars specifically designed, so popular and ill-informed legend has it (Australian legend loves a touch of the horrors), for the dreadful incarceration of convict servants.

Some of the old villas are lovely. Vaucluse House above its eponymous bay, which began as a simple cottage, and was aggrandized in stages into a country house, now feels to me remarkably like a West Indian plantation house, with its big windows and cool rooms, the corrugated iron roof of its veranda, the rattan screens that shade it and the great dark trees growing all around. On the other hand Admiralty House, on the north shore, may be Georgian and Victorian in architecture but is suggestively Italian Lakes in temperament. Its steps run down to moorings where lovers' skiffs should lie. Its gardens look across to Sydney Cove where Como ought to be. Twelve commanding admirals in succession used it as their residence when the Royal Navy was at the peak of its confidence and good taste, and now the lucky Governor-General of Australia lives in it when he is visiting Sydney.

There are some old stone houses in the northern suburbs which look like forest lodges, shady, woody, mushroomy, as though there are cut logs piled for the fire inside, though the kookaburras may be laughing and the dreary highway is only a few hundred yards away. Here and there one sees the delightfully absurd extravaganza of some late Victorian millionaire, all spikes and towers, probably converted into hospital, school or nursing home but still superbly *nouveau riche*. The main building at the Sydney Church of England Grammar School, known as Shore presumably because it stands on the harbour's northern shore, used to be the home of one such tycoon, Bernard Otto Holtermann, and is just recognizable as such, though heavily educationalized. Prominently mounted in its tower (and now removed to a library wall), a stained-glass window depicted the bearded magnate standing beside the gigantic Holtermann Gold Nugget, nearly five feet long and reaching to his shoulder, which had enabled him to build the house.

I never fail to be surprised by the bridge which leads across a wooded ravine to the suburb of Northbridge. There I am, driving along an unnoticeable stretch of standard suburban highway, 1930-ish, when turning a corner and descending a steep hill I find before me an enormously castellated mock-Gothic bridge, with hefty towers, arches, crests and arrow-slits, such as might have been thrown across a river in Saxe-Coburg by some quixotic nineteenth-century princeling (actually it was built by the North Sydney Tramway and Development Company, in 1889, to encourage interest in a flagging housing estate). I am invariably charmed by the little church of St Peter's above Watson's Bay, designed by Edmund Blacket in 1864 to be the very first building newcomers would see when they sailed through the Sydney Heads: with its belfry and homely porch it is uncannily like an English village church in a meadow somewhere, except that it stands histrionically on a windswept, sun-soaked, ocean-salted plateau looking over the wild Heads. I am naïvely thrilled every time I discover, up by the Hawkesbury River, the truly glamorous marina at Akuna Bay: deep in the bush on its silent creek, a glittering assembly of yachts and launches, attended by Mercedes and BMWs, with a swish restaurant and a boat hangar, with a forest of aerials and radar masts, suddenly revealed among the empty woodlands of the Ku-ring-gai Chase National Park.

Of all these suburban serendipities, my favourite happens at Lavender Bay, a small inlet of the northern shore just west of the Harbour Bridge. Long ago barrack ships were moored here, some to house stone-cutters and lime-burners, others waiting to take some of the more recalcitrant of the Sydney convicts to still worse banishment on Norfolk Island. Nowadays it could hardly be more innocuous. On its east shore are the dilapidated buildings of the once-famous Luna Park amusement centre, deprived now of the huge laughing face which constituted the entrance and was one of Sydney's trademarks, and left in a kind of stagnancy between purposes. On the west shore a suave restaurant stands at the water's edge. There are two ferry jetties and a sailing school, lots of yachts are moored offshore, and a couple of apartment blocks overlook the waterfront.

High above the bay rise the office towers of North Sydney, a formidable financial and commercial centre in its own right, but below them there is a settlement of a very different kind. There a handful of old houses tumbles down the hillside in the seclusion of a small and well-wooded park. This is a favourite artists' and actors' quarter, and the houses possess a strong sense of languid bohemianism. They are built variously of sandstone and clapboard, and one has a merry little tower. At the top there is an Indian restaurant, and this is apposite, for with their gables, bleached railings and balconies these houses have an evocatively Simla look. Clustered tightly together there, thickly shaded by the trees, embedded by ferns and jacarandas, almost out of sight either from the land or from the water, they ought to have white-robed bearers preparing tea on their verandas, and memsahibs in floppy hats.

Back we come, though, inevitably to the harbour itself, towards which all these suburbs, however remote and landlocked, instinctively seem to strain: in Sydney, the playwright David Williamson once said, nobody cares about the meaning of life – it's a harbour frontage that counts. The harbour was the original *raison d'être* of this city, and remains its visual saving grace. Trollope said of it, in one of Sydney's favourite quotations, that he thought it might be worth a man's while moving to Sydney just so that he might look at it 'as long as he could look at anything'. It is the Sydney standard, by which all else is measured.[1]

The harbour is ringed with sensuous delights, pleasant little coves,

[1] In many ways the Australian standard too: for example I learn that Australian engineers measure reservoirs by a unit called the 'Sydarb'.

waterside parks all green and welcoming, fine houses to look at, boats riding by, the tinkling of yacht fittings, the slap of ropes, the singing of the cicadas. Sometimes it reminds me of the Bosphorus – notably at Kirribilli, where the apartment blocks stand side by side at the water's edge, their inhabitants to be waved at from passing ferries. Sometimes the glitter of its waterside commerce is like Manhattan. Sidney Nolan once painted it looking like a lake in a barren desert, while the nineteenth-century watercolourists gave it a gentle Home Counties allure, alleviated only by the odd kangaroo, or by groups of natives ornamentally disposed.

All the same, the harbour seems to me less a spectacle than an event. It is like a perpetual pageant, punctuated by astonishments. Something is always happening on it, even in the small hours of the morning – always a ship passing, a helicopter flying by, unexplained lights wavering in the distance, dim white sails loitering. I looked from my balcony one morning to see an enormous pair of inflatable sunglasses perched high upon a wing of the Opera House as upon its nose: they had been placed there by a group of ecological activists, including the first three Australians to reach the summit of Everest, in protest against the depletion of the ozone layer, and I could see those adventurers scrambling over the high roofs pursued by policemen. The very next day, when I looked out again, I saw a man sitting on the gantry at the very highest point of the Harbour Bridge, threatening with angry gestures to jump off: policemen and white-coated medics were up there trying to persuade him to come down, a police helicopter hovered above him, a police launch cruised below, police cars and ambulances jammed the bridge approach, and on both sides of the harbour hundreds of people were staring up at that high arch, half-hoping despite themselves that the man would jump.

He never did, and the police soon deflated the opera house sunglasses, but anyway on Sydney harbour there is always another day, another drama. It is by no means always blithe and sunny there. When one of those sudden winds blows up, and everything is flying, scudding, racing, flattened, flecked with white, the whole pace of the haven seems feverishly quickened. When one of Sydney's thunderstorms comes raging in, suddenly all turns a bronze or ochre colour, the lowering clouds hang like doom over the skyscrapers, and the whole harbour seems to be catching its breath, waiting for the lightning and the rain.

I once crossed the harbour in a tossing small launch during one of the most ferocious of these downpours, described at the time indeed as Sydney's worst natural disaster, and seeing the place grotesquely distorted through our water-streaked windows, as in an old surrealist movie, now the bridge swooping above us, now the office towers crooked and bent, made me feel that another and altogether more sinister city had been conjured.

STYLE

Y EARS AGO, IN THE PUBLIC ICE-RINK NEAR THE CENTRAL
station, I came across a Sydney boy whose style I have never
forgotten. He was about five years old, tough, blond and capable.
He could not actually skate, but he was adept at hobbling about the
rink on his blades, and his one purpose was to gather up the slush
that fell off other people's boots, and throw it at more accomplished
skaters. Hop, hop, he would abruptly appear upon the rink, and
choosing a suitable target, staggering his way across the ice, zealously
he would hunt that victim down until splosh! the missile was dispatched – and quick as a flash he was out of the rink again, gathering
more ammunition.

I could not help admiring him. He hardly ever fell over, he seldom
missed, and he did everything with dexterity. When I asked him his
name he grimly spelt out GORGE with his finger on the rail of the
rink; and in my mind's eye I could see him thirty years from then,
exploding into a company meeting with an irresistible takeover bid,
relentlessly engineering the resignation of a rival, or (it occurs to me
now) bashing his way down the harbour in command of an 18-footer.

Of course he made me think of the convict children. It used to be popular to see penal origins to everything about Sydney, and occasionally I fall into this romantic fallacy myself – it is all too easy to fancy the mug of an eighteenth-century London footpad in a passing loveless face, or to imagine in a well-fed child at a skating rink some apotheosis of those poor little abandoned creatures in the streets of Sydney 200 years ago. The chances are remote indeed that Gorge is connected in any way with the transportees: if his grandparents were not homely souls from Macclesfield they were probably hard-working fishing folk from the Aegean. Still, it is fair to conjecture that the existence of the original penal settlement may have permanently affected the style of the city, and even of Gorge himself.

In many ways, indeed, Gorge's style is Sydney's style. He was a delightful boy, but not exactly tender; Sydney is a genial and generous city, but with a streak of malice to it. A well-recognized characteristic of the place is called 'the tall-poppy syndrome' – the tendency to cut you down to size, if you are seen to be too successful. This is the municipal equivalent of throwing ice-slosh at you.

The transportation policy was not all evil. Its methods were ghastly and its chief intention was certainly to rid Great Britain of as many unwanted persons as possible, but it was seen also as a chance for the miserable discards of British life to make a new beginning. Once their sentences were worked out they were 'emancipated'. They became free citizens of New South Wales, very likely with grants of land, and this gave thousands of people a better chance of success than they would ever have found at home. Many spent the second halves of their lives as respectable run-of-the-mill colonists, and a few became extremely rich. In the later years of the system, when the worst was over, convicts often looked upon exile as a kind of assisted emigration. Charles Darwin, in 1836, thought that transportation had succeeded 'to a degree perhaps unparalleled in history' in converting useless vagabonds into active citizens, and by the time the system ended the sons and daughters of the transportees had indeed proved themselves

remarkably law-abiding. A fine interesting race, the naval surgeon
Peter Cunningham called them in his book *Two Years in New South
Wales* (1828), intensely proud of their city, and only anxious to dis-
tance themselves from criminal association ('I should be afraid to go to
England,' one girl told him, 'from the number of thieves there').

Nevertheless Sydney grew up, like a child in a bad home, inured to
terrible facts, terrible sights. Penal Sydney was run in the first place
by officers of a brutalized Royal Navy – offending Marines were
punished even more horribly than convicts – and cruelty was endemic.
Prisoners were part of the street scene in the early years. They were
clanking about in irons, breaking stones, building roads, digging sand,
sometimes degradingly kitted out in frayed exotic uniforms taken
from foreign prisoners-of-war, sometimes in a ragged mixture of prison
dress and miscellaneous hand-me-downs. They were shackled like
beasts to wagons. They were bonded as domestic servants or as labourers on private farms. Between 1788 and 1840 huge works of development and reclamation – the Argyle Cut through the Rocks, the
Semi-Circular Quay, the road over the Blue Mountains – were accomplished by these slaves of the State, whipped mercilessly to their
labours.

There was no closing one's eyes to the truth, in this little town. For
the first decades of Sydney's history gaols, barracks and labour yards
were among its most prominent buildings – as one visitor remarked,
all the best buildings 'had something to do with convicts'. St Phillip's
Church looked more like a prison than a house of God, and even
Greenway's elegant St James's had arrows stamped all over its steeple
in case the copper sheathing was stolen. If you went to divine service
you shared your devotions with sullen prisoners on compulsory church
parade – 'the most miserable beings in the shape of humanity', thought
Tench when he went to church one Sunday, 'worn down with fatigue'.
As a matter of course artists included in their landscapes convicts
labouring in chains, or pulling carts in which the muslin-dressed and
sun-hatted women-folk of officers reclined.

Sadism was institutionalized, and must have given the infant city a
pervasive air of the macabre. The whistle of the scourge, the cries of

flogged men were familiar to everyone – you could be flogged just for the expression on your face, or for looking at a passing ship. The treadmill creaked and groaned the hours away. Women sat in the public stocks, or were ducked shaven-headed in ducking-stools. The very first court that ever convened in Sydney, on 11 February 1788, sentenced its first prisoner to 150 lashes (he had abused his guards), and sent its second to spend a week alone on Pinchgut. Forty years later two delinquent soldiers were committed to gaol with fifteen-pound fetters on their wrists and ankles, linked by chains to spiked iron collars riveted around their necks. On Goat Island, at the eastern end of the harbour, one is shown the rock to which a convict named Charles Anderson was sentenced to be chained for two years. An eighteen-year-old orphan, transported for smashing shop windows, during his time in Sydney he had already received 1,500 lashes for petty offences; now he was forbidden any human contact, made to sleep at night in a crevice with a wooden lid locked over him, and fed like a mad creature with food on the end of a pole.[1]

Inevitably the administrators of the place, and the free settlers, were contaminated by all this. Gently nurtured families found themselves the slave-drivers of felons. Priests who had given men the holy sacrament one day passed by them chained in road-gangs the next. Children grew up with a contemptuous disdain for working people – for all working people in those early years were convicts – and sometimes horrifying vocabularies. Gentlemen got used to employing shackled prisoners around the estate, and the servant who brought your dinner, as Darwin observed with distaste, might well have been flogged the day before at the instance of your hospitable host; George Allen, the Godly and teetotal owner of Toxteth Park, in the suburb of Glebe, thought little of ordering thirty-six lashes for a carpenter who took a day off, twenty-five lashes for a boy who drank.

[1] Though the local folklore and guide-books have him serving out this nightmare sentence, in fact the punishment went too far even for penal Sydney, and after some weeks Anderson was unchained from his rock; he was sent in the end to Norfolk Island, where he spent a few mercifully peaceful years as a cattle-guard and signalman, before fading from his vale of tears.

People went out in their boat-loads to stare at Anderson in his misery, and when a new gaol was opened at Darlinghurst in 1841 crowds of citizens jeered and catcalled as the convicts were marched bedraggled through town to their new quarters. As late as 1846, according to David Mackenzie, a local clergyman, anyone standing at the door of the Sydney police office on a Sunday morning would hear a barbaric sentence pronounced from the magistrates' bench every two or three minutes – 'Six hours to the stocks – twenty days to the treadmill – fifty lashes!' Another priest, J. C. Byrne, arriving in Sydney at about the same time, was shaken to hear that his assigned servant had received, at one time or another, an aggregate of 2,275 lashes.

For of course not everyone was desensitized. If children sometimes learnt to despise their convict fellow-beings, sometimes they learnt to sympathize with them, and even to side with them against their parents. We read of the Scottish wife of a farm superintendent, Margaret Wightman, crying herself 'almost into hysterics' because all night long she could hear the clank of chains as the convict labourers stirred in their sleep. And the writer Louis Becke, who lived as a child near the convict stockade on Cockatoo Island, at the mouth of the Parramatta River, remembered with compassion all his life the clanging of the bell on a foggy day that meant a convict had escaped, together with 'the sound of someone panting hard in his swim for liberty'.

Long after the ending of the penal system it remained a characteristic of Sydney that the genteel lived in intimate neighbourhood with the disreputable. For years the Domain itself, whose centrepiece was Government House, was infested by ne'er-do-wells, and the gentry of Darling Point were neighbours to miscellaneous ruffians living among the reeds of Rushcutters' Bay. The prime example of such cheek-by-jowl propinquity was the Rocks. In the upper part of this small peninsula, by the middle of the nineteenth century, the Sydney bourgeoisie had built itself those agreeable terrace houses, that pretty village green, which tourists are still taken to see at Argyle Place. Just over the ridge, though, the rest of the Rocks fell away towards the harbour in almost indescribable squalor. At Argyle Place, any evening in the 1850s, the children said their prayers before bed, the ladies did their embroidery, the gentlemen came home from the office in their spanking carriages. A few hundred yards away the pubs and stews were warming up for business in a bedlam of drunkenness, foul talk and illicit transaction. Goats, whores and footpads indiscriminately wandered the back alleys of the Rocks, whale-hunters and seal-killers thronged the taverns, rats were fought, opium was smoked, violent gangs flourished, drunken seamen were kidnapped, there was a rip-roaring Chinatown and a colony of destitute Maoris, and all down the steep lanes open sewers tumbled, 'maintained in a constant state of moisture', as was graphically reported in 1858, 'by new accretions of liquid filth'.

With violent contrasts went violent shifts of fortune. Suddenness always seems to have been a Sydney characteristic, and sudden wealth especially. Almost from the beginning an explosive capitalism erupted here. Although the original settlement was ostensibly a bureaucracy of the most absolute kind, the officers of the New South Wales Corps very soon made themselves masters of its economy. They established corners in rum and many other commodities, and one at least opened a retail store; most of his customers were his own soldiers, and if they ventured to complain about his extortionate prices (he worked to a 100 per cent profit) he merely threatened to have them flogged. In no time the cleverest of these moonlighters had been transformed from officers in perhaps the least fashionable regiment in the entire British Army to rich landed gentry. Taken out to Sydney at Government expense, paid Government salaries, given land by Government, assigned convict labour by Government, they sold their produce to the Government commissariat and became immediate aristocrats.

Speculators of other kinds made equally quick fortunes. Ships' captains, their holds crammed with goods from England, easily doubled their money on each voyage, and it is said that in the 1820s Sydney was a favourite and profitable outlet for stolen goods, smuggled from

London for sale by George Street jewellers. Some of the emancipated convicts became very archetypes of *nouvelle richesse*. One year they were poor bondsmen, the next they were bosses of great concerns. We hear of one emancipist, in the 1850s, leaning stately on a gold-headed cane in a phaeton drawn by four ponies and driven by liveried postilions; of another, aged and illiterate, 'dashing along in a perfectly appointed tandem, with a lovely girl beside him'. Sometimes they threw vastly expensive parties: at a dinner given for the emancipated forger John Tawell, in 1831, one of the guests took a moment off to calculate that thirteen of his fellow-diners possessed between them property worth £437,000 – perhaps A$30 million each by today's standards. The origins of great fortunes were well-recognized. One mansion was frankly known as Frying-Pan Hall, because its owner had made his pile in ironmongery. Another was Juniper Hall, expressing its proprietor's indebtedness to gin. Sydney doubtless laid a collective finger along the side of its nose when J. G. N. Gibbes, Collector of Customs, found the wherewithal to build the splendid villa at Kirribilli that is now the Sydney residence of the Governor-General of Australia, and it probably surprised nobody to hear that the well-educated and gifted Bradley of Bradley's Head, who had gone home to such a distinguished naval career, had been sentenced to death in London for his fraudulent practices, and very nearly shipped back to Sydney as a convict.[1]

From our distance of time it seems astonishing how quickly the struggling penal colony turned into a rich man's elysium. Everywhere comfortable houses sprouted – not vast English-style mansions, but agreeable neo-classical villas that fitted very well into the vaguely Mediterranean environment. All around the harbour they presently stood, and among the farmlands of the interior, with names like Curzon Hall or Tusculum, with terraced gardens and avenues of Norfolk pines, with elaborate outbuildings where the convicts toiled, with imported silver and furniture of polished cedarwood and even,

[1] Instead, since he was by then an admiral, he was allowed to go and live in France, where he died in 1833.

whether by inheritance or imagination, family portraits. By the 1840s, when one sailed up the harbour, these pretty buildings ornamented almost every bay and promontory of the southern shore. They looked urbane, but they all too often represented no more than crude opportunism. The early commerce of this city was elemental, and no-holds-barred. Its first industries were whaling and sealing. The booms that later enriched it were based upon wool and gold. These were abrupt, un-creative sources of wealth, and convinced Sydney people, perhaps, that they might thrive not by the old-fashioned means of making things, or even growing things, but by snaring, catching, grazing, swapping, digging things out of the earth or even, in later years, imagining things.

And how much of this old rawness, abruptness, bitterness of experience, keenness of opportunity, lack of scruple and abundance of gusto is really apparent in Sydney in the last decade of the twentieth century? One can only generalize, and I must start by saying that at its best the style of contemporary Sydney is delightful. Almost every foreigner thinks so (although almost every Sydney citizen is likely to say, as citizens say everywhere, that it's not like it was in the old days ...). To my mind it still displays the 'open sturdy manliness' that Alexander Harris, writing in the 1840s, thought characteristic of the plainer emancipists. Nine times out of ten the Sydney person in the street, in the shop, on the bus, will be friendly, polite and remarkably frank, and young people coming from Britain, in particular, immediately feel a sense of euphoric hope and liberty. The supra-national, supra-ethnic fraternity of kind, educated, open-minded people, which exists like a freemasonry in every city of the world, is powerfully represented here, and a palpable sense of fellowship is apparent, too, in the camaraderie of pubs and clubs, and in a penchant for reunions. There was a reunion recently of mothers, babies and grandchildren at one of the city's maternity hospitals, and there are often gatherings of descendants of particular nineteenth-century settlers, or immigrants from some Greek islet, or survivors of a destroyer crew from the Second World War: the reunion of the Anzac soldiers of 1914–18 is by tradition the one occasion of the year when the police turn a blind eye upon the old soldiers' gambling game of two-up, and the little band of veterans takes the chance, encouraged by all, to throw a bet or two in Hyde Park.

There is much goodness in Sydney. Every kind of charitable and altruistic organization flourishes here, bat-defenders and seal-supporters, environmental protest movements and Aboriginal protection leagues. Sydney people are hospitable to strangers rather in the way Americans used to be, before worldliness set in, and in most matters the city is outspoken and un-shockable. I always admire the impeccably lady-like shoppers who buy their groceries so imperturbably among the porn shops, strip shows and general scatologicals of King's Cross. Startled though I was, I was impressed when, pausing in Martin Place to sympathize with a young woman who seemed to have difficulty in getting up from her bench, she thanked me courteously but added confidingly that 'it was a good lay, anyway'. I liked the sound of the man who wrote in a Letter to the Editor: 'I always read Gittin's column, sometimes I wonder why I bother. I think February's effort was probably the biggest load of crap he's written so far.'

'Melbourne people come as you are,' said a Sydney card inviting people to a party in 1930s dress, and the joke exemplified this city's cocky and lighthearted self-regard. Most Sydney people seem immensely proud of their city, immensely proud to be its citizens, and this happy confidence is contagious; it makes the outsider, too, feel proud to be there – when I look out from my balcony across the harbour I feel positively possessive, and nobody is more invariably moved than I am, I swear, by the two floodlit flags that fly so bravely in the evening above the Harbour Bridge.

At its worst, on the other hand, the Sydney style can be disconcertingly nasty. This city is still more hardened to the brutalities of life than most of its peers. Can one imagine people in Copenhagen or Vancouver looking up, as breakfasters at a King's Cross café did one day in 1990, to see a man with a baseball bat clubbing a barking dog to death across a street? Would *Le Progrès* of Lyon include among a celebratory group of city worthies, as the *Sydney Morning Herald* recently did, a rugby player convicted of smuggling heroin from Thailand? Are there many opera houses, besides Sydney's, where a conductor in the pit has been seen pulling an imaginary lavatory chain when a soprano concludes an aria? On a single Sydney day the following local items find their way into my notebook:

¶ A television advertisement for a pick-up truck shows two louts hitting each other with crowbars, butting each other's heads and kicking each other in the testicles, until one clinches the dispute by applying an electric sander to his opponent's face.

¶ A sixty-two-year-old woman is accused of murdering her husband, binding his corpse from head to foot and concealing it in a brick crypt below her rumpus room.

¶ A former Premier of New South Wales having expostulated about the behaviour of the clientele at his local pub, who go in for vomiting, urinating, copulating and self-injection in the streets around his house, a gentle acquaintance of mine wonders what he is making such a fuss about.

¶ The mother of a recently murdered homosexual millionaire throws herself under a train.

¶ Walking through the suburb of Newtown in the afternoon I hear a girl call to her lover on the other side of the street, as she might remind him not to forget the mayonnaise: 'I work my fucking arse off for you, you don't even pay the fucking rent.'

¶ A private detective complains to the Press that policemen have been searching for a dead body under his tennis-court. 'It absolutely repulses me,' he says, 'that they would even suggest I have some poor soul buried in my back yard.'

There can be poison to this crudity, too. The unfortunate Danish architect Jøern Utzon, returning home in despair after months of controversy concerning the building of his Opera House, thought the débâcle as much malignant as incompetent, and called it Malice in

Blunderland. He was by no means the only eminent alien to feel himself savaged by Sydney, and there are still suggestions that when in 1956 Eugene Goossens the conductor was caught at Sydney Airport with pornographic literature in his suitcase, he had been shopped by ill-wishers. I was amused to watch the exchanges when one of the most celebrated of London newspaper harridans ran the gamut of the TV interviews in Sydney. Asked once why she was so unpleasant about people in her column she replied, 'I tell the truth, and that's why I'm famous, and not a little television reporter like you': but into the eye of that little television reporter there crept a gleam of loathing so pure, so well-honed, so evident and so rooted in history that we all knew who had won.

Sydney is notoriously racist. It was brought up to be so. Robert Hughes suggests, in *The Fatal Shore*, that the bigotry began with the convicts, despising the Aborigines 'because they desperately needed to believe in a class inferior to themselves'. In later years it was encouraged by membership of the British Empire, itself so racist and xenophobic that the official attitudes of this city were ingrained with fear of foreigners. Two World Wars sustained the suspicions, and they were powerfully encouraged by the national policy of White Australia, rigidly pursued for several generations. The spectre of the Yellow Peril was vivid here – 'We don't want to fight,' said a Sydney version of an old British *cri-de-coeur*, 'but by jingo if we must/We'll lick the yellow peril and leave it in the dust.'

These emotions are far from dead, and appear indeed to be self-generating: in the 1970s the children of Lebanese immigrants ('Lebs') found themselves horribly bullied at school, and even now women in Muslim dress are treated with open hostility and contempt. The immigrants of one generation project their own resentments on the immigrants of the next – sometimes of the one before too, as I realized when a Greek assured me one day that 'Poms are arrogant bastards, and ignorant too'. In 1989 there was a proposal for a new industrial satellite city, obscurely called a Multi-Function Polis, which would be built on the outskirts of Sydney and greatly increase its industrial and technological power; support soon soured when it was realized that most of the money behind it would be Japanese, and that some 30,000 yellow men might be coming to work there. I am still taken aback by the attitudes of some otherwise cultivated Sydney gentry to the Aborigines, whom they shamelessly call 'abos' – like calling American blacks 'niggers' – and whose very mention in a conversation can bring into the Sydney voice a disturbing steeliness, into the Sydney eye an involuntary glint of distaste.

So time and again one finds, exploring attitudes in present-day Sydney, that one is treading emotions of the past.

Land brought an early and lasting passion to the Sydney style. The Aborigines thought either that it was held in trust for everyone, or that it held everyone in trust. The whites thought it the one permanent and infallible source of personal wealth. The British authorities, disingenuously resolving that since the Aborigines did not appear to do anything with it, they had no right to it, declared it all at the disposal of the Crown, and distributed wide tracts among worthy white recipients. Since the land was mostly thick bush, entirely unworked, it sometimes came in very large parcels. Emancipated convicts were allowed only a few acres, and the more humble kind of free settler could expect little more: migrants of means were soon playing about with thousands, amounting to gigantic if originally hypothetical estates.

I know a man in Sydney whose family owns one of the very same patches of land granted to it at the turn of the nineteenth century – then a small country property, now the site of a row of terrace houses. Many such Sydney clans established their well-being upon land given them by Government (though not many still possess it), and the consciousness of land, its status as the ultimate form of wealth, runs deeply through the ethos of the city. The Lands Title Office swarms always with animated claimants and disputants, like a bank or passport office somewhere else. If there had ever been a Sydney constitution, an inalienable right to the pursuit of property might well have been written into it – also a right to the sale of property, for many of the original land grants were very soon split by their owners and sold off in lots: even Craigend, the Surveyor-General's lovely place on Woolloomooloo Hill, lasted only thirteen years before it was divided into eighty-six profitable segments of real estate.

The almost universal desire to own one's own house is part of this territorial instinct. So is the fascination, amounting almost to a public obsession, with house prices. Sometimes I think all Sydney life is governed by the price of property, so inescapable is the subject in conversation and the press, and so obtrusive the hyperbole of the estate agents: The Best Address on Earth, the Quintessential City Terrace, Possibly the Most Eloquently Contemporary Waterfront Residence in the World – Ever. Sydney realtese has a long and often irritating pedigree. When Vaucluse House went on the market in 1838 it was described as 'a splendid and unequalled Marine Estate, commanding a perfect view of the head lands and sinuosities of the various Bays and inlets of the truly romantic Harbour in which it is situated'. A century later D. H. Lawrence saw bungalows advertised as being 4 Sale or 2 Rent: nothing would induce him, he said through his surrogate character Richard Somers in *Kangaroo*, to live in a house thus advertised, especially when it was likely to have a name like Arcady or Racketty-Coo.[1]

Occasionally the fate of a house, its rising or falling value, its varying ownership and its future prospects become part of the general gossip. One recently was Swifts, a mansion on Darling Point said to be the most valuable house in the city. It was built for a nineteenth-century brewer in the Scottish baronial manner, was willed to the Roman Catholic Church as an archiepiscopal residence, and was bought in 1986 by a reclusive and enigmatic racehorse trainer. He paid A$9 million for it and was soon refusing offers of A$38 million, but got into the news when an eighty-four-year-old retired engineer threatened to foreclose on a large debt he said the man owed him. How the press loved it! A huge costly house with statues in the

---

[1] Though Somers did eventually rent Torestin, and the house that Lawrence himself rented at Thirroul, some thirty miles south of Sydney, was called Wyewurk.

garden, a man of mystery connected with the Turf, an aged com-
plainant ('ruining the last years of my life'), the Catholic Church,
padlocked gates, enormous mortgages, vast potential profits – it was all
Sydney wanted of a real estate affair.

Even more popular was the story of Paradis sur Mer, a lavish but
unlovely mansion on Point Piper – One of the World's Great Deep
Waterfront Properties, Unparalleled Panoramic Harbour Views,
Championship Tennis Court, Etc., Etc. This had become famous as
the home of a particularly well-publicized and amusing hostess, several
times married and always to celebrities.[1] It was bought for a fabulous
price, sold even more extravagantly, bought again by a speculator
who lived in it for only three months, at an estimated cost of A$2,000
a day, before selling it once more at a loss of A$3 million. All Sydney
waited to see what would happen next, but when on the following
Sunday people picked up their newspapers, they found that Paradis
sur Mer had been demolished overnight by its latest owner, who
planned to build several more lucrative buildings on the site. Enthusiasts immediately flocked to Point Piper by boat, helicopter and
jet ski, in the hope of picking up souvenirs among the ruins.

Nobody had time to protest about the extinction of Paradis sur
Mer, but furious rearguard actions have been fought in defence of
other properties. For a time the building unions refused to demolish
old buildings in the interest of property developers, and with reason,
for not many cities have been so implacably knocked about by speculators. Phillip wanted most of the present downtown area to be inalienable Crown land for ever, but he misjudged the nature of Sydney,
and two centuries of the market economy have seldom given the city
a breathing space. The old quip about Manhattan, that it will be a
fine place when it's finished, applies still more pertinently here, and I
know of no other city that seems so permanently incomplete.

Whole neighbourhoods were destroyed in the 1930s, when the Harbour Bridge approach-roads were built, and even now it is hard to

[1] When asked what had happened to the last of them, a titled New Zealander, she
said sweetly that he had gone down the plug-hole, back where he came from.

keep up with the topography of the place, so drastically and frequently is it altered in the name of progress or profit. Sometimes buildings disappear almost overnight, sometimes they remain for decades in a limbo of uncertainty. In my time Sydney Cove itself, the historical and aesthetic focus of the entire city, has stood always at half-cock. They spent a decade and more building the Opera House, on the eastern side. They spent years restoring, rebuilding and developing the Rocks, on the western side. They were ages building the new Ocean Terminal. They redesigned the park area. They put in new walkways. 'Revitalizing the Quay', said a sign they put up above an apparently permanently moribund building site near the Opera House. As I write they are completing a harbour tunnel underneath the cove, planning to do away with the tall ugly buildings on the eastern quay, and about to turn the former Maritime Service Board building into a museum of modern art, while from time to time there are suggestions that they might tear down the elevated railway and the Cahill Expressway, and start all over again.[1]

In 1990 a new 'heritage listing' plan proposed that more than a quarter of the downtown city should be declared protected property, not to be demolished: not a single city block would be without a protected building, which would probably make future commercial development more than ever subject to hook, crook and wheeler-dealing. For if some people watch all these developments so passionately because they are concerned about the condition of their city, many others watch because there's big money in it. Sydney people do not seem to me terribly interested in small money, money as such. Easy come, easy go was noted as a Sydney financial maxim at least as early as the 1850s, and foreigners today often marvel at the insouciance of Sydney taxi-drivers, who are not greatly concerned about tips, and indeed often reduce the fare to the nearest round figure. The political

[1] A consummation I myself thought would most satisfactorily celebrate the 1988 Bicentennial.

economist Andrew Wells recently suggested[1] that 'the Sydney style has now elevated all forms of individual accumulation to an ethical imperative'; on the other hand it is said to be relatively easy to push one's way to the top of the plutocracy in Sydney, because so few people can be bothered. I get the impression that citizens are chiefly interested in other people's wealth – not so much in the power of it, either, or the morality, but simply in its ability to dazzle and entertain. The great tycoons of Sydney, however disrespectfully they are treated in the gossip columns, are civic stars really, and the melodramatic spectacles of high finance, the takeover bids, the bankruptcies, the venal internecine feuds, are watched with insatiable fascination.

To be extraordinarily rich is a properly native ambition. In many callings there comes a moment, if you want to be really in the big time, when you must abandon Sydney to practise in Europe or the United States. You can, however, become supremely rich without ever leaving home. Some of the older rich families have mellowed into a conviction of ample superiority, requiring no exhibitionism. Some have put their money out of sight, so to speak, into estates in California, country houses in Hampshire or Paris apartments. But there is something about the flash of Sydney, the easy conceit and the lack of envy, that makes it the perfect setting for extravagance, and it is the lifestyle of the brasher wealthy that seems best suited to this city. The showy carriages of the nineteenth century displayed (as an observer wrote in the 1850s) 'luxury without refinement'; their truest successors are the power-boats which rampage around the harbour today, the perfect images of uninhibited wealth – ostentatious, deafening, socially defiant, totally unnecessary and fun.

Sudden wealth is the thing – not the long slog, but the bonanza. It was always so. The stupendously successful emancipist Solomon Wiseman was asked once if he did not regret his illiteracy. 'What's the use of education,' he retorted, 'when the acquisition of wealth is the main lesson on life?' In 1850 the discovery of gold at Bathurst, beyond the Blue Mountains, galvanized the city: citizens from clergymen to

[1] In *The Sydney–Melbourne Book*, edited by Jim Davidson, Sydney 1986.

labourers rushed off to the diggings, countless firms found themselves
without employees, and there is a splendid picture of the arrival of a
gold transport at the Treasury in 1851 – the clattering cart of treasure
with its top-hatted driver, bearded guards with rifles on their knees,
cavalry men cantering around, the populace gaping and the whole
scene informed with the excitement of instant riches.[1]

The last quarter of the twentieth century, with its emphasis on
theoretical money, has suited Sydney admirably. Fortunes built on
fantasy are very much its style, and in the 1970s and 1980s the whole
paraphernalia of monetarism flourished mightily in this city. When
the character then called the Yuppie first emerged in New York, he
very soon found his clones in Sydney, and long after he fell out of
mode elsewhere his local incarnation thrived. Nobody could be yup-
pier than a Sydney yuppie, nobody's BMW was more carelessly
parked beside the four-wheel-drive in the car-port, nobody's trousers
were more fashionably baggy, nobody flaunted his suspenders more
dashingly, or spoke with such fluency about such multi-digited sums
over cellular telephones in public places.

There is a place called Hopwood's Terrace, at Blue's Point on the
north side of the harbour, where I used to love to watch the yuppies
perform. It is a modest row of buildings of the 1920s, with a quaintly
ornamented roof line and shingled gables here and there, but it has
been trendified. There is an Expo Oz Design House, a boutique, an
advertising agency, Giuseppi's Italian Restaurant and something
called the Image Bank. There is also a pleasant pavement café, and
here the young executives, in the brave days of yuppiedom, loved to
gather for Sunday morning breakfast. One in particular always
engaged my attention. He was an ageing example, balding rather and
a little too plump for the squash court, but he sported a proper
Sunday-morning mode of T-shirt with whales on it, blue shorts and
bare feet, while his companion had her blonde hair in pigtails, and
wore khaki slacks and sandals. Suavely he drank his cappuccino and

[1] Edward Hargraves, discoverer of the goldfields, told his partner as they panned their
first dust: 'I shall be a baronet, you will be knighted, and my old horse will be stuffed,
put in a glass case, and sent to the British Museum.' None of it came true.

ate his croissant. Knowingly but condescendingly he read out bits in the paper about people he knew. If his cellular phone rang he would saunter over to his Porsche talking loudly into his telephone as he went. How largely his laugh used to echo down Blue's Point Road! How unsmilingly *soignée* his woman watched him as he returned still talking and joking across the road to the café, deftly flicking his diary pages as he came – successful, progressive, worldly, barefoot for all to see!

He was a gambler, I suppose, if only a gambler with other people's money, and Sydney has always liked a betting man. Sydney people will wager on almost anything, and as we have seen illegal off-course betting is a vice even among the most homely of linen-hatted senior citizens. Alone among the big Australian cities, except only Canberra the federal capital, Sydney has no casino, but this is not surprising, because in New South Wales there are more poker machines per head (fruit machines, as they are called elsewhere) than anywhere else outside Nevada. In 1976 the money that passed through these devices, the vast majority of them in Sydney, amounted to one-fifth of the entire disposable income of the State; so perhaps the best way nowadays to glimpse the instinct for immediate wealth is not to tour the opulent suburbs, looking for show-off houses, but simply to visit one of the Rugby League social clubs, where Sydney's working people stand hour after hour before the poker machines, the old one-armed bandits, hoping for the sudden thrilling clatter of silver coins that means jackpot: not an estate in the country, perhaps, not a flashy equipage or a power-boat, but at least money for nothing.

To gamblers as to all others, though, the tall-poppy syndrome applies. Many of the entrepreneurs who were Sydney heroes in the 1980s fell upon hard times at the end of the decade, and found themselves plagued by bankruptcies and criminal investigations: the press turned upon them then, and called them collectively Greed Inc.

Sydney has traditionally prided itself upon being a classless society. There are certainly no such obvious emblems of class distinction as

there are in England, no such fearful contrasts between rich and poor
as one sees in the United States. Slums are rare, the standard of living
is high, and there are no more than a dozen families of any dynastic
pretension. Houses generally pass from hand to quite unrelated hand.
There is one called Mort's Cottage, in Double Bay, whose history has
been meticulously recorded by its present owner.[1] Its owners and
occupiers have included a grocer, an umbrella-and-parasol-maker, a
celebrated industrialist, a pioneering woman physician and John
Tawell, the emancipated forger whose opulent dinner-party we
glimpsed a few pages back. Egalitarianism has always been a Sydney
brag: it was said of the Anzac soldiers in the First World War that
they had never in their lives known what it was to be given a direct
order, 'undisguised by a "you might" or a "would you mind"'.[2]

Nevertheless class always counted strongly in the style of Sydney, as
it did everywhere the British trod. Hardly had the colony been
founded than it evolved class distinctions of its own. There were the
administrators and military officers – the official Establishment. There
were the Sterlings or Exclusives, the English-born free settlers – the
colonial gentry. There were the Pure Merinos, the sheep graziers who
saw themselves as the county folk of Sydney. There were the Currency
Lads and Lasses, white people born in Australia, whose nickname
implied a coinage good only in the colony. There were the emancipists
who were ex-convicts, and their sub-kind the more modest Dungaree
Settlers. There were the Ticket-of-Leave men who were more or less
on parole. There were the convicts, who included gentlemen-felons
called Specials, and who preferred to be known as Exiles, Government
men or Empire-builders. And there were the Aborigines, grounding
at the very bottom in that lowest of the lowest of Sydney society, the
black woman. 'Ladies, Gentlemen or Others', was the formula used in
the small advertisements of the day.

Much of all this was based upon English precedents, and English
social values were often anomalously applied – one can imagine how

---

[1] In *Mort's Cottage*, by Jill Buckland, Sydney 1988.
[2] By C. E. W. Bean, in the *Official History of Australia in the War of 1914–18*.

bitter was the sense of caste among the twenty-seven free women
who arrived with the 750 felons of the First Fleet, and how reluctant
they must have been to employ convict wet-nurses. Those
gentlemen-convicts were put into a special camp, where unfrocked
clergymen, cashiered officers, disgraced lawyers and exposed bankers
got special treatment. One such was the naval officer John Knatch-
bull, member of an ancient Kent family.[1] Dismissed the service for
behaviour unbecoming an officer, this patent psychopath was transported in 1825 for picking a pocket in London, but was not
deterred. He beat a man to death on the voyage out. He tried to
poison the entire crew of the ship taking him to Norfolk Island. He
murdered a woman with a tomahawk. Yet he was given his own
servant on the journey to Botany Bay (the man he beat to death)
and to the very day of his eventual execution, by hanging in Sydney
in 1844, he was surrounded by suggestions of aristocratic privilege.
Lady Gipps the Governor's wife herself was supposed to have
agitated for his reprieval, and when he went to his death nevertheless he was wearing a handsome new suit allegedly supplied, for the
sake of his class, by Her Excellency.

Then there was Sir Henry Browne Hayes, an Anglo-Irish squire
transported for fourteen years in 1801 for having abducted an heiress.
As one of life's irrepressible rebels Hayes did endure hardships during
his sentence, spending some time in the penal coal mines at Newcastle,
100 miles up the coast from Sydney, and some on Norfolk Island; he
once complained querulously that St Patrick took no more notice of
his prayers than if he were 'some wretched thief in a road-gang with
manacles on my legs'. For the most part, though, he was allowed to
live as a gentleman should, attended by the valet he had brought
with him from Ireland. He bought some land on the southern harbour
shore, used the labour of fellow-convicts to build an agreeable stone
house upon it, and filled a ditch all around with 150 tons of specially
imported Irish peat, to keep the snakes out. Pardoned in 1812 by the
intervention of the Prince Regent, Hayes returned none the worse for

[1] Into which Lord Mountbatten later married.

his experiences to live happily ever after at his delightful family mansion in County Cork.[1]

On the other side of the legal fence, but equally advantaged by his rank, was Sir Frederick Pottinger, Baronet, a Pottinger of the Berkshire Pottingers, whose father was the first Governor of Hong Kong and whose cousin Eldred, 'Pottinger of Herat', was a celebrated hero of the Indian frontier wars. Sir Frederick seems to have been a true-born failure. Getting into money difficulties in his late twenties, in 1860 he resigned his commission in the Coldstream Guards and enlisted as a trooper in the New South Wales Mounted Police, employed in rounding up the outlaws known in Australia as bushrangers. Although very soon promoted to sub-inspector, when his baronetcy was inadvertently discovered, he was famously ineffective in this role, his failure to catch one popular villain being immortalized in a Sydney ballad:

> Sir Frederick Pott shut his eyes for the shoot
> And missed in the usual way.
> But the ranger proud, he laughed aloud,
> And bounding rode away!

But if Pottinger seldom succeeded in shooting a bushranger, in the end this hapless toff succeeded in fatally shooting himself, accidentally with his own revolver while boarding a coach. Through it all he remained the patrician anyway, and Sydney recognized it. His deathbed was in his own room at the Victoria Club, and his funeral was attended by the Premier of New South Wales.

Some of the colonial gentry were bemused by English social pretensions. It was wonderful how many of the early free settlers in this remarkably uninviting colony seem to have been related to lairds and baronets at home, or had grown up on grand family estates. In 1853 William Charles Wentworth, one of the colony's most forceful politicians, actually proposed the establishment of a formal New South Wales aristocracy, with its own ranks of nobility ('Botany Bay Barons',

[1] Vernon Mount, more recently the headquarters of the Munster Motor Cycle and Car Club.

his opponents mocked); and when in the following year a Voluntary Artillery Corps was formed 'among the young gentlemen in the service of Government', it was assumed that paid help would be found to clean the guns. Landowners, in particular, very soon acquired lofty airs. In 1838 a new church was opened at Cook's River, four miles from Sydney Cove, the celebratory buffet was served in three sessions, just as in Old England – the first for the carriage folk, the second for the local farmers, the third for the workmen who had built the church.

Many shoots of snobbism took root, from a general toadying to visiting nobility to a preoccupation with suitable dress. The apparatus of visiting cards and proper introductions was rigorously upheld. The Bank of Australia (founded by graziers) was the bank for gentlemen, the Bank of New South Wales (tainted by convict association) the bank for the people. It was not the done thing to walk in the Domain on Sundays, because maidservants and their boyfriends went there. In 1838 a citizen was ejected from the Queen's Birthday Ball at Government House on the grounds that during his military service he had been only a sergeant-major: he argued in vain that he had married the daughter of a lieutenant. When in 1843 the first Lord Mayor of Sydney threw a popular fancy-dress ball on behalf of his newly formed City Council, many of the city fashionables declined to come – they were, as a contemporary satirist wrote,

> All pure merinos, trained to keep
> Their distance from your coarse-woolled sheep.

There is plenty of snobbery still, too, whether it be expressed in footling dress codes at jumped-up pubs, or in the parade of bigwigs in medals, orders and tiaras which preens itself whenever royalty is around. It is not entirely a desire for an excellent education, we may be sure, which ensures that the great Sydney private schools have waiting lists of thousands, and anyone who thinks this is a city beyond convention should read the ten-page dress code issued to women lawyers in 1990 by one of its best-known firms. Long-sleeved blouses, says this ineffable directive, 'convey the most credible image', and with them suits must be worn, preferably navy-blue, black or charcoal-grey (their jackets to be buttoned when standing, unbuttoned when sitting) together with anti-static slips five centimetres shorter than their skirts . . .

One of the sillier Sydney modes, copied like many another from Manhattan, divides restaurants into fashionable and unfashionable segments – some tables desirable and frequented by the famous, some (collectively nicknamed Siberia) absolutely unacceptable if you have any sense of status. On the face of it one table generally looks to the uninitiated very much like another, and it was fun when a mischievous journalist published table-plans of the trendiest Sydney eating-houses, clearly demarcating their Siberias, and puncturing not a few complacencies.

Where one lives is also more socially important in Sydney than in most cities of my acquaintance. It was a long time before an emancipated convict, however rich, was able to build himself a house on the harbour front, and those sprawling suburbs are largely identified by class.[1] I am told the districts used to be less homogeneous, most communities including people of all ages and all kinds. Now sociologists say that to a degree unexampled elsewhere they specialize in old residents or young, rich or poor, immigrant or native-born. Social maps of the city, delineating its character by blodges of colour, show heavy concentrations of blue (the rich colour) in the northern and eastern suburbs, wide examples of red ('relatively poor' is as far as the sociologists will go) in the south and west. Even within the blue there are differentiations – the north-shore suburbs are the place for high earning power, the eastern suburbs for great assets.

Some suburbs are of course still socially mixed: opposite an attractive row of small villas in Newtown I noticed one day a graffito saying GARBAGE-SUCKING SCUM LIVE HERE. Others are in a state of fierce social flux, as the energy of the market shifts their condition: the sociologist Peter Spearitt wrote in 1986 that 'when Sydney gentrifiers

[1] Hence the old Sydney nicknames for first and tourist sections on aircraft – 'Vaucluse' and 'Woolloomooloo'.

invade a working-class Sydney suburb they know no mercy'.[1] Others again maintain their social reputations more or less inviolate down the generations. La Perouse, down on Botany Bay, has never been able to escape its multiple social disadvantages (an Aboriginal settlement, a prison, toxic inductions and an unlovely setting) while any Sydney citizen has a mental image of the kind of person you are likely to be, if you say you live in Double Bay, St Ives or Granville.[2] 'This is not a baby area,' an acquaintance of mine was told decisively by a shop assistant, when she asked for bottled food in North Sydney.

A charmer among these perennials is Hunters Hill, one of the most self-contained and gentlemanly of the suburbs. It is not on the flashier reaches of the harbour, but lies west of the bridge, where the Lane Cove River meets the Parramatta, and is compactly tucked away on a spit of land between the rivers. It is ranked only twenty-eighth in the suburban-opulence roster, and is the smallest local-government area in Sydney, but it is said that hardly anybody moves out of the place, so stable and village-like is its character. It has a town hall, and a tea-shop, and a post office with a postmaster in blue shorts and spectacles. It has lots of trees, verandas, cats, garden-seats and narrow bosky lanes, together with a bowls club and, inevitably, CRUSH – Concerned Residents Under Siege in Hunters Hill. In Hunters Hill you see very old ladies being helped through garden gates by solicitous sons, and high-spirited children with trim satchels being met at school by personable young mothers in Volvos. After the Beijing massacre in 1989 the municipal council of this civilized community predictably declined to endorse a planned visit to China by one of its staff members: the People's Republic of China accused Hunters Hill of interfering in Chinese affairs and being friendly to criminals and law-breakers – charges received with perfect equanimity, I would imagine, by its burghers, and described by its Mayor merely as being 'a little harsh'.

Nothing much changes in Hunters Hill. Everything has changed in

[1] In his contribution to Jim Davidson's *The Sydney–Melbourne Book*.
[2] Double Bay very glitzy; St Ives very conservative; Granville – well: Q. What's there to do in Granville? A. Go up to the Parramatta Road to watch the cars go by.

Balmain, which occupies another peninsula not far away across the harbour. Balmain began life as the first commuter suburb, to be reached by boat from the city centre, and in mid-Victorian times it was a favoured residential area for the bourgeoisie. In the 1850s, however, a shipyard was opened there, with a dry dock and large repair yards, and Balmain was proletarianized. Hundreds of workers' cottages were built, dozens of pubs arose. By 1920 the Balmain Council was ambiguously declaring that Balmain's 'industrial qualifications far surpass those of its residential claims' – which meant that it had become dirty, smoky, over-crowded and of low taxable value. By 1953 all the aldermen of the local council had been removed from office because of corruption, and a powerful criminal underworld had set up shop in the place.

Now the dry dock is only a memory, the Balmain Mafia is said to be dispersed, and the suburb has once again been transformed. It is still an untidy congeries of hilly streets, pub-speckled and poor in parts, but long ago the lift-off of gentrification occurred. Little workmen's cottages are pretty with trellis-work and bougainvillaea. Pubs are popular with young accountants. Authors write novels, and at the bottom of steep lanes down to the water handsome launches stand on slipways. Chic invests the town centre, where there are Japanese restaurants and real-estate offices and gourmet shops and alternative-medicine surgeries and a Float-Tank Centre. When I looked in one morning to catch an assault case in the magistrate's court, in this once notorious hive of criminals, the victim failed to appear, the defendant could not be found, the police had no evidence to offer and I was the only spectator in court.

Bondi, on the ocean, is another readily categorized suburb.[1] Densely clustered around its celebrated sand and surf, a mass of red-tiled bungalows and modest high-rise apartment blocks, it has long been strongly Jewish and is now popular with New Zealanders, especially Maoris. Its famous promenade is dull and shabby – to most foreigners,

---

[1] Its name is pronounced Bon-dye, and is said to be an economical Aboriginal word meaning 'the sound of waves breaking on the beach'.

one of the great disappointments of Sydney – but it remains on the whole a frank, hail-fellow kind of place, where fundamental Oz survives the assaults of gentrification, cosmopolitanism and changing morality: middle-class, middle-income, middle-of-the-road, and for all its plethora of faces and languages, unmistakably Australian.

On the other hand Chippendale, an enclave near the University of Sydney, is decidedly *un*-classifiable. This a small oblong bounded by four noisy city streets, and though its own main street is called Myrtle Street, and is crossed by Rose Street, and bounded by Pine, it is uncompromisingly urban. Originally industrial, its architecture is unnoticeable, but its atmosphere is famously tolerant and eclectic. Chippendale is very tight-knit, very much its own place, coloured on those maps a poorish red but in fact housing people of all kinds. I went to dinner there one evening at the house of one of Australia's most distinguished authors. My fellow-guests, all near neighbours, included a politically active lawyer, another writer and two artists, and the food was brought in from the take-away Lebanese restaurant around the corner. After dinner my host took me a little way down the road to show me the site, perfectly located between a side alley and one of those busy boundary highways, of a well-publicized recent murder.

The name of Mount Druitt, in the west, has lately been adopted by the press as a synonym for working-class Sydney – distinctly red on the social map, where the poor bloody taxpayer lives, where the archetypal voter waits to be polled, where the cannon-fodder would come from in a war. It is quite a pleasant place on the way to the Blue Mountains, but has an obscurely makeshift feeling to it – something messy, something temporary, with muddled shacks here and there, and more rubbish than is usual in this city. I take this to be because it is out here in the western suburbs that Sydney's newcomers generally settle, on their way they hope to bluer parts. Some such western suburbs have been utterly metamorphosed by the latest waves of Asian immigration. Cabramatta in particular seems for the moment at least to have been altogether detached from the rest of Sydney. Its centre is an ordinary enough commercial fulcrum in a lightly modernist style, but walking through it is precisely like walking through a provincial town in one of the more stable and prosperous countries of east Asia. Hardly a face, young or old, is not oriental. Whole classes of Vietnamese schoolchildren pass by. Vietnamese housewives emerge from every shop. There are smells of Asian cooking, sounds of Asian music. The population is very young, scrupulously clean, and impeccably tidy, as though it has been expressly selected to inhabit a model town. Here and there one sees elderly white Australians bewilderedly wandering, as if in foreign territory.

Still, when all is said, on the whole this is a naturally sociable and egalitarian city. There is a statue of Burns in the Domain, and though he might have laughed at Sydney's streak of social sycophancy, and would probably have been shocked by its racism, I think he would have agreed that here a man generally is a man for a' that. 'Now girls, remember they're not all for you,' said a waiter at an excessively modish Sydney banquet, placing a box of dessert chocolates between me and an even maturer and far grander dame. Before very long those Cabramatta Asians will doubtless be talking Sydney English, and stylistically this famous dialect is the great binding force of the city. To foreign ears its sinewy sounds perfectly vocalize the place, and also seem more absolutely Australian than any others. The Australian vernacular was born here, after all, and it was Professor Afferbeck Lauder of Sinney University who first codified it.[1] Sydney English is strong, strident and lively – not as creative as the street-talk of California or black America, but still always on the move.

It began with Cockney thieves' slang of the eighteenth century, the half-secret argot of the English underworld. This was brought out in many varieties and in full flow by the convicts of the First Fleet, and was doubtless crossed *en voyage* with elements of Anglo-Irish and English provincial dialects. Tench called it the 'flash' or 'kiddy' language. It was 'infatuating cant', he thought, so obscure that it was sometimes

[1] In *Let's Stalk Strine*, Sydney 1965, a book described in its foreword as 'above all, minatory and warmly human'. The Professor's *alter ego* is Alastair Morrison.

necessary to have interpreters in courts, and its eradication among the convicts would 'open the path to reformation'. Not a hope! The language of their origin, craft and brotherhood was the one possession the convicts inviolably held, and they bequeathed its vigour and its potency to the free generations that succeeded them – perhaps its guild qualities too, for when in 1990 a crooked doctor and a bent solicitor were taped talking to each other about criminal ventures, they were found to converse in a semi-illiterate underworld jargon. In earlier years the Sydney dialect included cryptic elements of rhyme, like the East End slang of London: to go to the barber was to go down to Sydney Harbour, Jimmy Grants were immigrants.[1]

Sydney English has never lost its Cockney twang, though its vowels have grown broader as the generations have passed, and its inflections have shifted.[2] The language is perhaps not so witty as Sydney citizens often suppose it to be. Much of it consists of an infantile preference for cosy abbreviation, so that a can of beer is a tinny, a bathing-costume is a cozzy, a U-turn is a U-ie, sickies means sick leave, a pollie is a politician, a lippie is a lipstick, a westy is someone from the western suburbs, a Greenie is somebody supportive of natural conservation, a ute (short for utility) is a pick-up truck, Darlo is Darlinghurst, Paddo is Paddington, and brekkie, bikey and boaty are perhaps sufficiently puerile to be self-explanatory. Nor is the vocabulary of man-in-the-street discourse very striking, its chief characteristic being an ineradicable fondness for the endearment 'Mate'. The humorist Nino Culotta (alias John O'Grady) published his book *They're a Weird Mob* in 1957,

[1] It also included, of course, lots of homely English idioms. When in the 1890s the infant son of the British commanding admiral in Sydney heard a coachman say 'Ups a daisy' as he lifted a bag, he asked his elder brother what it meant. 'He told me, with a certain scorn at my not knowing, that it was a very nice thing to say & you always said it on such occasions.' (From the unpublished memoirs of Sir David Montagu Douglas Scott, 1985.)

[2] Semanticists believe it to have been influenced recently by the presence of so many New Zealanders in the city, so that Sydney people are more likely nowadays to drop their Ls, saying 'miuwk' for example instead of 'milk', and to flatten their vowels in some special way, so as to pronounce 'six fat fish' as 'sux fet fush'. These are permutations too subtle for my ear.

but his reported greeting between two working men still rings true
today:

> ''Ow yer goin' mate orright?'
> 'Yeah mate. 'Ow yer goin' orright?'
> 'Orright mate.'

Nicknames and idioms are far better. Sydney has always loved
them. Long ago immigrant girls used to be given the names of the
ships they had arrived on, like Matilda Agamemnon, or Susan Red
Rover, while for years Sydney policemen were nicknamed Israelites
because most of them had sailed out from England on board the
Exodus. Criminals, hermits and general originals have always been
given colourful sobriquets, too, from old ones like Whaler Joe, Sudden
Solomon, the Earl and Rock Lizard to Tom the Terror, Abo Henry or
Disco George today. I like the words 'bubbler' for a drinking fountain,
'bludger' for lazy, 'chook' for a chicken, 'hoon' for a street hoodlum
(formerly 'larrikin'), 'Cocky' (short for cockatoo) for a small farmer,
and hence 'Cockies' Joy' for golden syrup.[1] I am intrigued by the use
of 'identity' to mean 'personality' – a TV identity, a Colourful Racing
Identity. A sly-grog shop beautifully describes, it seems to me, premises
illegally selling alcohol. Nine Nuns in a Rugby Scrum nicely sums up
the Opera House, the Coathanger is perfect for the Harbour Bridge,
the Sydney Tower really does look just like a Plunger. To perve
almost onomatopoeically expresses looking at someone libidinously.
Silvertails is a good word for the well-heeled, rorting is horribly
expressive of fiddling the accounts, dobbing someone in is better than
telling tales on them, Pom really does fit many kinds of Englishmen,
Dinky-di encapsulates the purest kind of Australianness, and I know of
no handier way of explaining your daughter's resident boyfriend than
calling him her *de facto* – a euphemism which seems to have been in
use since the first days of convict registration. Often and again Sydney
citizens surprise one with a quaint or apposite usage. 'Take a squiz,'
says the shopgirl, inviting you to look around. 'She's a rural,' says a

---

[1] Although the farmers share this enthusiasm with the Aboriginal people – and
emphatically with me.

schoolgirl of a friend visiting from the countryside. 'It's ticking like buggery now,' says a patient after a heart operation. 'Sydney's going down the gurgler,' says a businessman complaining about interest rates. 'Rugby's getting a bit robust,' says a sportsman who disapproves of violence on the field. Sometimes such turns of phrase are given sanction, if not permanency, by the news media – weather forecasters prophesying a beaut, a bonzer or a bottler, or the *Sydney Morning Herald* reporting on the problems of bikies in city traffic.

Built into this language is a caustic humour that is as old as the city itself. Sometimes it shows itself in pungent invective – a politician may be likened to a human suitcase, characterized as an archetypal son-in-law or be accused of having 'all the menace of a tea-urn'. Sometimes it is just gently sardonic. When there was a search for an official tourist slogan for Sydney, someone suggested SYDNEY - SUN, SIN AND SEWAGE: and the pupils of one of the Sydney schools have themselves translated their school motto, 'I Hear, I See, I Learn', into the Latinism 'Audio, Video, Disco'.[1]

Donald Horne the political scientist called Australia the Lucky Country, and except during the city's cyclical periods of depression most Sydney people would probably accept the description. They are lucky and they know it, to live upon this generous and generally even-tempered shore. 'No worries', is Sydney's habitual nonchalant assurance, 'not a problem'. Fortunately the consciousness of good fortune has not made the people smug, and even now they are inno-cently anxious to cast a happy impression, to show their city in the best light and prove it World Class.

The chief people-watching site in Sydney is unquestionably Circular Quay, which offers a kaleidoscopic view of the generic Sydney style, leavened by coveys of tourists, but representative of most kinds and classes. Here we may see the last of the Dinky-di Aussies, in their

[1] Though to be honest I suspect the most truly contemporary Sydney phrase I came across during the writing of this book was displayed on a board by a girl waving goodbye to a departing warship: LUV YA BRUGIE.

shorts and long socks, sometimes wearing bush hats and bearing themselves with a touch of bravado, like the kilted and sporraned Scotsmen who parade the streets of Edinburgh. Here we may see the Sydney office population *en masse* – on the whole a healthy, good-looking population, moving vigorously, laughing a lot. There are workmen with majestic beer-bellies, sitting on their haunches eating fruit, and ladies who are dressed as for royal garden-parties, but are probably just going shopping. Groups of semi-punks sometimes meander through, with yellow hair, silver-buttoned jackets and T-shirts incomprehensibly sloganed. A postman lopes past in bush hat and shorts, with a rucksack of mail on his back. Here and there along the quay solitary fishermen, in anoraks and baseball caps, bait their hooks with chunks of fish from plastic buckets. Around the corner at the oyster-bar businessmen are getting slowly and pleasurably sloshed on wine, beer, prawns and sunshine.

It is a great place for buskers. There is a Japanese playing *Danny Boy* on a kind of zither, and a very slow-motion go-go dancer in a yellow straw hat. A serious young woman plays Bach on her clarinet. A black comedian raises a burst of laughter along by Pier 4, and an evangelist maintains that One Cannot Live Without God ('quite untrue', loudly and briskly retorts a man in a dark suit as he hastens by without a pause). Somewhere somebody is winding up his bagpipes. Towards the Opera House we may see a dark-haired girl, ten or eleven years old perhaps, playing *Waltzing Matilda* earnestly on her violin; her even smaller brother waits to turn over the page of her music (bound, we may note, in the Australian flag) while looking up into her face in just the pose of a small Renaissance cherub, in the foreground of a masterpiece.

All around us people are pottering about, or enjoying a late breakfast with the morning paper, or consulting their guide-book maps, or exchanging computer files over omelettes and white wine, or strolling with beach gear and snorkels towards the Manly ferry. Except at rush hours, when waves of commuters come pouring through the ferry turnstiles, people are not half so agitated here as they are at most such city hubs. If they miss one boat they can always get the next. There is

a train every few minutes. Another coffee? Why not, the office can
wait. All through its history Sydney has been characterized as essentially easygoing, and easygoing it remains. It is a metropolis of the
lucky country – lucky to get away with it.

PEOPLE

1. Majorities

THE PEOPLE OF SYDNEY ARE SOMETIMES CALLED SYDNEY-siders. Nobody is quite sure why. Some theorists believe it originally meant people living on the north or Sydney side of the Murray River, as against the south or Melbourne side, while others think it merely referred to transported convicts – they were sent to the Botany Bay side of the world, and later the Sydney side, as American servicemen went home Stateside. Whatever its origins, it suits them. The word is sturdy, explicit and satisfied, and so on the whole are the people. Sydneysiders *en masse* are more easily recognizable, I think, than the inhabitants of most big cosmopolitan cities. Stylistically, historically and topographically theirs is a town of potent personality, and two centuries of settlement have created a citizenry to match.

Once almost entirely of stock from the British Isles, now embracing Greeks, Italians, Yugoslavs, Vietnamese, Maltese, Thais, Turks,

Lebanese, Russians, Hungarians, Syrians and scions of almost every other race you care to mention, *homo Sydneyaticus*, whether male or female, has been moulded generation by generation into a species of its own. Sometimes I think it is the natural successor to the New Man travellers thought they found in the North America of the nineteenth century; perhaps it is even the celestial race that the poet Bernard O'Dowd hoped might evolve in Australia.[1] The climate of this city, the food, the fresh air, the space and the general ease of living soon mutates peoples of very disparate roots into a recognizable kind – small island Greeks become husky, women whose parents lived wan in Lancashire become marvellous golden girls, and it seems to take no time at all for a slender Italian to become a whole-hog beer-swilling Aussie. If I spend too long in Sydney I sometimes develop recognizable Sydneyside symptoms myself.

By now this is a self-generating species. Immigrants still come, but since 1981 more than half the people of Sydney have been Australian-born to two Australian parents. Short of some cataclysmic ethnic convulsion or climatic reverse, the young native-born Sydneysider of today is likely to be, so to speak, definitive. The mutation is, however, as much temperamental as physical. Sydney's origins have influenced the city's style, and I suspect they have profoundly influenced its psyche too. It took guts to get to Sydney in the first place, whether you came free or manacled in a convict ship. It took patience or cunning to endure captivity, and spirit to defy it. Force of character, if nothing better, was necessary to administer the convict community, and a thick skin, if nothing worse, to act as its gaolers. Complex feelings of rivalry, scorn and rejection governed early relations with the Aborigines. Only a keen eye for the main chance could exploit Sydney's early disadvantages, and a fine discrimination between anarchy and discipline was necessary to evolve a free society out of a prison. All these characteristics are still apparent among the mass of

[1] Last sea-thing dredged by sailor Time from Space,/Are you a drift Sargasso, where the West/In halcyon calm rebuilds her fatal nest?/Or Delos of a coming Sun-God's race?

the Sydneysiders, passed down the generations through the collective
unconscious.

D. H. Lawrence said that Sydney had no rulers. He meant that it had
no hereditary élite, but of course it always had a governing stratum of
rich and powerful people. In the very beginning they formed a military
oligarchy – the first nine Governors of New South Wales were all
naval or military men – and later they evolved into a tough civil
Establishment of officials and private citizens. They were the recognizable progenitors of contemporary Sydney's upper crust, and they are
often honoured in retrospect, at least by the more old-fashioned popular historians, with the sobriquet Father of This or That. Here are
half a dozen examples:
¶   The unchallengeable Father of Sydney was Arthur Phillip, RN
(1738–1814). His power over the original community was absolute,
thousands of miles as he was from the nearest superior authority,
and his commission was described at the time as 'a more unlimited
one than was ever before granted to any governor under the British
Crown'. He could be arbitrary when his temper was aroused; when
one of his servants was murdered by Aborigines he ordered a puni-
tive expedition to behead ten natives in reprisal, bringing the heads
back to him.[1] On the whole, though, he exerted his autocracy tem-
perately. A small man, with a small, sensitive, melancholy face,
childless from two marriages, he was the son of a German language
teacher and his English wife, and during periods of half-pay in his
long naval career had twice been seconded to the Portuguese Navy.
This perhaps gave him a wider perspective than most of his con-
temporaries (and experience as it happened of transporting convicts
– to Brazil). From the start he saw Sydney as potentially 'the most
valuable acquisition Great Britain ever made', and, sticking to this
conviction against all odds, he went home to London sick and ex-

[1] Later he relented, and said that two should be shot and four sent to Norfolk Island;
but the only native the Marines of the expedition could find was an old friend of
theirs, so nobody was punished at all.

hausted after four years on the job. When he died in Bath in 1814
Sydney was well on the way to a fine future, but he seems to have
died a sad man anyway, by crashing his wheelchair through an
upstairs window, perhaps on purpose.[1] 'A good man', is how Lord
Nelson simply described the Father of Sydney, and 200 years later
Sydney generally agrees.

¶ Lachlan Macquarie (1761–1824), the first soldier-Governor, was
a Hebridean with a sufficient conceit of himself: there are twenty-
three streets named either Lachlan or Macquarie in Greater Sydney,
together with nine Roads, seven Avenues, five Places, two Groves, a
Drive, a Close, a Terrace, a Circuit, a University and a Shopping
Centre. He had served in the American War of Independence and for
many years in India, and sounds a pompous but generally kindly
man, of relatively liberal views, who believed that the future of the
colony lay above all in the hands of the emancipated convicts. He
invited ex-prisoners to functions at Government House, he patronized
the forger-architect Francis Greenway, and a blackmailer-poet named
Michael Massey Robinson became his unofficial poet-laureate.[2] Macquarie was sporadically sympathetic to Aborigines and beautified the
colony with his building programme. Nevertheless he made many
enemies – among the free settlers and the military officers, who
thought him soft on criminals, sentimental about blacks and a threat
to their own fortunes, among his superiors in London, who thought
him irresponsible and extravagant. In the end he was accused by an
imperial Commissioner of unwarranted expenditure on public works,
and went home bitter and disappointed, though fulsomely remembered in modern Sydney: he looks from his portrait a Scotsman
through and through, and he lies on the Isle of Mull beneath the
appositely presumptuous inscription FATHER OF AUSTRALIA.

[1] Certainly he is not buried in his own parish church in Bath (he lived in Bennett
Street, near The Circus), but at Bathampton on the outskirts of the town, now the
site of an annual Australia Day pilgrimage.
[2] And his eulogist – 'His glowing Heart, at Mercy's Pleadings mov'd,/Shares, as He
yields the Boon to Worth approv'd:–/Wipes the big Drop from Sorrow's glittering
Eye,/And opens the blest Path to Liberty . . .'

¶ The first, most thrusting and most unappealing of the Sydney tycoons was John Macarthur (1766–1834), Father of the Australian Sheep Industry. Son of a Plymouth draper, he came to Sydney in 1790 as paymaster of the New South Wales Corps, and soon made himself a fortune on the side. He became a landowner, a hugely successful businessman and a pioneering sheep-breeder. He built Elizabeth Farm, which we visited at Parramatta two chapters back, naming it for his much more engaging wife Elizabeth Veale, and he had visions of himself as a dynastic gentleman – the Macarthurs considered themselves descendants of King Arthur. He behaved all his life, though, like a vulgar parvenu. He quarrelled constantly, fighting a duel with his own commanding officer, leading the rebellion against Bligh, plotting against Macquarie and calling those he disliked Reptiles, Bloodsuckers or Cockatrices. He himself was nicknamed The Perturbator. Abnormally splenetic always, he went mad in the end, estranged from his unfortunate wife but able to fulfil his last ambition by supervising the building of the great mansion, Camden Park, which he envisaged for his descendants – a properly Sydney denouement to an archetypically Sydney life.

¶ Benjamin Boyd (1800–51), who might be called the Father of the Sydney Takeover, breezed into the city terrifically in 1842, sailing his magnificent armed yacht *Wanderer* through the Heads with an escort of four less glamorous vessels carrying his supplies and possessions. He had launched a bank in London to finance development in Australia, and he fell flamboyantly upon the New South Wales economy, acquiring thousands of acres of farmland, promoting whaling and export–import businesses and importing South Pacific islanders as indentured labour. For a few years he was one of Sydney's heroes, like one of the fabulously successful corporate raiders of the 1980s, but before long his whole showy construction began to unravel. Of course he turned out to have been cooking the books, his ventures were spectacularly in debt, his bank presently collapsed, his indentured-labour scheme was exposed as the next worst thing to slavery, and he sailed away again in the *Wanderer* for the California oilfields. Sydney never saw him again, for in pursuance of a later dream to establish a private kingdom among the Papuans he vanished without trace in the Solomon Islands, very likely eaten by cannibals.[1]

¶ Robert Campbell (1769–1846), very Scottish, very canny, very pugnacious, very efficient, was the Father of Australian Commerce. Campbell arrived in Sydney in 1798. He had family interests in Calcutta, and based his fortune upon the growing trade between Sydney and British India. His ships became familiar throughout the eastern seas, and his warehouses and fine house on the western arm of Sydney Cove were dominant buildings of early Sydney – Campbell's Cove it remains to this day. Campbell bred Arabian horses, imported Brahman cattle, kept peacocks, supported Bligh in his squabble with the officer corps and was in general an unimpeachably useful citizen, besides being enormously rich – the sort who gets honorary degrees nowadays from the University of New South Wales, and attends gala performances at the Opera House.

¶ Thomas Mort (1816–78) celebrated his twenty-first birthday on the ship coming out from England. 'Of a truth,' he wrote then, 'the sun had put on his most splendid and magnificent attire to grace my manhood's dawn. I hoped it was a bright omen of future Success.' He gave it a capital S, and it came true. Mort became the Father of the Australian Meat Industry by introducing refrigerated ship services to England, and he built the dry dock at Balmain, and founded sundry marine repair companies and engineering works and auction houses and real-estate concerns, and built himself a mansion at Darling Point. He had advanced ideas for the welfare of his workers, and was considered a model Sydneysider – there is a grateful statue of him in downtown Sydney still. For myself, all the same, I am rather haunted by his report on a visit to the Destitute Children's Asylum in the suburb of Randwick, which he contemplated as the convenient nucleus of a silk industry. The Asylum offered three great advantages, he told his fellow-promoters: ground for the planting of mulberry trees, a big room for the silkworms, and 'the labour of the children free' – three very important items, emphasized the philanthropist.

*

[1] The lovely *Wanderer* sailed on without him, to be wrecked off Port Macquarie, north of Sydney, and coveted by putative salvagers ever since.

There are still no Sydney rulers in quite Lawrence's sense. There are
people with non-hereditary British titles, bestowed upon them before
New South Wales abandoned the imperial honours system, and people
who are members of the Order of Australia, and put the letters AC,
AO, or AM after their names. There are people, naturally, who are
richer or better educated than the average. But except among first-
generation immigrants there are no obvious distinctions of accent or
physique, and stripped of their clothes on a beach Sydneysiders look
beyond social analysis; gone are the stooped shoulders and rickety legs
of the European poor, and a patrician presence means nothing in a
crowd of magnificently bronzed and muscular surfers. Physically at
least this really is a city of equals.

But here as everywhere there is an élite all the same, and I often see
in it shadows of the early Sydney society. The first thing that strikes
me is its proximity. It is not in the least remote. The political Establishment is as immediately to hand as it was in the days when the
Governors occupied their first little mansion above the Cove. Three-
quarters of the population of New South Wales lives in Sydney, its
capital, and this makes the place much like a City–State, with its
Head of State always on view, if not actually next door. Everyone
knows the Premier, knows where he lives, knows his origins, knows a
tale or two about his imprudences or his peccadilloes and seldom
hesitates to tell it. Also there are generally a few ex-Premiers around,
making the presence of power more familiar still, and it is surprising
how often women one meets turn out to have been, at one time or
another, their wives.

The very rich, too, are as inescapable now as they were in the early
days. People talk of them familiarly. They are not distant figures of
legend, as they so often are in London or New York. They are like
bank managers in some much more modest city, or perhaps squires in
an English market town, so that the X. family house is pointed out to
visitors in passing, the Y. family boat seems known to all, and the
very day I lunched with one of Sydney's more influential editors he
got a personal note from his proprietor, one of the richest men in
Australia, giving him the immediate sack, effective that afternoon –

what could be more proximate than that? In a downtown department store I once came across the former châtelaine of Paradis
sur Mer, making a charity appearance at a cosmetic counter and
surrounded by admiring middle-aged women. She welcomed them
like the lady of the manor at a fête, and they responded, it seemed
to me, with familiar affection. 'There's our Susan,' I heard one
woman say to her companion, as they hastened excitedly towards the
presence.

The moneyed and powerful of contemporary Sydney are often
almost allegorically moneyed and powerful. When I first went to
Sydney its rich women, in particular, had a famously scornful expression of face, noted by many observers: it was said of the novelist
Patrick White's mother (née Withycombe and granddaughter of a
Somerset inn-keeper) that her mouth was 'permanently set at twenty
past seven'.[1] Above the main door of the Customs House, on Circular
quay, the architect James Barnet put a bust of the young Queen
Victoria which immortalizes that particular Sydney look, and it is
also to be seen in some of the portraits in the New South Wales Art
Gallery (including at least one self-portrait). It is mercifully out of
fashion now, but there is still no denying a predatory character to the
Sydney élite. A hint of steel-within-the-velvet-glove characterizes its
social style, and I would not care to make enemies among the Sydney
jet set. I met a young man at a banquet once who was introduced to
me as having just bought a television channel: 'Two, actually,' was all
he said, without a smile. There is a dauntingly veneered and lacquered
look to many of these people, who often seem rather too absolute to
be true – too well coiffured, too expensively dressed at the wrong time
of day, rather too glittery and enthusiastic. Gush is a well-known
Sydney society failing, but so is the habit of interruption: among the
upper crust here the art of conversation is mostly the art of competitive
monologue, and I have seen souls from gentler milieux reduced to
stunned withdrawal because they have never been allowed to conclude

[1] From David Marr's biography *Patrick White*, London, 1991.

a sentence.[1] Nor is delicacy a quality of the Sydney *hoi polloi* (as
Sydney people, in a curious semantic inversion, call their society folk).
I was proudly introduced one evening to a woman descended from
one of the oldest and most eminent Sydney families, and never in my
life have I encountered such an overbearing, loud-mouthed, over-
dressed, sozzled and insensitive old hag.

This raw but effective aristocracy is extremely well-travelled, often
owning properties abroad and sometimes sending its children to
Europe or America for their education. There was a time when it was
also passionately Anglophile and royalist, and one comes across sur-
vivals of the convention – any visiting peer is soon adopted by the
party-going classes. A Sydney novelist once told me that a prime
characteristic of Sydneysiders was their ability to tug a forelock and
spit abuse at the same time, and the dichotomy is apparent even
among the sophisticated, who are by no means unaware of their own
elevation, but curiously susceptible to the altitude of outsiders.

With all this, there is something undeniably attractive about
Sydney's higher society, in a cynical, glittery, hospitable way. It gives
me the disarming impression that it enjoys life hugely, and if I tread
warily in its generic presence, I tread with pleasure too. It is a small
society. It meets frequently, knows itself intimately and is made homogeneous by common success. At a single party in the city I met, one
after the other, two Premiers of New South Wales, two of Sydney's
most notoriously expensive barristers, its most famous living architect,
one of its most celebrated authors, the headmistress of its most fashionable girls' school, the director of its greatest library, the chairman of

---

[1] During my research on this book I came across the following quotation: 'There is no
modesty, no attention to one another. They talk very fast, very loud and all together.
If they ask you a question, before you can utter three words of your answer, they will
break out on you again – and talk away.' It might well have been somebody writing
about Sydneysiders, 1991; it was really John Adams writing about New Yorkers,
1774.

On the other hand I read about a Sydney man who put this message on his
telephone-answering machine: 'They say life comes down to a few moments. This is
one of them. Let's see what you can do.' Hardly any of his callers, he reported, could
think of a word to say.

several of its most profitable companies and the man who had just
bought the television channels. Almost all were equally charming to
me, though some kept their eyes on the door behind my back, in case
somebody more important walked in – Robert Campbell perhaps, or
(far better at a party) Ben Boyd of the *Wanderer*.

Sydney's original society was polarized simply enough between the
gaolers and the gaoled, but gradually there came into existence a
powerful middle class of professional people, functionaries and politicians, and down the generations this was to produce some of the city's
most memorable characters. Six of them, now:

¶ John Piper (*c.* 1773–1851) first arrived in Sydney in 1792 as a
member of the New South Wales Corps, but so clearly realized the
potential of the place that he returned in 1812 to take the job of
Naval Officer – part harbourmaster, but more importantly part
customs collector, which gave him 5 per cent of all customs due. He
was an enthusiastic Scot, despite (or perhaps because of) German
paternal origins. Handsome, dandyish and extravagant, he married a
convict's daughter and lived headily, breeding and racing horses,
throwing money around, while steadily making himself rich on the
strength of his 5 per cent. By the 1820s he had built himself so grand a
mansion that he was known as the Prince of Australia: twin-domed
and colonnaded, Henrietta Villa stood at the tip of one of the most
delectable harbour promontories, and was the scene of glorious junket-
ings. Piper had his own band, and his guests danced quadrilles beneath
the verandas, being seen off in the morning with ceremonial salutes
from miniature brass cannons on the lawn. Behind the house, as if in
expiation, a huge Cross of St Andrew was laid out in clipped hedges
on the hillside. Alas, this endearing hedonist over-reached himself.
Obliged to resign his office because of inexact accountancy, burdened
with frightful debts, one day he was rowed out into the harbour with
his kilted piper, and jumped overboard to the playing of a lament. He
was fished out anyway with a boathook, but his glory days were over.
Henrietta Villa was sold to pay off the debts, and Piper retreated

from history to die in altogether more bathetic circumstances.[1] All that remains of him is the name of the promontory he made so fashionable – Point Piper, which at least is *soigné* still.

¶ Two violent clergymen bring zest to the old Sydney annals. The Rev. Samuel Marsden (1764–1838) was a gross eighteenth-century figure, a Fielding character. He was the son of a Yorkshire blacksmith, had a Cambridge degree and came to Sydney as assistant chaplain in 1794. He looks in his pictures a perfect horror – fat-faced, bull-necked, sour-mouthed – and he made himself a squarson of the old English school, at once landowner, magistrate and vicar of Parramatta. In 1807 he took to London the very first bale of Australian wool, and was presented to King George III wearing a suit woven from his own fleeces. He is remembered in Sydney, though, chiefly as an exponent of corporal and capital punishment – Flogging Sam. He ordered floggings at the drop of a hat, he fervently wielded a whip himself, and he ordered hangings without compunction. It is said he used to drive parishioners to church with a dog-whip; he certainly sentenced one of his own servants to death for absconding, and then attended him on the scaffold. He was a famous proselytizer of the Maoris, but saw no salvation for the Sydney Aborigines, declaring them to have 'no Reflections, no attachments and no wants'. Sam Marsden was a pillar of society, as a clergyman must be, a member of the Turnpike Trust, president of the Benevolent Society, committee member of the Bible Society, but even the generally temperate Macquarie was once goaded into calling him a Mendacious and Vindictive Cleric.[2]

The other memorable man of God was the Presbyterian John Dunmore Lang (1799–1878), who was violent in a more forgivable kind. He was a flaming Scottish Calvinist who came to Sydney in 1823 especially to reform its morals. For nearly half a century he thundered and raged about them, attacking everybody from venal bankers to

---

[1] At Bathurst, New South Wales, in 1851, supported by the charity of friends.
[2] In his poem 'Five Bells', 1939, Kenneth Slessor put a prayer of thanksgiving into the mouth of this cruel hypocrite, engraving his own Testament upon the bloodied backs of miscreants: Not, mine, the Hand that writes the weal/On this, my vellum of puffed veal,/Not mine, the glory that endures,/But Yours, dear God, entirely Yours.

delinquent Governors. He built his own Scots Kirk, he started two newspapers, he founded a college, he wrote innumerable pamphlets, he was a vociferous member of the Legislative Council. At his own expense he brought out about a hundred Scottish craftsmen and their families in order to elevate the quality of the Sydney proletariat.[1] He was a Napoleon of the manse! Nothing could restrain him in his headlong pursuit of the right. He infuriated officialdom by publishing a series of parodies supposed to be intercepted dispatches to London, and at the height of his fame spent four months in Parramatta gaol for libel. But he was undaunted, and carried on in just the same way, God's rabble-rouser, until his death.

¶ William Charles Wentworth (1790–1872) was Sydney's proto-typical politician. His mother was transported for theft. His father was a physician who had been charged with highway robbery in England, but had escaped punishment by volunteering as a surgeon for the colony, where he had greatly thrived and sired at least eight children by various women. W. C. Wentworth became famous in his early youth as one of the first three Europeans to cross the Blue Mountains, in 1813, and when he went up to Cambridge he became something of a poet: in 1823 he was runner-up for the Chancellor's Medal for his poem 'Australasia', dedicated to Macquarie and full of apostrophe'd Sydney images (throng'd quay, lengthen'd street, column'd front, glitt'ring heaps and vent'rous tread). All his life, impelled perhaps by his slightly disreputable origins, he stood for the New Man, the self-reliant Australian-born. He called himself The First Australian, and started a newspaper called *The Australian* which argued vehemently for self-rule in the colony, and was perpetually at odds with Government House. Wentworth had inherited a fortune from his father, and used it with brio, making his house Vaucluse the Henrietta Villa of his generation. It was there that the Constitution Bill was drafted, giving responsible Government to the colony of New South Wales, and there that Wentworth cocked a famous snook at one of his chief

[1] True to form they built themselves a little Glasgow around Clyde Street, in the midst of the Irish Catholics of the Rocks, with McAusland's General Store on the corner.

opponents, the martinet Governor Ralph Darling: when Darling sailed for home in 1831 Wentworth invited 4,000 guests to a rollicking celebratory party on his lawns, the climax of the evening being a fire-work display which spelled out the words DOWN WITH THE TYRANT triumphantly across the night sky. 'Australia First' was one of Went-worth's slogans, but it was not Australia to the Last for him, because he went to England again in 1862 and died there ten years later.

¶ The two most celebrated Sydney politicians of later years were Sir Henry Parkes (1815–96) and William Morris Hughes (1862–1952). Both were born in Britain, the one of English parents, the other of Welsh. Parkes was six times premier of New South Wales and the dominant Australian politician of his day. Hughes was Prime Minister of Australia during the First World War, the Antipodean Lloyd George. They were both unforgettable figures, and both began their careers humbly in Sydney – Parkes worked in an ironmongery and kept an ivory knick-knack shop, Hughes mended umbrellas and ran a general store in Balmain. The huge, richly bearded and lavishly whiskered Parkes looks in pictures remarkably like an Aborigine. The small, jug-eared and gnome-like Hughes had long droopy moustaches and melancholy eyes, and was known universally as Billy. Parkes's voice varied peculiarly from deep bass to falsetto, and he bore himself like an actor–manager, sometimes adopting a visionary expression of the eyes and sometimes falling into what was once described as a 'vast and inexpressive weariness'. Hughes became in his prime an ardent British imperialist – 'what fields are left for us to conquer?' he demanded rhetorically of the King's subjects after the victory of 1918. 'We are like so many Alexanders.' Parkes, who was accused in 1885 of 'an inane and tedious vulgarity of rhetoric', was married three times, went in and out of bankruptcy and died very poor at the age of eighty-one. Hughes, who was a famously entertaining orator, sat in one assembly or another without a break for fifty-eight years, chose his first Sydney constituency because it was the only one within a penny tram fare of Parliament House, and was given a State funeral in Sydney, in 1952, which was attended by 100,000 people.

*

And here now on a North Shore pier stands a modern Sydney bourgeois, waiting for the ferry. Is he a Wentworth, one wonders, is he a
Piper, is he at heart a Flogging Sam? He is in his early forties,
perhaps, slim but florid. He wears an Italianate three-piece suit with
double vents to the jacket and four buttons on each sleeve, together
with a stiff white collar above a blue-striped shirt, and a tightly
knotted tie of the old school sort. His brown hat, tilted forward, has a
wide and slightly curled brim. Under his arm he carries a not too
bulging briefcase, and he walks up and down the pier, one hand in
pocket, with a preoccupied air. Perhaps he is preparing a brief, we
may speculate, or weighing a prognosis. But then we notice his shoes.
They are expensive-looking, highly polished shoes, but if we look
closely at them, when his back is turned, we may see that they are
pathetically down at heel. He is not what he seems – his clothes are a
bluff, his briefcase probably contains nothing but the morning tabloid,
and he hasn't the cash to get his shoes heeled. Let him be a lesson to
us: the contemporary Sydney bourgeoisie, of which we thought him
so substantial a member, is extremely hard to pin down.

This is because it ranges, as it always has, from the criminal to the
genteel, freely mixing. We are quite likely to meet the man with the
worn shoes at tonight's sixtieth birthday party for the Professor, but
equally we might run into him taking illegal bets on the 4.30 at
Randwick. If fashionable Sydney is almost incestuously tight-knit,
middle-class Sydney seems to me generously heterogeneous, and is the
least obviously Australian of the city's social layers. It has its fair
share of glorious southern physique; but I once went to a Sydney
theatrical occasion, attended in particular by young intellectuals, and
thought that all in all, with their pale exhausted faces, their lounging
postures and their generally lacklustre or perhaps hungover attitudes,
they were the weediest theatre-goers I had ever seen.

Let me take you to a dinner-party among the better-off Sydney
middle classes – a composite picture, so to speak, true in the detail but
fudged in the whole. The style of the apartment is trendy – everything
new, everything the newest in fact, pictures by the most admired
Sydney figurist of the day, furniture in the latest Slav-Mexican mode,

tulips in Chinese vases, fabrics in the muted cerise, streaked with green, which has recently been decreed by Australian *Vogue*. The food is excellent, the wine terrific. The conversation is partly about last night's *La Bohème*, and partly about real-estate prices, and predominantly about other people, and is very catty.

One of the guests tells us without embarrassment that among her family connections are some of the best-known members of the Sydney criminal classes. Another recalls his happy time as a Rhodes Scholar. A third explains the anti-corrosion system which has made his family business so successful around the world. A fourth is that awful old harridan of eminent pedigree. Two more are, before the pudding is served, sitting on each other's laps in a corner of the room. A seventh is the man we saw at the ferry pier, who presently spills his glass of red wine over the brand-new and gleaming white carpet. They all laugh a lot, ignore those they choose to ignore, interrupt freely, eat wholeheartedly and repeatedly congratulate our host upon the rapidly rising value of his property. We enjoy it all tremendously. We are sitting among truly historical figures, clearly recognizable in the Sydney annals, and bringing to that well-appointed apartment on the North Shore resonant echoes of old habits and intentions.

It seems to me that the professional, artistic and business classes of Sydney have only recently found themselves. When I first encountered them, thirty years ago, they were still patently subject to what used to be called the Cultural Cringe – the general assumption that things foreign, and in particular things British, were necessarily superior. Today this old complex is mostly dissipated, and the middle classes are generally confident of their own merits – as well they might be, since they have produced in the last couple of decades an astonishing stream of distinguished representatives. They are proud and fond of their city, too: during Sydney's annual day of clean-up in 1990 some 40,000 people, most of them undoubtedly from the bourgeoisie, volunteered to help.

The best of these people are fluent, idiomatic, friendly and enthusiastic. They are also delightfully accessible. Cherishing a romantic but purely frivolous desire to see the actual botanical specimens collected by Joseph Banks during Cook's visit to Botany Bay, I called the Botanical Gardens and asked if I might. In no time at all two devoted botanists were producing from their drawers those aged plants and flowers, with no sign of resentment at my jejune motives.[1] I scarcely had to mention an interest in inner suburban arrangement, than I was the guest of a lively lawyer at his own suburban house. Hardly had I met my first Sydney politician than I was eating oysters with him in the restaurant of Parliament House. I expressed one day my curiosity about Sydney social mores, and in a trice I was being entertained by a group of academic sociologists – two young research fellows of progressive views, a scholar of Russian origins and a fluent command of the Cantonese language, a veteran head of department dressed, in speckled scarf and safari suit, more or less as for the Battle of Britain.

If there is a generic failing to this class of Sydneysider, it is perhaps a tendency to the omniscient. *What* a lot they know, and how they talk about it! Do not even try to raise the subject of abstract expressionism – your host is certain to have just returned from the current de Kooning exhibition in Manhattan, and is very likely the author of a monograph on Jackson Pollock. You think you know Roussillon well? Not half as well as the woman at the cocktail party, who will very soon put you right about the origins of Catharism. Just back from Prague – great chum of Gore Vidal – living in Paris then – not as good as the Connaught – bumped into Tom Wolfe – surely it should be pronounced Portmyrion, should it not? – bottomless is the experience, liberal the advice, of the Sydney intelligentsia. I kept a note during one stay in the city, and found that in two months I had been helpfully instructed on the rules of cricket, how best to cook rice-pudding, the Sykes–Picot Agreement, the architectural accomplishments of the Royal Navy, bats, post-modernism and the role of the Privy Council in the Common Law.

Of course there are some very conservative families in this varied

[1] The plants looked to me perfectly fresh and new, and would be as useful as specimens now, the botanists told me, as they were 200 years ago.

milieu. The private schools of Sydney seem staunchly traditional still, and produce alumni of ordered and stoic mould. On a very hot day I once overtook a long line of girls from one such school labouring up the steep track to South Head, wearing thick school blazers over their cotton dresses: breathless but uncomplaining they climbed, too well-disciplined to remove their jackets, until I heard a lady-like call come winging up the hill behind – 'You can take your blazers off – pass it on – You can take your blazers off – pass it on' – up the line and past me, speeding on its way like a watchword, while one by one the girls dutifully peeled off their blazers in its wake.

There is also, though, a potent stratum of the unorthodox, if not the anarchic, among this bourgeoisie. A sizeable proportion of it is homosexual, which gives it an agreeable element of the raffishly defiant, and there is much of the exhibitionism which has always been endemic to this city. One of the most extraordinary houses I know is an unassuming small villa in Neutral Bay whose flamboyantly individualist owner has turned it into a kind of grotto, its walls painted all over with *trompe-l'oeil* and tomfoolery, where an apparently constant succession of casual, unannounced and sometimes it seems totally unknown guests drops in at random for drinks or meals, at all hours of the day, heartily welcomed by the owner, his dogs, and unidentified acolytes.

No need to find individual precedents for the Sydney proletariat. Its founding antecedents were a social condition and a historical phenomenon. Far more than the Establishment or the rentiers, it is still the blue-collar working people that set the tone of the city. Their bounding but indolent optimism strikes almost all visitors, and this is surely a legacy of old trials. To endure the road-gangs without losing one's spirit, to emerge as so many convict families did into competence and respectability, to have overcome the old unfairnesses of life, to feel oneself the equal of one's former gaolers, to have defied the law by surviving the worst it could do, to be able to sit back at last without being bullied or flogged – just to have achieved all this, the common experience, was surely to achieve a permanent spirit of euphoria. No other populace on earth has grown out of such handicaps, and survived them with such panache.

Often the convicts were heroically scornful of the authority that had them so terribly in its grasp. I am proud to say that the only Morris who arrived in Sydney with the First Fleet (seven years for stealing a pair of breeches and a waistcoat) absconded within five days and was never seen again, giving me the tantalizing fancy that somewhere among the Aborigines there may be cousins of mine. Many others escaped too – it was easy to abscond from this prison without walls. Some just wandered hopelessly about the bush for a few days, but a few got away in epic style. In 1808 a gang of convicts seized a trading-brig that was lying in Sydney Cove itself, beside Campbell's Wharf and in full view of Government House; they got as far as the South China Sea before they were caught. More inspiringly still, one night in 1791 Mr and Mrs William Bryant, with their two small children and seven other convicts, stole the Governor's own cutter and rowed it down the harbour past the sentries, through the Heads and out to the open sea. Mary Bryant, a sailor's daughter from Cornwall, was the captain of this desperate enterprise. It took them ten weeks to sail 3,000 miles in one of the great open-boat voyages of history – repeatedly blown helplessly off-course, once stranded on the Great Barrier Reef, once pursued by cannibals, only to be arrested in the end in Dutch Timor and shipped back to England. Mrs Bryant lost her husband and both her children in the course of the adventure, but lived herself to be unconditionally pardoned, and became a seven-day wonder in Britain as The Girl from Botany Bay.[1]

We read of marvellous courage in the suffering of punishment – men and boys who had been mere hooligans in Britain became stoic champions in Sydney, enduring year after year chainings, floggings and every kind of bullying. Their insolence could be indomitable. Maurice

---

[1] A £10 annuity was settled upon her by a particularly enthusiastic fan, James Boswell. One of her comrades in the escape celebrated his survival and pardon by volunteering for the New South Wales Corps and becoming a Sydney gaoler.

Fitzgerald, for instance, an Irishman sentenced to 300 lashes for his part in an insurrection in 1804, knocked both of his warders down the moment he was unstrapped from the triangle, inspiring his namesake the poet Robert David FitzGerald to write:

> Could I announce
> That Maurice as my kin I say aloud
> I'd take his irons as my heraldry, and be proud.

When in 1834 John Jenkins, an absconded convict, was found guilty of murder and asked if he had anything to say before the death sentence was pronounced, he told the judge that 'he did not care a bugger for dying, or a damn for anyone in court, and that he would as soon shoot every bloody bugger in court'.[1]

To be obedient or to be intractable were alternatives, to be fatalist was almost obligatory. You could keep your head down and count the years, you could spit at the system and suffer the consequences. Either way, an acceptance of destiny must have been part of the communal ethos. The convict Matthew Eberingham, transported for the most forgivable of all crimes, obtaining books by false pretences, died in 1817 after twenty-three years of exile, and expressed it on his Sydney tombstone:

> Farewell vain world i have had enough of thee
> and am Carless what though canst say of me
> thy smiles i court not nor they frowns i fear
> beneath this turf my head Lies quiet hear.

Doubtless all these miseries bred jealousy, treachery and sycophancy, but they also bred in a few people an irresistible determination to win, however rotten the hands life had dealt them. A handful of convicts, almost the moment they had served their terms, launched themselves into careers of full-blooded capitalism, and became extremely rich.

For example they called Sam Terry the Botany Bay Rothschild, so

---

[1] 'The judge sat,' reported *The Australian* convincingly, 'in mute astonishment.'

wonderfully did he prosper after his time with the labour gangs (for
theft, the records say, though his descendants preferred to think it 'for
political offences'). Emancipated in 1809, Terry began his free life as
a publican, having married a usefully endowed wife. He went on by
astute usury to be a landowner, with scattered properties all over
Sydney and 19,000 acres in the country, worked for him by 100
assigned convicts. He was a rough crude man, only just literate, plain
of appearance and miserly of instinct, but he built himself one of the
largest houses in Sydney – it had stables, a coach house and a central
courtyard, and somewhere within it, so legend said, Terry kept much
of his vast fortune locked away in hard cash. Into it the Botany Bay
Rothschild (by then himself proprietor of several convict transport
ships) withdrew when he was paralysed by a stroke in 1834; from
then until his death he could move only with the help of two servants,
making rare excursions, 'pale and bloated', through the streets of the
wondering town. Although his business methods were decidedly shady,
if not actually criminal, Terry was buried with Masonic honours, and
a regimental band played a funeral march for the old rascal.

His contemporary Simeon Lord was a more sophisticated entrepreneur, and looks back at us from his portrait with a disturbingly
calculating gaze. Lord was transported for theft in 1791, aged twenty.
At the end of his term he set up a retail business, dealing in everything
from soap to sheepskins, and became one of Macquarie's token emancipists. He was appointed to the board of magistrates and shown off
at Government House receptions. In time he came to have a hand in
almost everything, every kind of business, every category of import,
export, production or investment. He owned 18,000 acres of farmland
and eighteen blocks of Sydney town. He had a mill at Botany Bay. He
managed a fleet of whalers, sealers and transport ships. He manufactured beaver hats, he experimented in paper production, and he built
himself a house which outdid even Sam Terry's – a three-storey
building, with verandas on two floors, which towered above everything else like a portent of things to come.

Most formidable of all, among these felon-plutocrats, was Mary
Reibey. If it was hard for a male convict to become a millionaire in

penal Sydney, it must have been almost inconceivably difficult for a female, yet Mary Reibey did it. When she was thirteen, in 1790, this Lancashire girl was sentenced to seven years' transportation for stealing a horse (or borrowing it without permission, as she preferred to say). When she was seventeen she married a free businessman, and opened her own retail store. When she was thirty-five she was a comfortably-off widow with seven children and a thriving general business. When she was fifty she owned two ships, eight farms, many houses and a very large bank account indeed (the Bank of New South Wales was one of her tenants). When she was sixty she was one of the best-known people in Sydney, often to be seen driving stylishly around town in a carriage drawn by two white stallions. When she was seventy she had built herself a mansion and could be characterized by the Anglican Bishop of Sydney as being 'praiseworthy in the highest degree for her exertions in the cause of religion'. When she was seventy-five she died, a round-faced, pink-cheeked, bonneted, bespectacled and beribboned old matriarch, leaving heaps of money and a grandson to become, in the fullness of time, Premier of Tasmania.

Could such careers be paralleled anywhere else on earth – not just rags-to-riches, but actually manacles-to-millionaires?

More fundamentally, the penal experience gave rise to an egalitarian staunchness that has become traditional to the Sydney character. Volumes have been written about the Australian condition of 'mateship', the male bond of working-class camaraderie which is thought to have been born in those penal days, and was certainly strengthened in war. To foreign sensibilities it always sounds a little sickly, but alongside it there did grow a philosophy of simple loyalty which was articulated by many a colonial poet and balladeer, most nobly for my tastes by Adam Lindsay Gordon:

> This life is mostly froth and bubble,
> Two things stand like stone:

Kindness in another's trouble
Courage in your own.

The sentiments survive in Sydney still, if not always in comradeship, at least in communality. Trade-union power is greatly diminished in Sydney nowadays, but fishermen, surfers, bowlers, policemen, criminals, yachtsmen, gamblers – all seem to work and play together with an uncommon intensity, as though they are kith and kin. The club spirit is strong, and so is the sense of brotherhood. BE READY, MATES, THAT'S ALL, says an epitaph I admire in Sydney's Rookwood Cemetery.[1]

For modern mateship at its most vigorous one need only go to one of the innumerable working-class social clubs – Rugby League Clubs, Workmen's Clubs or clubs of the Returned Services League. Originally, I imagine, these were much like British Legion clubs in Britain, or Veterans' Posts in the United States, but in 1956 the legalization of gambling machines in New South Wales fabulously transformed them. They became extremely rich, and around the batteries of poker machines that became their cores they built themselves lavish new premises, with excellent restaurants, glittering bars, dance floors with resident bands and every manifestation of popular hedonism. Some of them have splendid sports facilities too, and swimming-pools. Hardly a rock star is too expensive to be beyond the fees of these clubs, and though they often stand in dingy streets in dingy suburbs, and sometimes look from the outside pretty dingy themselves, inside they greet you with a most hospitable verve. They are the Workers' Paradise sublimated, offering history a lesson in what Communism might have achieved, if it had not been so priggish.

Not long ago the Sydney proletariat was altogether homogenous, being almost entirely of Anglo-Saxon or Celtic origin.[2] This was the citizenry that made the reputation of Sydney – to this day, when the world imagines this city, it imagines your cheerful, boozy, prejudiced,

---

[1] Another just says STREWTH.
[2] Even now it is claimed that every fourth Sydneysider has had a Scottish grandmother.

lazy, brave and disputatious Ocker male (your Ocker female is somewhat mistier in the mind).[1] He still exists. You see him a thousand
times a day, in his stubby shorts and singlet, heaving crates about,
mending telephone wires, reading the tabloids at ten in the morning
with his feet up in the cab of his delivery van, or squatting on his
haunches with his mates outside pubs at dinner-time.[2] In him the
Sydney male physique reaches its excelsis – no longer tall and stringy,
but more solidly powerful – the thick-set brawn of the surfer or the
rugby player, the drinker's pot-belly. His accent is rank and twisted.
He can be horribly oafish and ill-educated, especially when young,
and is not always much fun on holiday in Bali, but in general his
manners are blunt without being discourteous, and his humour is
agreeably caustic. He seems, whatever his years, more or less ageless,
and he possesses still a certain crude charisma that D. H. Lawrence
attributed to another generation of Sydneysiders – 'that air of owning
the city that belongs to a good Australian'. In many other great cities
the populace has outlived its old sterotypes: the Sydney masses remain
just as we expect them to be.

2. Indigenes

Here since the beginning of Sydney, likely to be still hanging around
if it ever comes to an end – here stand the indigenes. Today's Sydney
Aborigines are not people of the Iora tribe, which may well have been
living here before there was a Sydney Harbour, but was extinct
within half a century of the British arrival. They are migrants from
other districts, drawn here like everyone else by the magnetism of the

---

[1] Ocker: the archetypal uncultivated Australian working man (*The Macquarie Encyclopedic Dictionary*, Sydney 1990).
[2] As long ago as 1825 he was described as 'making no efforts beyond what [is] necessary to supply [his] own animal needs'. This is how Anon. put it, in a contribution to *A Book of Australia*, edited by T. Inglis Moore, London 1961: Me and my dog/ have tramped together/in cold weather and hot./Me and my dog/don't care whether/ we get any work/or not.

big city, and often by now with strong infusions of white blood. Australian Aborigines they are, nevertheless, by conviction and by perception, and thus spiritual and historical descendants of the original inhabitants. They are at the heart of Sydney's meaning, they bring out the worst and the best in it, and they have a right to an allegorical position in this book – a central position, that is, in its central chapter.

I did not always think like this. I used to consider the Aborigines a marginal people, empty, pathetic and almost irrelevant, and I remember two episodes in particular which seemed at the time to sustain this sad conviction. One occurred at La Perouse ('La Per' to the locals), the suburb on the north shore of Botany Bay which contains Sydney's oldest Aboriginal settlement. I drove out there one morning just to look around the place and, finding myself in a decidedly unwelcoming cul-de-sac, where mangy dogs bit at my tyres, and groups of young blacks stared at me with a kind of listless suspicion – turning hastily around at the end of the street with a less than confident grinding of gears, I was just in time to see something that I had never anywhere in the world seen before. One Aborigine knocked another out, there and then, with a massive punch to the jaw before my very eyes. The man went down like a log, the attention of the bystanders was momentarily but still apathetically diverted, and I got out of the place before anything worse happened.

The other occasion, years ago, was an Aboriginal rally at Alexandria Park in Redfern, where many of the black people live. This was to have been the conclusion of an Aboriginal Rights march through town, but it went sadly awry, and by the time I reached Alexandria Park seemed to have fizzled out altogether. All I found was a huddle of dark-skinned people around an open bonfire, surrounded by rubbish on the edge of the park. They greeted me with concern, offering me beer out of an ice-bucket, sidling around me and occasionally winking. A small thin boy with cotton wool stuffed in one ear wandered here and there with a black puppy on a string. Others kicked a football about in the gathering dusk, and around the fire a handful of old women looked sadly into the flames. A strong smell of

alcohol hung over us, and the man with the bucket repeatedly urged
me to have one for the road. Had the rally been a success, I asked?
'Yeah,' they said, and looked into the fire.

These dispiriting experiences, if they no longer illustrate my own
feelings about the Aborigines, probably still confirm the views of most
Sydneysiders – the indigenes are predictably reviled by the more
racialist of the whites, and widely thought to be beyond redemption.
But many citizens are sympathetic to their causes, and I imagine that
few people nowadays would deny the unfairness of their destiny.

The first words the Europeans ever heard uttered by the Sydney
Aborigines were *Warra! Warra!*, which meant 'Go away'. Cook himself said that all the natives apparently wanted from his men was their
immediate departure. They viewed the goings-on of the new arrivals
first with fear (they thought they might be devils), then with super-
stition (they thought they might be the ghosts of their own ancestors),
then with curiosity (seeing them swarm up the riggings of their ships,
they thought they might be giant possums), then with apparent indifference (David Collins, of the First Fleet, says that during the first six
weeks of the settlement only two Aborigines ever bothered to visit the
camp), and finally with mingled responses of opportunism, disillusion-
ment and hostility (Phillip himself was once speared by an Aborigine,
and for years there was sporadic fighting in the countryside around).
The Iora seem to have behaved rather like cats, fading in and out
of view, sometimes pretending not to notice events, sometimes ingratiat-
ingly participating, sometimes scratching and spitting.

At first the British called them Indians, and thought them hardly
more than animals. They seemed to have no abstract ideas. They
apparently had no notion of property. They could not weave. They
had never put a sail on a boat, let alone a wheel on a wagon. They had
never built a hut. Their one attempt at agriculture was the cultiva-
tion of yams. They lived by hunting, by scraping shellfish off the
rocks and by the most elementary methods of fishing. They went
stark naked, and were smeared all over with rancid fish oil. 'In no

part of my voyages,' wrote the botanist Joseph Cavanilles, who went to Sydney with a Spanish expedition in 1793, 'have I seen our nature more degraded, or individuals more ugly or savage.'

Could they possibly have souls? More improbable still, could they seriously be considered, now that the Union Jack flew above their hunting-grounds and oyster-beds, to be British subjects? The convicts by and large thought not, robbing and violating the Iora without much compunction. The more imaginative of the officers recognized human qualities in them, Spartan qualities in particular, and often befriended them. There was a time, according to Captain John Hunter of HMS *Sirius*, when 'every gentleman's house was now become a resting or sleeping place for some of them every night', and the commander of the 1793 Spanish expedition, Alessandro Malaspina, reported fastidiously that he and his officers had been guests at the same table with Aboriginal men and women 'entirely naked and disgustingly filthy'. Watkin Tench recorded with admiration a moment when an Aboriginal woman, attending the flogging of a convict who had robbed her, broke into tears at the sight of the terrible punishment, while another woman grabbed a stick to threaten the scourger. Richard Johnson the chaplain gave his daughter, born in Sydney in 1790, the Aboriginal name of Milbah, and George Worgan, surgeon of the *Sirius*, summed up his own views on the natives thus: 'active, volatile, unoffending, merry, funny, laughing, good-natured, nasty, dirty . . .'[1]

Governor Phillip's attitudes to the Aborigines were ambiguous. Bloodthirstily though he responded when they killed his servant, he forbade retaliation when he was speared himself, and gave Manly its name in tribute to what he called the Aborigines' 'confident and manly bearing'. He had three tribal males kidnapped and brought to live at Government House, as he might have trapped a few kangaroos as pets. One died of smallpox, one escaped, but the third, Bennelong, became a popular member of the household and a favourite of the

[1] Worgan might well be honoured as the Father of Australian Culture – he took a piano with him to Botany Bay.

Governor, who built a hut for him on the point – Bennelong Point – where the Opera House now stands, and later took him on a protracted visit to England.

An unlimited supply of convict labour meant that the Aborigines were not needed as workers or servants, as indigenes generally were elsewhere in the British Empire. Nor did they pose much threat or competition to the infant colony. They could within reason be indulged. Macquarie settled sixteen families at South Head, vainly trying to make agriculturists of them, and he instituted an annual feast and corroboree at Parramatta. John Macarthur, perhaps imagining himself another Duke of Argyll, dressed some of them up in scarlet shirts, blue trousers and yellow neck-cloths, and paraded them as a private bodyguard.

Whether out of naïveté or opportunism, some of the Iora played along with these attitudes, and became well-known characters of early Sydney. A few achieved a sort of official status, and wore crescent-shaped brass breastplates as tribal representatives. The most assertive of them was Bungaree, nicknamed the King of Sydney, who habitually met ships coming into harbour dressed in a cocked hat and an admiral's jacket, but shirtless and barefooted. Bungaree circumnavigated Australia as interpreter to the navigator Matthew Flinders in 1802, and was chosen by Macquarie to preside over the South Head farm village, together with his wives Boatman, Broomstick, Onion, Pincher and the paramount Queen Gooseberry. In his prime Bungaree was not only merry, but also dignified, and he was painted by many artists. Every Governor knew and greeted him, and Admiral Sir James Brisbane, RN, gave him that cocked hat and jacket. When he died, in 1832, his obituary occupied a full page in the *Gazette*.

But if he died a celebrity, he died ravaged and defeated – an alcoholic buffoon, slung around with trumpery emblems of mock-authority, greeted by all those Governors and Admirals not with real respect, but with amused condescension. One of his later portraits shows him with a basket of beer bottles at his side; the last, by the Frenchman Charles Rodius, presents a face tragically sunken, degraded and reproachful, all its humour gone. In theory, in those early years, Government policy aimed at non-interference in native affairs – royal instructions to Governors said there must be 'no unnecessary interruption in the exercise of their several occupations'. In practice European civilization fatally interrupted all the occupations of the Iora. Its good aspects, hard enough to detect anyway in early Sydney, had little effect upon them, while its evil cruelly rotted them. Even Phillip's friend Bennelong, having been lionized as a Noble Savage in England, returned to Sydney to die rum-soaked in 1813.

They had no chance – from the very first landing in Sydney Cove they were probably outnumbered by the newcomers, and they had no means of countering what Robert Hughes has called 'the malignant gravitational field' of the penal colony. How could one reconcile the mores of a settlement largely of thieves with the customs of a people who left their canoes lying around for anyone to take? Early representations of the Iora, virile and interesting in the foregrounds of watercolours, presently gave way to more contemptuous images: of drunken men, bloated degraded women, pot-bellied children, brawling, swigging liquor at street corners and begging from passers-by. Squabbles with the Europeans soon became more common, as the tribespeople came to seem less quaint and more irritating, and the Europeans turned out to be not ancestral spirits or possums, but bullying landgrabbers. Smallpox was endemic among the Iora, it seems, before the Europeans arrived; cholera, influenza and venereal diseases further decimated them. Their traditions were disregarded, their pride was destroyed, and the last successors of the Bennelongs and the Bungarees, dressed up still in the frayed remnants of their fineries, went ruined to their graves. Queen Gooseberry was last heard of begging opposite the Emu Inn in George Street, and by 1857 a man who habitually sat outside the house of the Speaker of the legislative Assembly could be pointed out as the very last survivor of the Sydney tribes; people used to throw him coins, as they passed by in their carriages.

'Well Mister,' the last of the original Botany Bay Aborigines told an official investigator, 'all black-fella gone! All this my country! Pretty place, Botany! Little piccaninny, I run about here. Plenty black-fellow then; corroboree; great fight; all canoe about. Only me left now!'

Sydney has never been without its Aborigines, because there has always been a steady coming and going of black people from else-where; but paradoxically they have become the one group of Sydney-siders who do not, like Lawrence's workmen, look around the city as though they own it. The city has generally considered them unimprov-able nuisances – the inn-sign of a pub called The Labour in Vain used to show a white man vainly scrubbing an Aborigine in a bucket of soap. In 1859 the writer F. Fowler described a group of them coming into town on the steamer from Newcastle, nearly all drunk, and tumbling about the boat 'like so many hogs'; the women gave intoxicated boxing displays while the men went around begging for money. By the 1880s black families were directed into an official camp at Circular Quay, where they were given Government rations to keep them off the streets; the compound became a spectacle of entertainment for the white people of Sydney, who went down there in their hundreds to gape at the prostitutes, the drunks and the brawlers. Then in 1895 an Aboriginal reserve was set up on the seashore at La Perouse, far from the city centre. Methodist missionaries worked hard to make Christians of its residents;[1] many of its young girls went away as indentured house servants under the auspices of the State Aboriginal Protection Board; but the Aborigines did for a time re-establish an element of tribal tradition down there, living by fishing and by the desultory practice of crafts – as was reported in later years, a man might make one boomerang one day, three the next, two the day after and then take the rest of the week off. La Perouse also became in time a popular afternoon's outing for Sydney people. The Aborigines sold them tea-sets or slippers ornamented with shells, gave them boomerang displays and mystified them with their ability to identify incoming shoals of fish by species: 'mullet, bream, blackfish', spotters would sing out from the headland above, and sure

[1] Ambivalently defining the task, in their journal in 1901, as 'the evangelization of the perishing people'.

enough, when the boats came back with their catch, mullet, bream or blackfish were what they had caught.

The official reserve came to an end in 1931, but the Aborigines remained, living first in shacks on the beach, then in fibro houses built for them by the State, and many Sydney people of a certain age remember family housemaids from La Perouse. Today people still go out to 'La Per' on a Saturday afternoon to buy wooden and shell trinkets, to watch the young men throw their boomerangs, and to see the Snake Man tip his assorted reptiles out of their sacks in the sunshine, as his father tipped them out before him. By now few of the residents are full-blooded Aborigines, and the streets in which they live, where I saw the man knocked out, have a gypsy-like air to them. Windows are often covered in blankets or rugs, scavenging dogs lope here and there, rubbish blows down the sidewalks. Nevertheless if there is a traditional centre of native life in Sydney, a place where you may just imagine a link with the song-lines and the rites of initiation, it is down there on the shores of Botany Bay, in the lee of the oil refineries, windy, sandy and raw.

Aboriginal consciousness of a more contemporary kind is concentrated in Redfern, whose name has become a metaphor for black activism in Sydney. There is no claiming that the black part of Redfern is very reassuring. Parts of the suburb are fast being gentrified, but the Aborigines' patch of it looks like a disaster area – like a bomb site, or a no-go area of Northern Ireland. In a couple of dilapidated streets, the doors of their houses opening directly into rutted potholed roadways, a community that appears to be half-stoned, or half-drunk, stares blankly at the passer-by. Some of the residents are more white than black, some more black than white, but most are classed as Aborigines, and upon them is concentrated the distrust and dislike of Sydney's racist whites. A palpable sense of morose resentment hangs upon the air, heightened by the fact that every now and then the police raid the district in search of drugs, stolen property or wanted criminals.

For half a century this has been a haven for Aboriginal drifters, but more recently it has also been the symbolic focus of a black revival movement. The world has come to recognize that there was always more to the Australian Aborigines than met the western eye, and for myself I have come to think of them, as I have come to think of Sydney itself, in an entirely new way. A proper supplement to a visit to Redfern is a trip out to the West Head, not far from that shimmering marina at Akuna Bay, to see some Aboriginal drawings on a rock there. Nobody knows for sure how old these are, but they seem to have sprung out of a society marvellously confident and exuberant. High above the sea in a clearing in the bush, they are a vivacious gallery of portraits animal and human, not at all like the patternings and eerie X-ray pictures we have come to expect of Aboriginal art. Wallabies bound, fishes squirm, birds flap, and a triumphant human figure in a tufted headdress holds a big fish in one hand, a boomerang in the other. Nothing could be further from the image of Bungaree with that wretched breastplate slung around his neck.

We realize now that, far from being the hapless incompetents the first settlers thought them, the Iora were perfectly adapted to their environment. They were superb hunters, and they had a masterly knowledge of herbal medicines and wild foods: scholars have listed eleven kinds of shellfish, thirty-two kinds of fish and seventy-four plants Aborigines ate in the Sydney region then, not to mention crustaceans, reptiles, marsupials of many kinds, innumerable birds, platypuses, grubs and bats.[1] Charles Darwin, meeting a party of tribespeople in 1836, thought they showed 'wonderful sagacity' in the arts of survival in the bush.[2] Their boats, dismissed by Lieutenant Bradley, RN, as by far the worst canoes he had ever seen or heard of, could be made in a single day, and even the Lieutenant had to admit they were wonderfully manoeuvrable. What the settlers thought of as terrible wilderness was friendly and familiar territory to the Aborigines, and it was largely by using old tribal tracks that the Europeans

---

[1] A menu presented in *A Difficult Infant*, edited by Graeme Aplin, Sydney 1988.
[2] 'Some few degrees higher in the scale of civilization than the Fuegians', was his final evolutionary assessment.

found their way out of the Sydney beach-head into the Australian interior. Only now are we beginning to appreciate the subtlety of the Aborigines' spiritual ideas, their conception of land as possessor rather than possessed, their visionary grasp of the relationships between place, man and the rest of nature – the 'incomprehensible ancient shine' that Lawrence detected in the Aboriginal eye.

The Sydney Aborigines themselves, so bludgeoned by destiny, seem gradually to have re-awakened to a sense of their own worth. In 1938 the La Perouse community held a Day of Mourning to protest against 150 years of colonization. In 1973, when the Opera House was ceremonially opened on Bennelong Point, at the height of the festivities an Aboriginal actor appeared dramatically at the apex of the building to represent the spirit of poor Bennelong himself. In 1988, when Sydney celebrated its bicentenary, a popular graffito said INVASION DAY, 1788, and a convoy of Freedom Buses brought protesting Aborigines into town. Today, as I have only belatedly discovered, one can meet in Sydney some formidably articulate, talented and well-read blacks, confined to no ghetto, half-castes probably more often than not, but fiercely proud of their Aboriginal origins and traditions.

The Aborigines' one claim to respect used to be the all-too-often repeated reminder that they had lived in Australia for 40,000 years, but now they are liable to speak in very different tones. They speak of secret tribal initiations; they tell tales of long-forgotten battles against the British; legends of fearless guerrilla leaders feed the Aboriginal confidence, and convince the activists that they are descended not from passive primitives, but from resistance heroes. The status of the Australian Aborigines is beyond the power of Sydney, and beyond the scope of a book about this city, but more and more I have come to feel that their presence here in some way *charges* the place; and finding myself greatly moved one evening during the performance of an Aborigine play, I recognized that in them above all was personified Sydney's nagging suggestion of transience or yearning – its one glimpse of epiphany.

*

Yet there are very few of them – perhaps 20,000 in all – and they do
not often show. To the stranger their presence is mostly embodied in
memory: in place names like Allawah, Coogie or Parramatta;[1] in rock
carvings here and there around the harbour, often so worn by time as
to be almost invisible except at sunrise or sunset; in the reputations of
a few long-dead collaborators, Bennelong, Bungaree or Jacky-Jacky,
who is honoured in an inscription in St James's Church as having
'tended his leader Edmund Besley Court Kennedy during his fight
against aborigines in 1848'; in the reputations of a boxer or two –
there is actually a memorial to the most famous of them, Dave Sands,
in the suburb of Glebe.

They seldom appear on the downtown streets. Rumour says that
property developers are trying to force them even out of Redfern, and
indeed their quarter there is so small, so ramshackle, so apparently
irrelevant to the affairs of the city, that I would not be in the least
surprised, when I go there another time, to find it all vanished.
Occasional drunks and layabouts haunt the city's more raffish quarters; around the harbour one sometimes sees the distant figures of
black fishermen, scrambling over the rocks with strings of dangling
bream, or poised statuesque at the water's edge. Some Sydney people
would not mourn if even these fragile reminders were expunged. If
the Aborigines are a blot on the conscience to many citizens of the
city, to others they are just a pain in the neck. 'The only Aborigines I
ever see are the ones who hang about King's Cross,' one gently
brought-up Sydney lady told me, 'and I hate them.'

3. Minorities

Aborigines apart, when you think of Sydneysiders you probably think
first of white (or brownish) males – the image of this city is overwhelm-
ingly masculine and European, and its attitudes are endemically mass

---

[1] The first meaning 'Stay Here', the second 'Stinking Place', the third either 'Head of
River' or, preferably to my tastes, 'Place Where Eels Lie Down'.

attitudes. But of course it is never unanimous really, still less totally homogenized, and powerful social minorities stand beyond the civic stereotypes.

Demographically Sydney's women may not be a minority, but historically, here as everywhere, they have formed an underclass. International legend has it indeed that Sydney women live in a permanently downtrodden state. Perhaps they did in the days when the mateship cult was at its apogee, between the World Wars, and when a woman's wage was seldom more than half a man's. Tacitly or explicitly the Sydney of those days, Slessor's bunch-of-bananas, tramride Sydney, excluded women from most of its favourite public pursuits – drinking in pubs, watching cricket, playing rugby, reminiscing in servicemen's clubs, life-saving on the beach – except in ancillary or decorative roles. Even when I first knew Sydney, the segregation of the sexes was very apparent, women still being confined to ladies' lounges in most pubs, and banished to the far end of the room at many social functions. A Sydney symptom that struck strangers then was the feminine habit of ending almost every phrase with a doubtfully interrogative inflection, as though anything a woman said was tentative, possibly rather foolish and vulnerable to mockery. Latin has an interrogative, *nonne*, which expects the answer yes: Sydney women's English most decidedly expected the answer no.

The earlier annals of this city, all the same, were full of boldly self-reliant women, ever since the days of Mary Reibey and the Girl from Botany Bay. Many of the earlier female convicts were desperate people. They were desperate in anger and sorrow, one imagines, when one remembers the scores of babies who died on the voyages out, or hears for example (in 1838) the voice of poor Ann Mackintosh, terribly drunk, smothering her own child to death while crying to anyone who would listen, to life itself one feels, 'you shan't have my pretty dear, no, you shan't have my pretty dear ...' But they were also desperate in defiance. The officers of the First Fleet seem to have agreed that the women convicts were more intractable, foul-mouthed and lascivious than the men. A fifth of them were probably prostitutes, it has been academically estimated; in 1802 an Irish political prisoner writing home to his sister said: 'In this country there is Eleven Hundred women I cannot count Twenty out of that number to be virtuous. The remainder support themselves through the means of Ludeness.' But at least one is left with an impression of spirited independence, and some of the early Sydney women transcended their vile circumstances to be remembered ever after.

Jolly Grace Lynch, for example, seems to have been the life and soul of the Parramatta Female Factory, a combination workshop, lying-in hospital, old-age home, refuge, reform-school and prison for the early women convicts. In this depressing place Ms Lynch proved utterly irrepressible. We see her, coming across a chimney-sweep in the factory kitchen, instantly throwing her arms around him and kissing him, covering herself with soot and sending the other inmates into screams of laughter. We hear her letting loose a flood of 'dreadful Oaths' when her skimpy dinner is laid before her. Who she was, why she was there, where she came from history does not tell us, but it recalls her with a smile.

Then there was Ann Smith, who arrived in Sydney with the First Fleet at the age of thirty (she had allegedly stolen a pewter pot). She was evidently an old lag, and she was certainly no wimp. On the voyage out she told everyone that as soon as she could she would abscond, and hardly had she landed than she did so. Like Peter Morris, she was gone within a few days. She was never recaptured, but tantalizing clues about her fate have reached us. In 1790 a piece of linen found near Parramatta was supposed to be part of her petticoat. In 1798 fishermen sheltering in a cove at Port Stephens, about 100 miles north of Sydney, were told of a white woman living with Aborigines. And in 1803, when a whaler was attacked by pirates somewhere off Alaska, among those killed was a woman said to be named Ann Smith, and to have come originally from Sydney.

Many another woman tried with less success to escape her circumstances. We read of a poor soul called Elizabeth Power, illiterate, probably alcoholic, married for twenty years to an ex-convict, who walked out on her violent husband one day in the 1820s, taking with her £500 he had just earned from the sale of cattle. She planned to

get away to Tasmania, where her married daughter lived, but everything went wrong. Friends let her down. She kept getting drunk.
Crooked policemen relieved her of the £500. She was caught by her
husband, ran away again, was caught again, was beaten, laid a
complaint against the police for taking the money, and finally it seems
accepted her destiny with a certain wry dignity. According to her
husband he found her having a glass of rum and ginger-beer with a
neighbour at a pub, and as he walked by she stretched out her hand
and said: 'Shake hands old man and kiss me, everything is all right.'[1]

A more lurid figure was Angelica Hallett, who attached herself in the
1840s to the well-known local artist Samuel Elyard. Elyard was a
chronic depressive, and he claimed that Angelica, having dismissed
his doctors, brewed for him a medicine of her own which not only
made him curiously befuddled and excited, but also persuaded him to
marry her. She threatened that unless he signed over his property to
her, she would have him committed to a lunatic asylum, and she
eventually drove him to madness. Worse, however, was to come.
Abandoning Elyard, the appalling Angelica now stunned Sydney by
revealing that she had all along been the mistress of the Governor
himself, Sir Charles Augustus FitzRoy, whose dear wife had lately
been dashed to her death against that tree in Parramatta. Sensation!
FitzRoy found himself pilloried as an immoral hypocrite, and for a
decade and more the name of Angelica Hallett sent horrid *frissons*
through respectable Sydney society.[2]

Every Sydney decade has produced its memorable ladies. In the
1820s a resourceful Irishwoman known as 'Pig Mary' lived by extract-
ing lumps of offal from the swamp by the slaughterhouse at the head
of Darling Harbour, and selling them from door to door. In the 1830s
some of the old women of the Rocks were said to be so rum-soaked
that when they lit their pipes blue flames flickered from their lips. In
the 1850s, reported an English visitor, when young women of Sydney

---

[1] I take this tale from *Australians 1838*, edited by Alan Atkinson and Marian Aveling,
Sydney 1987.
[2] Though Elyard, I am happy to report, recovered from his wife's potions, lived to a
ripe old age, and spent his last years painting windmills and cottages in the country.

went walking 'you hear the tinkle of their bunches of charms and nuggets, as if they carried bells on their fingers and rings on their toes'. In the 1880s teams of women cricketers played in the Domain, wearing peaked caps and long striped skirts, and Grace Fairley Robinson, defying the opinion of the Dean of the University Medical School that 'she would be better employed if she got a nice frock and a nice man', graduated as a Bachelor of Medicine. In the 1890s Ms Val van Tassell, 'the only lady aeronaut in the southern hemisphere', having parachuted out of a balloon over Bondi beach, landed safely in the middle of a cricket match at Coogee. In the 1920s two women were among the most powerful bosses of Sydney's organized crime, rivals in the drug trade and in the management of prostitution in Darlinghurst:[1] if one can judge from the police photographs they were a tough pair indeed – Kathleen Leigh from Ireland wears a fetching silk scarf and looks murderous, Latilda Devine from London wears a cloche hat and buckle shoes and looks speciously humble. In the 1930s six women pilots took their biplanes into the air to greet Amy Johnson at the end of a record-breaking flight from England. In the 1950s Mary Gilmore, poet, teacher, political activist, folklorist, feminist, Dame of the British Empire, reached the climax of her career as one of Sydney's most celebrated citizens, with streets, schools, scholarships and awards named for her, and a portrait in the State Art Gallery by William Dobell which, like Queen Victoria on the Customs House, memorably demonstrates the Sydney sneer (she was ninety-two when it was painted, and said it 'captured something of her ancestry').

Sydney remains rich in women of forceful character. Occasionally one still notices the old feminine inflection – listen at a café table, and the baritone demand for a beer will end in a downward cadence, the soprano asking for a white wine will rise. By now though it is a dying habit, and seems to me purely dialectal, rather than sociological. Today Sydney women seem as emancipated as women anywhere else

[1] Then the vice quarter of Sydney, and variously nicknamed Razorhurst, Gunhurst, Bottlehurst and Dopehurst.

in the western world, and indeed the city has perhaps more than its fair quota of decisive if not pugnacious ladies, ladies of society, ladies of the TV screen, business executives and academics. They are often wonderfully adept at the monologic system of converse, and sometimes resort to a particularly penetrating timbre of voice, once daringly described by John Douglas Pringle as 'a strident saw-like whine'.[1] They can be very impressive, and they can be unfortunately lofty, like the wife of the politician who, looking around for a waiter after a gala performance at the Opera House, peremptorily handed her empty glass to the conductor.

I found myself recently at a school reunion at the former Fort School, above the Rocks, where a crowd of old girls were greeting one another as old girls do. How admirable they were, I thought! How nice to each other, how kind to me, how homely, how full of smiles, how breezily be-flowered of dress and carefully permed of hair, how jolly, how open and assured![2] They looked likely to live for ever, so free of stress they seemed, and indeed one hears of some truly splendid veterans in Sydney – the ninety-year-old woman who, during the First World War, addressed a letter to 'Any Wounded French Soldier', and who has been corresponding faithfully from that day to this with Monsieur Georges Temel; the seventy-nine-year-old ballet dancer who appears in the Australian Ballet's productions, and who made her debut in classical ballet when she was sixty-three; the celebrated actress who, besides appearing regularly in stage plays, offers a popular cabaret act at the age of ninety-one.

But then many of the younger women are formidable too. No incorrigible transportee could cock a snook at destiny more

[1] And instantly recognizable anywhere in the world. Thinking I caught a snatch of it recently above the polyglot hubbub of the Piazza San Marco in Venice, I sought it out through the crowds for curiosity's sake and found, sure enough, a woman in a T-shirt emblazoned SYDNEY YOU'RE BEAUTIFUL. Mr Pringle was writing in his book *Australian Accent*, London 1958.

[2] And Sydney being Sydney, I could not help thinking, how perfectly possible that some of them might be going on that evening to the all-male show advertised in the morning paper as Australia's Hottest Ladies' Night Out – 'They're Australian, They're Handsome, They're Yours!'

effectively than some of the strapping girls one sees, in stubby shorts and shirts, cleaning the streets of Sydney; and one of the most impressive people I know in this city is the woman pilot who flies, in tandem with her husband, the Aquatic Air seaplane services up the coast to Newcastle – immensely competent, dapper and good-looking, to be seen at the seaplane jetty between flights, her blonde hair pinned up with a blue ribbon, simultaneously joking, drinking tea, checking the log and smoking a cigarette, like an image of Australian Womanhood in a propaganda poster.

Originals, male and female, have always been a well-recognized Sydney minority. The great mass of the Sydney population is probably as conformist as any other, but it likes to think of itself as a society of individualists, and has always cherished its exceptions. I suppose the convict system, which tried to reduce all its subjects to numbers, engendered a backlash which has never died.

Affectionate tribute is still paid for instance to William King, the Flying Pieman, who came to Sydney as a free schoolmaster in 1829 but became a seller of hot pies and a virtuoso walker – he walked from Sydney to Parramatta and back twice a day for six consecutive days, he walked 1,634 miles in five weeks and four days, he pulled a woman in a gig for half a mile, he picked up 1,000 corn-cobs set a yard apart in less than an hour, and he performed various esoteric feats of pedestrianism while carrying goats, dogs, cats, rats and mice. William Bland, a convict surgeon who became the most fashionable physician in Sydney in the 1830s, is fondly remembered for his famous flying machine, a kind of airship called the Amotic Machine (*sic*); it never actually flew, but was to be propelled originally by manpower, later by steam, and was supposed to be capable of carrying five tons of cargo from London to Australia in five days. In one of the official publications of the Royal Botanic Gardens a large photograph honours William James Chidley, one of the most peculiar of all the peculiar public speakers who have mounted their soapboxes in the Domain; for many years in the early part of this century he was always to be found there, dressed in a white Roman tunic, declaiming wild ideas on sex and healthy living, and periodically detained either on suspicion of lunacy, or on charges of indecent language and offensive behaviour.

Sanctioned by such illustrious examples, oddballs still seem to be generally tolerated in Sydney, and numerous eccentrics of one kind and another wander the Circular Quay, or sprawl magnanimously on the Hyde Park benches. Quirks and anomalies abound, and there is nothing wrong with showing off in this city. One often sees people in the street, old as well as young, rich and poor, blatantly soliciting the public amazement. When I first came to Sydney there was a local celebrity whose life and reputation gloriously exemplified these attitudes. In her time Bea Miles, who died in 1973, was certainly one of the city's favourite identities. She had been expensively educated (Abbotsleigh Church of England School for Girls), but had made herself into a walking emblem of bloody-mindedness in the heroic tradition of the early convicts. A burly woman of genial countenance, supported by private means, she stood for everything free, disrespectful and entertaining, and detested, as she said, all 'priggery, caddery, snobbery and smuggery'. Everyone knew her. She was usually dressed in an old cotton dress, a sun-visor and men's black shoes, carried a satchel containing books by fellow spirits like Swift and H. L. Mencken, and was often found declaiming Shakespeare by heart in the Domain. Sometimes she was seen diving into the ocean with a knife in her mouth, looking for sharks. For years this magnificent original maintained a personal feud against bus-conductors (too officious) and cab-drivers (too arrogant): sometimes she spent all day riding provocatively around on buses, chivvying bus-conductors but greeting admirers everywhere, and once she hailed a taxi and told the driver to take her the 2,600-odd miles to Perth – which he did.

There is a café at the opulent suburb of Double Bay ('Double Pay' to the wags) which Sydneysiders from Central Europe frequent. I like to go there too, to observe in his fulfilment a minority figure who was not so long ago called The New Australian – the first-generation immigrant, that is, from a country other than Britain. On the terrace at the Cosmopolitan the New Australians are no longer new, and have clearly prospered since they first came to Sydney thirty or forty years ago. Their children are absolute Australians by now, but they themselves behave just as though they are in their distant capitals of long ago. Here four men with coats slung over their shoulders smoke small cigars and passionately argue about politics – generally in still heavily accented English, sometimes in Ruritanian. Here a couple of leathery ladies, furred and proudly diamonded, sit in lofty silence over aperitifs. There is a smell of coffee and continental cigarettes. A few solitary men with signet rings read papers that ought to be called something like *Y Sblygod*, but are really *Sydney Morning Herald*s.

Yet there in the winter sunshine they all look complacently at home, and they are indeed essential to the Sydney idiom. I engaged a couple of them in conversation once. They were Hungarians, who had come to Sydney half a lifetime before out of a shambled Europe, had astutely enriched themselves and lived happily ever after. When I remarked that they seemed very fortunate people, they heartily agreed: they were extremely fortunate, Sydney was incomparably beautiful, and Australia was without question the Best Country in the World.[1]

Thirty years ago the New Australian was still an exotic and possibly a threat, even though in those days the immigrants all came from Europe. When the Sydney Municipal Board took to advertising itself in the various languages of its tax-paying citizenry – MESTSKA RADA SYDNEY, or SYDNEY VAVOSI TANBACS – old-school Sydneysiders thought the worst had happened. After all, I was told at the time, some of the immigrants had come from 'the kind of country you take pills for'. Yet in fact foreigners had always played important roles in the development of Sydney – beginning with the half-German Phillip himself. Phillip's Surveyor General, Augustus Alt, was a native of the

---

[1] All the same I suspect some of them still pine for lost luck of a different kind. 'How grand you all were,' I said when another Hungarian told me why he had never learnt to drive a car – in his youth they always had chauffeurs. 'Yes,' he simply replied.

Duchy of Hesse (and liked to call himself Baron), and his Superintendent of Convicts was a Rhinelander named Phillip Schaffer, who went on to start a thriving vineyard and was thus the Father of the Australian Wine Industry.

There were foreigners among the First Fleet convicts, too. Scooped out of the London underworld, their lives took a queer turn indeed when they found themselves shackled and confined on the other side of the world. There were two Swedes, two Frenchmen, a Norwegian, an Indian, a pair of unfortunates classified as 'probably Scandinavian' and 'probably Dutch', and at least twelve black men of various provenances. One of these, Black Caesar from Madagascar, was among those who never did knuckle under to authority. Transported for seven years for theft, he was twenty-three when he arrived in Australia, and he remained defiant until the day he died. He stole things, he ran away, he robbed Aborigines and white settlers alike. Whether in chains or in solitary confinement, he never gave in. Nothing, he proudly declared, could 'make him better'. Finally he led a band of absconding toughs into the bush and became the first of Australia's bushrangers: and so, free to the end despite everything, contemptuous still of all officialdom, he was shot dead by another convict, in 1790, there being a reward on his head of five gallons of rum.

Another famous black man was Billy Blue, a favourite character of Macquarie's Sydney. He is variously said to have arrived in Sydney in 1810 on board an American ship, or to have been transported as a convict from England in 1796, but then much about him was equivocal, for he was an enthusiastic liar. Macquarie, who employed him as a boatman, or perhaps a water bailiff, or perhaps in the Government stores, found him as entertaining as everybody else did, and gave him eighty acres of land on the north shore, almost immediately opposite Sydney Cove. This made Blue's fortune. He started a ferry service across the harbour, and on the strength of it, like his exact contemporary the ferry captain Cornelius Vanderbilt in New York, was known to everyone as the Commodore – later the Old Commodore. He was a great clown. Sometimes he made his passengers row the ferry-boat themselves, just for fun, and even in his prosperity he was a shameless beggar – he habitually carried a sack over his shoulder to accommodate the takings. Nobody knew how old he was, but he himself claimed to be seventy when he married, and he was popularly thought to be a centenarian when he died. Blue's Point is named for him, and there is a pub up the road from his ferry-station called the Old Commodore still.

Americans have frequented Sydney since the eighteenth century. They had just acquired a nationality of their own then, had seen their own penal colonies absorbed into the freest of Republics, and were perhaps given a certain *schadenfreude*, or alternatively a certain fellow-feeling, by the spectacle of the transportees. They also very soon saw chances to be grasped. American trading ships were among the first to find their way to Sydney, and Americans were prominent in Sydney's early whaling and sealing industries – who but New Englanders would have called an inlet in Sydney Harbour Chowder Bay? They have made themselves at home in Sydney ever since, and the countless Americans living in the city now are almost undetectable. The author Paul Theroux once wrote that only in Australia – perhaps only in Sydney, I would guess – could Americans abroad convincingly submerge their nationality in another, and American women especially seem easily assimilated into the civic style, cheerfully putting on weight and developing opinions well beyond the conventional perimeters.

As we shall later see, Frenchmen were the first foreign visitors ever to set foot in British Sydney, and they have often cropped up in the city's life. One of the ablest of the convict artists was the Frenchman Charles Rodius, who had been fool enough to get caught stealing a suitcase while on a visit to London in 1829; in Sydney he produced a series of lithographs of Aboriginal notables – perceptive, compassionate and haunting, but actually intended for the information of phrenologists. Hunters Hill was founded by two French émigrés in the 1840s, as a speculative project, and was for years almost a French enclave – the French Consul had a house there. French chefs have always been in demand, of course, until recently French restaurants were always the most expensive, and it was a French valet who committed one of the most notable crimes of early Sydney. In 1845 Jean Videll, having quarrelled with his employer Thomas Warne, bludgeoned him to death, dismembered him with an axe, stuffed him into a sea-chest and tried to set the house on fire: failing in this intent, he enlisted the help of a couple of friends and took the chest down to the harbour, where he hired a boatman to row them into the middle of the harbour. But Mr Warne was smelling badly by then, his blood was oozing from the box, the boatman was disinclined to believe the French explanation that it contained bad pork, and Videll was hanged outside Darlinghurst Gaol, watched by a large and appreciative crowd.

Many Greeks and Maltese have been driven to Sydney by tough times at home, and of these the most historically interesting are the immigrants from the Greek islet of Kastellorizon, which lies a few miles off the southern coast of Turkey. Kastellorizon's first contact with Australians occurred in 1915, when its entire fleet of caiques was sold to the British for the Dardanelles campaign, and helped to carry the Anzacs to their beach-heads at Gallipoli. After that war the islanders so enthusiastically emigrated to New South Wales that there are more Kastellorizians in Sydney ('Kassies') than there are in Kastellorizon, and they have a famous club in the suburb of Kingsford. As for the island itself, most of its people are now Australian citizens returned home in their retirement, and its economy is largely sustained by contributions from down under.

Some foreign settlers have added exotica all their own to the Sydney scene. It was a West Indian Creole named George Howe – 'Happy George' – who started the first Sydney newspaper in 1803, not only writing the whole of the often scurrilous *Sydney Gazette*, but editing it, setting it, printing it and personally selling it. Sydney's Superintendent of Police in the 1830s was the romantic and mysterious Captain Nicholas Rossi, an anti-Napoleonic Corsican who was popularly supposed to have got his job in return for some unexplained secret service to the British State – perhaps (and it sounds his style) in connection with George IV's divorce proceedings against Queen Caroline. Baron Carl von Beiren, a dubious nobleman variously described as Dutch, German and Dutch-American, turned up in the 1890s and founded the Australian Gunpowder and Explosives Manufacturing

Company – the suburb of Inglewood is named after his ever-hospitable house, Powder Works Road after his factory; but though the words ADVANCE AUSTRALIA were inscribed upon the gates of Inglewood, no munitions ever seem to have been produced, people came to suspect that the Baron was a confidence trickster or even a German spy, and the last we hear of him he was in gaol for embezzlement.

Then there were the Chinese who started a fish-salting works at Barrenjoey in the 1850s, and the seven Greek pirates of Hydra (captured by the Royal Navy off Libya in 1827) who worked the vines at Elizabeth Farm.[1] There was Mary Reibey's formidable female Fijian bodyguard Foo-Choo, and the otherwise unidentified Dr Brandt who lived with his baboon on Garden Island in the 1790s, and the magnificently named Russian Nicolai Nicolaevich de Miklouho-Maklay who started a marine-biology station at Watson's Bay in 1881. There were the brightly dressed Maoris and Portuguese who used to row the pilot boats, and there were any number of miscellaneous wanderers, dropouts, adventurers, deserters, mountebanks and beachcombers of every nationality under the sun, forever jumping ship, trawling Sydney for pickings, smuggling contraband or finding oblivion in the city's tolerant taverns.

Two minorities of un-British origin have played particularly fateful and permanent roles in the history of Sydney – the Irish and the Jews, both of whom have been represented here since the beginning.

There is a biographical dictionary of Australia's earliest Jews, and thumbing through its pages is a moving experience. Most of the first Jews were petty thieves from Fagin's world, the underworld of London.[2] They had usually been tried at the Old Bailey. Very few

---

[1] Five of them returned to Greece when the Greek Government, questioning the legality of their transportation, agreed to pay their passages home: two preferred to stay.

[2] But the man popularly supposed to have been Dickens' model for Fagin himself, Isaac (Ikey) Solomon, was transported not to Sydney but to Tasmania, where he was eventually freed and became in his old age relatively respectable.

had been charged with anything violent, and most of them were from the poorest of the poor – pedlars, fruit-sellers, old-clothes dealers, chimney-sweeps, hawkers, errand boys, slop-sellers, though we see an occasional silversmith and engraver, and at least one dentist. They were generally small dark people, and were likely to be well tattooed – Lewis Joseph, for instance, a moulder and founder, transported for theft in 1829, sported the tattoos 'Love', 'Hope', 'Love me little, love me long', an anchor, a sprig, a heart, and the initials EK and LJBK. Often they lived out their sentences in obscurity, eventually disappearing into the Sydney populace, but often enough they never submitted. Here is Samuel Lyons, a well-known pickpocket transported in 1815, twice trying to escape and once trying to rob the Government Stores (200 lashes, four years in the Newcastle coal mines). Here is Lewis Lazarus, tailor, transported for theft in 1818, further convicted in Australia of robbery, absconding, assault, receiving stolen property, drunkenness, absconding again, theft again – 136 lashes, six weeks on the treadmill, speared five times by Aboriginals. Bernard Levy, transported for robbery with assault in 1813, was described as 'the most notorious thief and pocket picker the colony has ever produced' – so beyond redemption that when he was pardoned at last in 1862 members of the Sydney synagogue suggested the congregation should raise the money to ship him back to England.

Turn a page or two of the biographical dictionary, though, and here we find James Simmons, convicted in 1813, aged seventeen, of having broken into the home of the Dowager Duchess of Devonshire, in very short order the owner of an inn and a store, a prosperous auctioneer, a charterer of ships and an alderman of the City of Sydney. Remember Sam Lyons, who tried to rob the Government Stores? Only twelve years later, home and free from the coal mines, here he is a spectacularly successful property developer, active in the synagogue, well-known for good works, driving around Sydney behind a pair of his Arab thoroughbreds. Esther Abraham, a London millinery apprentice transported for attempted theft, had attached herself and her baby to a ship's officer, George Johnston, even before she reached Australia; he became one of the colony's best-known citizens, she became mistress of a mansion and a great estate. Solomon Levey, transported in 1813 for accessory to theft, was pardoned within four years and became one of Sydney's most respected capitalists, purchaser of Piper's Henrietta Villa, pioneering patron of West Australia and founder of a distinguished dynasty in Australia and in England.[1] And sometimes if the Sydney Jews failed in their lifetimes, their descendants made up for it: Michael Davies, for instance (false pretences, 1839) came to nothing himself and saw one of his sons hanged as a bushranger, but his grandson became Speaker of the Tasmanian House of Assembly, while Cashmore Israel (theft from his own family's house, 1817) was father to the Auditor-General of the Commonwealth of Australia.

The convicts were soon followed by free Jewish settlers, and the very first male among these is perhaps the most celebrated. Barnett Levey came to Sydney in the wake of his immensely successful emancipist brother Solomon. He is remembered chiefly as the founder of Sydney's first theatre, but he had many other interests too. He started a lending library. He issued bank notes backed not by gold or sterling, but by Indian rupees. He launched a housing project. He owned the Royal Hotel, a grandiose building, designed by Francis Greenway, which was in its day the tallest in Sydney – a 'frightfully lofty temple' is how George Howe described it in the *Gazette*. Levey was frequently in trouble, legal or financial, but after endless altercations with officialdom, and repeated financial setbacks, in 1833 he achieved his chief ambition and opened the Theatre Royal; there he put on a racily eclectic repertoire of operas, operettas, classic plays, melodramas and sometimes bawdy farces. Alas, he squandered his profits away in drink and extravagance, and died poor but ever-mourned in 1837, aged thirty-nine – the Father of the Australian Theatre.

Since those days Jews have become ubiquitous in the business, artistic and financial circles of the city, and in general they have thrived. There have been occasional spasms of anti-Semitism – in recent years particularly, the vandalizing of graves – but it has not

[1] One member of which, the lawyer–dramatist Harold Rubinstein, a century later wrote a play, *To the Poets of Australia*, about the family's early days in Sydney.

been one of Sydney's habitual bigotries. Today the community is
60,000 strong, its rabbis are prominent civic figures, and it is worthily
represented by the magnificent Great Synagogue in Elizabeth Street,
consecrated in 1878. A grand structure in mingled Gothic and Byz-
antine manners, this has two towers, fine wrought-iron gates, and
a big rose window overlooking Hyde Park. I went there for a
guided tour once, and a most relaxed and entertaining member of
the congregation led us into the fane, whistling as he went, while
a video of the presiding rabbi, projected hugely on a screen above
the pillars, told us all about it. On another occasion, in an alfresco
restaurant beside Sydney Cove, I happened to sit at the next table
to a party assembled for a wedding at the synagogue next day.
Some of its members had not met each other for years, if ever, and
as I eavesdropped over my John Dory fillets I thought the snatches
of conversation I heard – 'he lived for a time at Breslau' – 'You
must be Reuben's daughter! My!' – 'Between Hampstead and Shep-
herd's Bush' – 'That was before 1939, of course' – 'Do tell us, did
you ever hear what became of Ruth?' – I thought it seemed like a
very orchestration, at once tragic and exhilarating, of the Diaspora
itself.

   And what can I say of the Irish? They have been in Sydney since
the beginning too, and they have remained as Irish here as they
remain anywhere outside their own island – weakening in their style a
little now, I think, as memories fade, religion falters and organized
labour loses its predominance, but exceedingly Irish still. About a
third of the convicts transported here were Irish, and they were often
different in kind from the rest – older, more likely to be married, more
rural, the women thought to be better-behaved than the English, the
men more often politically charged. Ireland was endemically in turmoil during the transportation era, and many a young Irish patriot
found himself sent to the other side of the world for waving the green
too exuberantly.

   Some of the Irish convicts were extremely simple. They were leading
progenitors of the theory that China lay just out of sight over the hills,
and that a quick walk through the bush would get you there; the

most ingenuous carried with them a home-made compass chart without a needle, believing that the compass points themselves would give them magic guidance. But there were some able and remarkable people too, especially of course among the political prisoners. The nearest Sydney can claim to a saint is William Davis, an Irish rebel transported in 1799, who for more than a year sheltered an illegally immigrated priest, Father Jeremiah O'Flynn; secret masses were held in his cottage on Church Hill, perilously close to the George Street guard-house, until in 1818 O'Flynn was discovered and expelled. Irish ex-soldiers led the only concerted armed rising of convicts at the Sydney settlement, the so-called Battle of Vinegar Hill in 1804.[1] They were mostly men transported after the Irish rebellion of 1798, and put to work clearing forest and building roads north of Parramatta; they hoped to raise a general convict insurrection, but were deceived by a false flag of truce and put down with many casualties, floggings and hangings.

You can still be very Irish in Sydney, if you want to be. There are Irish pubs. There is Irish music. There is a Blarney Street on Killarney Heights, and though it is true that Irishtown is no longer called Irishtown, it is still called Kellyville. The fifteen directors of the Australian Ireland Fund include two McGraths, two Burkes, two Cosgroves, two O'Reillys, one O'Neill and the Earl of Portarlington. I went once to a St Patrick's Day breakfast, held in a big marquee outside a pub in the Rocks, and saw the Sydney Irish at their jolliest. Pipes played, flutes tootled, stout and Gaelic coffee flowed, all the best-known Irish citizens were caught by the TV cameras tucking into a hearty ham and eggs or dancing vigorous jigs. 'Is there anyone here from Belfast, now?' rang the band-leader's inquiry fruitily across Sydney Cove, or 'Here's a little song for all you good people from County Waterford.' I had intended, since the breakfast cost $50 a head, to watch these proceedings economically from the outside, peer-

[1] One of the two pitched battles between Europeans on Australian soil, the other being the affair of the Eureka Stockade in Victoria in 1854, which lasted only ten minutes.

ing through a flap in the tent, but a couple of cheerfully tipsy waiters soon pulled me inside and gave me a Guinness.

And all these people are immigrants, every one, if only by descent – even the Aborigines have come from somewhere else. Thirty years ago it was easy enough to forget the fact, so settled and homogeneous was Sydney's population. Now reminders are everywhere. Kilioni Uele, charged with the attempted murder of Haumomo Uepe of Homebush outside the Tonga Taboo nightclub, is arraigned before Mr Alex Mijovich, Her Majesty's Justice of the Peace. Passionately defending the wearing of tartans on behalf of Comhairie Oighreachd Albannach (the Scottish Heritage Council) is Mr R. Nicolson Samios. A black shoeshine boy in the Queen Victoria Building struts around his stand like a dancer in a musical. Multi-racial larrikins race their bikes hilariously through the Botanic Gardens. Rahmat Ullah, seventeen, defects from the Bangladesh National Dancing Group and vanishes into Sydney, leaving a note for his producer: 'Uncle, my luck in Bangladesh is very poor. So, I am out to search for my fortune.'

I hope he has found it by now, and become a New Man like all the rest, or one of the Sun-God's race.

CONSOLATIONS

IT IS A NICE PARADOX THAT SYDNEY, A CITY BORN IN MISERY, should be blessed with a true gift for self-consolation. In 1850 Charles Dilke was already commenting upon its high capacity for personal pleasure, and it long ago developed a very different communal ethic from that of the more religion-bound and work-obsessed cities of North America. Nowadays the arrival of Friday arvo is a Sydney institution – the sanctioned moment when, at noon on the fifth day, much of the populace subsides into hedonism; but no matter what day of the week it is, or what time of day either, more than most cities Sydney seems to enjoy itself.

There were few Puritans, of course, on Australia's First Fleet, and a general lack of religious zealotry or remorse has undoubtedly helped to foster the Sydney euphoria. It could never be said that religion is the opiate of the Sydney masses – I know of no city where it seems less obtrusive. A century ago it was recorded that orthodox Christianity had little hold on the local mind, 'neither belonging to the country nor yet adapted to its peculiar requirements': the 1986 census showed that apart from the faiths of immigrants, the fastest growing denomination was the one classified as No Religion. The Baha'i Temple stands proudly enough among the woodlands of the north, Greenway's St James's church is prominent, the Great Synagogue is resplendent, St Mary's Cathedral is vast, but on the whole places of religion play an unusually minor part in the city's aesthetic ensemble.

For some years they played no part at all. An outdoor Anglican service was conducted on the first Sunday after the landing at Sydney Cove, the text of Chaplain Johnson's sermon being taken from Psalm 161 – 'What shall I render unto the Lord for all his benefits towards me?' No church went up, however, for another five years, until Johnson had one built at his own expense on a spot (in Johnson Place) now marked by a memorial. Its convict congregationalists were flogged if they failed to attend without good cause: wondering perhaps what they could best render unto the Lord for his mercies, they habitually spat, coughed and hiccuped throughout the services, and it was almost certainly some of them who burnt the building down in 1798. A second church was soon built – the one that looked like a prison – but in 1826 Barron Field was still complaining that Sydney was 'a spireless city, and profane'. The first three Catholic priests, allowed into the colony at the start of the nineteenth century, were soon expelled on the grounds that they were inciting rebellion; the fourth arrived illicitly in 1817, began his underground pastorate under the protection of brave Mr Davis, and was thrown out in 1818. It appears to have been only in the middle of the nineteenth century that religion assumed the social role it played in most English-speaking cities around the world, and even then it was largely an instrument of class – English Anglicans on one side, Irish Catholics on the other. Today it is administered by a Catholic Cardinal, an Anglican Archbishop, and countless ministers, rabbis and mullahs; yet it seems to me, as an agnostic outsider, relatively muted still.

Like any great English-speaking city Sydney has its quota of cults and enthusiasms, encouraged here perhaps by the quasi-Californian climate, but it has never been a great place for revival movements or sectarian bitterness.[1] There was however one famous example of religious ecstasy in Sydney, and its improbable focus was on the beach promenade in the suburb of Balmoral, on the Middle Harbour. This is now a very model of suburban contentment. It has a little white pavilion, a bathhouse and a rotunda for a band. An ornamental bridge leads to a public garden on a spit, and there a club of local friends meets every day of the year to have breakfast as the sun goes up. This modest esplanade was to acquire unexpected prominence when the mystical Theosophical Society declared it a site of profound sacred significance. The Theosophists were convinced that a World Teacher would soon be coming to rescue mankind from its ignorance, and some of their seers also believed in the existence of the lost continent, Lemuria, which lay beneath the Pacific and would eventually give up its ancient secrets for the salvation of mankind. After the First World War they determined that Sydney was central to these truths. It was, they said, 'the occult centre of the southern hemisphere'. They acquired a large many-gabled mansion at Mosman on the northern shore, and Theosophist pilgrims came there from all over the world – including the young Indian, Jiddu Krishnamurti, whom some of them believed to be the World Teacher in gestation. They established a school and a radio station, 2GB.[2] They arranged publicity in the press. They attracted influential sympathizers, including Walter Burley Griffin up the road at Castlecrag. By the 1920s their Lodge in Sydney was said to be the largest in the world, and in 1924, on the unassuming beach at Balmoral, they built a great white holy amphitheatre. It could hold 2,500 people in twenty-six tiers of seats, and it looked magnificently across the harbour, through the Heads and out to sea. Here was a place of Coming, it was said, where the World Teacher would reveal all when the time was

[1] Though the nineteenth-century Welsh sculptor W. Lorando Jones must have felt at home in Sydney when, refused commissions because he had been convicted of blasphemy, he was reduced to making tombstone pedestals.
[2] The GB standing for Giordano Bruno, the sixteenth-century philosopher who was claimed as one of Theosophy's progenitors.

ripe; and through those mighty bluffs would flow the knowledge of
Lemuria.

The conviction faded when, in 1929, Krishnamurti publicly
declared that he was not the promised Teacher, and in 1939 the site
of the Coming was sold – an apartment block stands on the site now.
Today it is hard to find signs of religious fervour in Sydney. I once
saw a shirtless boy march into St Andrew's Cathedral and fall in
passionate prayer before the altar, but it seemed forlornly out of
character. I went to the lying-in of a much venerated Irish Catholic
priest, expecting to find scenes of histrionic distress, but the mourners
were restrained, tearless and altogether devoid of black veils. A group
of charismatic Christians recently fed their conceptions of Jesus into
the Sydney Police Crime Unit's Image Generator – its Identikit. He
looked like a cross between the Bondi life-saver and a small-time
crook, with short hair back and sides.

Spiritually the most rewarding place in Sydney seems to me
Rookwood Cemetery, which is one of the largest in the world, and
includes graves of every denomination. It was founded in 1867, and
by the end of the century was the very latest thing in cemeteries,
eventually embracing 777 acres of land (well away from settled
areas, we read, 'so that adjoining land would not be devalued').[1]
It had its own railway stations, and twice a day trains from Sydney
stopped at stations *en route* to pick up 'corpses, mourners or clergymen', the mourners and clergymen having to buy tickets but the
corpses travelling free. It was splendidly landscaped, with gazebos
and canals, and was famous for its flower-beds – a green rose
used habitually to blossom there. A park ranger lived in a lodge
with a tower, wore a peaked cap with RANGER on it, and carried
a revolver for the extermination of stray dogs and goats. People
of all sorts were buried in this ideal necropolis. The very first was
an eighteen-year-old Irish pauper, and among those who followed

---

[1] It was clearly modelled upon Brookwood Cemetery, outside London, which was
opened in 1854 – and surely named after it too, though the Sydney theory is that it got
its name from a local prevalence of crows, this city's second-best substitutes for the
rooks of the old world.

him were politicians, artists, bushrangers, entertainers and tycoons.[1]

The trains stopped in 1948.[2] The showplaces fell into decay, and today Rookwood is a more realistic allegory of the natural condition. In its centre it is still well-kept, and the adherents of many creeds lie there in trim oblivion – disciples of Shintoism, or Assyrian Catholicism, or the Salvation Army, or Hinduism, or Judaism, or Islam – Greeks and Latvians and Hungarians and Assyrians and Italians – all in their own clearly demarcated and appropriately scripted plots. Joggers and cyclists pass among them, here and there are people tidying up graves, or laying fresh flowers, but as you wander away from the heart of the place an organic decay sets in. Obelisks become more tottery, gravestones are cracked, iron balustrades stand bent and rusted, until finally the great place of death is regenerated at its edges into life. The remotest parts of Rookwood are pure bushland, and there snakes, frogs, tortoises, ginks and geckos flourish, hares and foxes hide, figbirds and honey-eaters flutter vivaciously among the gums.[3]

Secular consolations have been more boisterously pursued. Sex in

<hr />

[1] Not to mention, since this is a passage about religion, Jacob Pitman, died 1890. He was a religious pioneer whose brother was Isaac Pitman, the spelling reformer, and his epitaph at Rookwood says he woz the ferst Minister in theez Koloniz ov the Doktrinz ov the Sekond or Niu Kristian Church.

[2] One of the burial stations was turned into a restaurant, another now forms the beguiling Church of All Saints at Ainsley, Canberra, where its congregation is summoned to worship by a bell taken from a railway engine – sustaining the motif, as it were. In previous years passing the Redfern mortuary station was the signal to railway travellers that they were approaching Sydney Central. 'No hurry till you see the mortuary station' – how many people had made that remark, wondered Kylie Tennant in her novel *Ride On Stranger*, 1943, as they folded up their newspapers ready to leave the train?

[3] More than a million people are thought to be buried at Rookwood, and in 1981 the Society of Australian Genealogists transcribed all their surviving epitaphs on to microfilm. It took ninety people seven years to do the job, and their labour is recorded in a book, *The Sleeping City*, edited by David A. Weston, Sydney 1989, to which I am much indebted.

Sydney, for example, began with a bang on the night of 6 February 1788, when the female convicts were disembarked to join the males already ashore at Sydney Cove. No doubt in the fortnight since the raising of the flag the married officers and wives had comforted each other in their beds, and perhaps a few people of initiative had already found comfort among the Aborigines. For the mass of the convict population, though, the barriers were lowered when the women at last came down the gangplanks on to Australian soil. It was a rough night. Violent winds and rain swept the settlement, lightning streaked across the harbour, but the moment the women stepped ashore the penal community threw itself into orgy. After eight months at sea, cooped up in sexual segregation and cruel confinement, both men and women were ready for it. The officials and marines were unable to control them – perhaps they did not even try – and the diarists seem to stand back aghast, as they view the commotion beside the Tank Stream. Tench preferred not to mention it at all. Arthur Bowes Smith, surgeon on one of the transports, said it was beyond his abilities to give a just description of the scene. We can only imagine it, reading between the lines and remembering human nature: around the soggy tents and shacks of Sydney Cove that night, watched from a cautious distance by officialdom and the less impetuous of the felons, several hundred couples writhing and twisting in the mud, while oaths, drunken songs, laughs, groans and the clankings of irons compete with the thunder.

It is a scene not at all appropriate to Sydney. This is not a very orgiastic city. In modern times the relationship between men and women here has traditionally been self-conscious, while homosexuality, though prevalent among the convicts and common now, has only recently become socially acceptable. It is true that the history books are full of licentious suggestion: 'detestable vices' that could be satisfied in the Sydney of the 1790s, 'scenes of immorality beyond description' in the Domain of the 1860s. However when in 1838 rumour said that Richard Davies was 'doing something improper with a pig', his neighbour Mrs Holland retorted indignantly that he

was 'not a man of that description', and most Sydney males today are
not of that description either.[1]

Wowserism has never been as powerful here as in Melbourne – its
name, indeed, was invented by a Sydney man of permissive instinct,
John Norton the editor of *Truth*.[2] Still, the city has had its share of
killjoys, and anyway the general delight in the sun, the sea and the
sand has perhaps kept libidos in restraint. I recently analysed a column
of twenty Strictly Personal advertisements in one of the suburban
newspapers, and found that twelve of those seeking soul-mates required
a commitment to sailing, bush-walking, surfing or simply the beach:
the Cultured Lady, 49, who admitted that she was chiefly fond of
anything fattening, expensive or sedentary seemed to me to be casting
her bread upon unpromising waters. When the magazine *Tracks* asked
its readers which was better, surfing or sex, 62 per cent said surfing. To
be sure 80 per cent admitted they thought about sex when surfing,
but then 51 per cent said they thought about surfing during sex.

It says something about the survival of innocence in Sydney that its
people are so touchingly proud of King's Cross. Originally called
Queen's Cross, in honour of Queen Victoria's Diamond Jubilee, the
suburb was renamed when Edward VII came to the throne, and it
used to be the centre of bohemia in Sydney, the one cosmopolitan
part of town before the New Australians arrived. It was given a sleazy
reputation by the American servicemen who flocked there during the
Second World War, and later during the Vietnam War, and at night
nowadays it suggests a red-light quarter in some kind of sociological
exhibition, so compactly assembled are its strip shows, its pornographic
bookstores and its upstairs massage parlours. The necessary hard-
looking unshaven men hang around the Alamein fountain, a whirling
floodlit device like a dandelion head. The essential emaciated prostitutes parade the shadowy sidewalks of Victoria Street. There is the
statutory scattering of drug-addicts, transvestites, tourists, drunks,

[1] Though Mrs Holland was wrong, unfortunately: Davies was later caught in the act
in his peach orchard, and sent away to life imprisonment on Norfolk Island.
[2] Supposedly, I learn from *The Macquarie Encyclopedic Dictionary*, as an acronym for his
ironic slogan 'We Only Want Social Evils Remedied'.

sailors and miscellaneous layabouts from around the world. You would have to be very unworldly to be surprised by the all-too-familiar sights of King's Cross; yet Sydneysiders habitually recommend it to foreigners as a prime metropolitan spectacle, not on any account to be missed.

Anyway, if you go back to the Cross in the morning you will find it charmingly village-like. The GIRLS! GIRLS! GIRLS! signs are out, the adult movie houses are closed, those jowly men are still in bed, and now you find flower shops and grocery stalls, pleasant houses in back streets, one of the best bookshops in Sydney and some of the most agreeable coffee shops. Along Victoria Street, now revealed as a delightful leafy thoroughfare, dropouts and addicts of the night before sit demurely beside the blistered Volkswagen campers they are trying to sell, before going home to be chartered accountants.

Far more than sex, the delight and the despair of Sydney has been strong drink. Hardly a passage of this city's history is without a reference to it, from the very earliest days when convicts always seemed to be able to get hold of it, to the fearful drunken-driving records of today. So far as I can discover the Australian Aborigines, almost alone among the peoples of the earth, never learnt to make fermented drinks – or perhaps never needed to, their elaborate otherworld of dreams, song and legend being quite intoxicating enough. Hardly had the British arrived, however, than alcohol became an essential adjunct to life, and rum, a generic name for hard spirits of all kinds, assumed the importance of money itself. Goods were bought in it. Labourers got their wages in it. Chaplain Johnson paid for his church in it. The rebellion against Bligh was named after it. The 44th Regiment mutinied for it. The New South Wales Corps, its officers having acquired their monopoly in it, became known as the Rum Corps, and for years the Sydney general hospital, which was largely financed by it, was called the Rum Hospital.

The original rum was all imported, from England or from India, but the settlers were soon making their own, together with wines, beers and more peculiar liquors. A spirit made of fermented sugar bags soaked in buckets of water proved popular among the Aborigines. The leaves of the Sticky Hop-bush, chewed by the Iora as a cure for toothache, were adopted by the Europeans to flavour their ale. A beer sampled at the Parramatta fair in 1824 was said to be so strong that 'reason was de-throned and madness and folly reigned in its stead', while an early settler of the North Shore, experimenting with fermented peaches, reported that 'one glas put parson in the whelebarrow'.[1]

In the nineteenth century there was a proliferation of pubs (called hotels in the city to this day). They were socially important in the early years because so many men were without families or decent homes, and later they became nests of mateship, being generally out of bounds to respectable women. With their quaint inn-signs and particular reputations, the taverns greatly enhanced Sydney's sense of picturesque antiquity, and they often had piquant names: the Help Me Through the World, the World Turned Upside-Down, or the Keep Within the Compass (kept by a former policeman). Sometimes they had resident fiddlers, often they were frequented by gambling schools and haunted by whores, and they came in many specialities. There were pubs where soldiers were not welcome, and pubs where convicts were not liked, and snug pubs that catered to the country trade, and rough pubs popular among the boxing fraternity. The massed taverns and sly-grog houses of the Rocks were so uproarious in their heyday that their cumulative noise could be heard miles out to sea. The bar rail of the Shakespeare Tavern, in the 1880s, had an electric wire running through it, enabling its puckish landlord to galvanize his customers. The Marble Bar at Adams' Hotel was a prodigy of coloured marble from France, Italy and Belgium, supplemented by American walnut panelling, chandeliers, stained glass and lubricious wall paintings.[2]

---

[1] He is quoted by Ruth Park in *The Companion Guide to Sydney*, Sydney 1973.
[2] And still to be enjoyed in a new home at the Sydney Hilton Hotel: as a pamphleteer wrote in 1893, 'the globe-trotter who visits the bar for his glass of whisky looks round him with astonishment'.

The pubs were open from six in the morning until eleven at night, and of course there were objectors to all this jollity. Temperance movements waxed and waned in Sydney – as early as 1837 the Quaker merchant John Tawell, whom we have met before, ostentatiously poured a large quantity of spirits into the harbour.[1] The real blow to the city's drinking habits, however, did not occur until 1916, when there was a mutiny among the troops at a training camp in the western suburb of Casula. Objecting to a new and demanding training programme, several thousand soldiers raided the camp liquor stores, looted some pubs of their drink, and set off on a dishevelled progress across the city, smashing windows, breaking up food stalls, seizing cars and wagons, attacking clubs and stores and terrifying civilians wherever they went. There was no denying that drink was the cause of this rampage, and so there came into force one of Sydney's most depressing institutions, 'the six o'clock swill'. For nearly forty years every legal pub in the city shut its doors at six in the evening, leading not only to a plethora of speakeasies, but also to a headlong consumption of liquor in the last moments before closing time, when people came out from work. The Sydney pubs acquired a new reputation for lavatorial crudity, and were mostly re-decorated accordingly, with tiled walls for the easier cleansing of spilt beer and vomit. Everything most philistine, provincial and misogynist about Sydney was epitomized in the six o'clock swill: at the end of each working day (as citizens of vivid memory have described it for me) a tide of inebriated men came rolling out of their ghastly taverns, staggering into railway stations, barging on to buses or being sick over ferry rails.

The rule was mercifully abandoned in 1955. Nowadays the pubs have mostly softened their ambiences, and welcome women with more or less good grace. Although beer and Sydney still go together in the world's mind, the per capita consumption of alcohol has lately declined, perhaps because of the new proportion of abstemious Italians, Greeks and Asians. Despite the neighbourhood problems of

[1] A watching seaman cried out 'That's real murder,' and this was a curious form of prophecy, for when the pious Tawell went home to England in 1838 he poisoned his mistress, and was hanged for it.

that former Premier a couple of chapters back, for the most part public drinking in Sydney is temperate enough – even rather apathetic. I looked at one pub across a suburban street on a summery Friday, and this is what I saw: upstairs, in a window with a wilted potted plant in it, and a faded awning outside, an elderly shirt-sleeved man with spectacles, all alone with a pint of beer; downstairs, through the open door of one bar, four slump-stomached workmen over the tankards at the counter, through the open door of another, two women watching an American chat-show on television. The general decorative impression was of a faded yellow. The television flickered dimly. A chalked blackboard offered Beef-and-Mushroom Pie or Chops with Mushroom Sauce. Catching sight of me scribbling these notes across the road, the man upstairs allowed his gaze to rest upon me for a moment or two, but soon lost interest.

On the other hand Friday evening down on the Rocks, traditionally the quarter of chaos, can still be sufficiently rumbustious. Then the young people come into town from the outer suburbs, determined to live metropolitan life to the full, and the mounted police regularly move in to keep things in check. I was at a reception one evening at the Regent Hotel, the most luxurious in Sydney, which was a paragon of discreet conservative elegance. The older people were dressed expensively but not gaudily, the younger ones were in properly tempered derivations of street fashion. The music was provided, as is habitual at the Regent, by an elegant flute-and-piano duo. The refreshments were suave. Needing a breath of fresh air I took a couple of sandwiches and wandered through the foyer into the street outside; and there, not a hundred yards away, in the shadow of the expressway, I found Saturnalia in full swing. A couple of dozen young people, reconditely dressed and impossibly drunk, were singing obscene songs in the half light. There were beer cans in their hands, beer cans lined up for future consumption, empty beer cans rolling over the sidewalk. A youth in a wild and scraggly beard played the guitar. Three or four girls danced an abandoned go-go on a ledge. The men were husky and flushed, the women looked half-crazed, and they were all singing, shouting, waving their arms about, sloshing their beer and sometimes breaking into hilarious dizzy dances, like people in a dream.

I was rather sorry to leave this Bosch-like gathering and return to the reception in the hotel, where a waitress instantly offered me a small shrimp canapé, and the flautist was into a Telemann sonata, I think.

Except for that brief grim period in the 1780s, almost nobody has gone hungry in Sydney. The Iora were always capably self-sufficient, the convicts were quite well fed. Perhaps it was this tradition of general plenty that made the city for so long indifferent to cuisine. Even twenty years ago the food, whether private or public, was a desperate approximation of English provincial cooking, its one famous dish being the Pie Floater – a meat pie floating in pea soup which has been sold since 1945 at the Woolloomooloo food stall called Harry's Café de Wheels. Fish generally turned out to be fish and chips in the old greasy style, few Sydneysiders were keen on oysters and the cooking of kangaroos was illegal.

It is illegal still, innumerable patriots holding that to eat a national symbol would smack of treason, or perhaps sacrilege, but by now food has become almost a national symbol itself, and is certainly one of the prime Sydney consolations. The influx of foreign restaurateurs has changed everything – starting with the tea, now generally metamorphosed into espresso coffee. The restaurants have burgeoned sidewalk tables at last, besides climbing several hundred feet up the Sydney Tower and spreading themselves all around the harbour front. I can think of no national cuisine which is not represented somewhere in the city nowadays, and at private tables the food may be anything from roast beef to couscous. For a time the *nouvelle cuisine* in its silliest forms seduced fashionable Sydney, and everything was stuffed with artichokes or grilled over herb-scented charcoal. Today the fad is over, and the best of the restaurants have come to realize that the true Sydney speciality should surely be fresh fish and shellfish, simply served. At Watson's Bay, on the harbour, the Doyle family restaurant has been preaching this gospel for several generations; now it has been joined by dozens of others, to be dropped in at while waiting for a ferry at Circular Quay, or flown to by seaplane on the Hawkesbury River, and serving Moreton Bay Bugs, Mud-Crab Salad, Sydney Rock Oysters and all manner of fish washed down with good New South Wales wine beside lovely watery prospects.

It is sadly true, however, that to many foreign palates even the freshest and most straightforward Sydney food, even the juiciest Bug or most perfectly steamed Hawkesbury River Teraglin, seems disappointingly flavourless. It is glorious in the idea, enticing in the appearance, but it tastes as though it has been cooked in unsalted water – or in the case of the sea-fish, caught in unsalted oceans. Only the Sydney Rock Oyster, surely the best in the world, lives up to its promise. I am sorry to say this, because I first learnt the pleasure of gourmandcy in Sydney, thirty years ago. Until then I had been as indifferent to the subtleties of food as any six o'clock swiller, but I was given lunch one day by a friend in his apartment on the south shore, with a glorious view ᴜp the harbour to the city. The food was nothing elaborate – a crusty roll, as I remember, some pâté and salad, perhaps a cheese, a glass of white wine – but my host served it all with such sensuous grace, broke the bread with such crispy decision, drank the wine with such an almost lascivious slurp, that suddenly in Sydney I realized what a transcendental delight eating and drinking could be.

For years I remembered every detail of this seminal occasion – the food itself, my stalwart epicurean host, the blue Australian sky above us, the olive-green of the trees, the white sails of the harbour yachts and, crowning it all like a benediction upon the experience, the soaring white wings of the Opera House. Only quite recently did it dawn upon me that the Opera House hadn't been built yet.

'Seven Miles to Manly', it says above Pier 3 on Circular Quay, 'A Thousand Miles from Care' – or, as an earlier publicity tag put it, 'Fourpence Spent on the Trip to Manly is Better than a Pound on Medicine'. Essential to the full enjoyment of Sydney is a taste for the out-of-doors. The climate may not be as perfect as foreigners generally suppose it to be, but it is never really cold, and every year contains

days of such unsurpassable beauty, such glory of freshness and stimu-
lation, that they colour all perceptions. For myself, though I have
experienced this city in moods surly, dismal and almost alarming,
when I think of a Sydney day I think immediately and deliciously of
a rather northern kind of brilliance, as though the pale white clouds
have drifted across the blue up there from Iceland or Helsinki.

And the setting is perfectly matched, providing the citizens of
Sydney with unbeatable pleasure-grounds. The harbour itself might
almost have been designed for recreation, and there has probably
been hardly a daylight moment, for 200 years, when there was not
somebody fishing somewhere on its shores, sailing on its waters or
having a picnic around its perimeter. The first registered owner of a
Sydney pleasure-boat was Robert Campbell the merchant, back in
Macquarie's day, and in 1827 the Royal Navy officially sanctioned
the delights of the harbour, as it were, by holding the city's first
regatta: all the local worthies were among the guests, quadrilles were
danced on board the warships in the harbour, and the Sydney professional watermen had their own race. By the mid-nineteenth century
people of all ranks were out in boats, and swimming and rowing
contests had become great Sydney spectator sports; 30,000 people
went to the funeral of 'Varney' Kieran, a champion swimmer of the
fin-de-siècle, and an obelisk on a rock in the Parramatta River still
honours Henry Searle, a star of late Victorian sculling.

Fleets of excursion boats now indulged the Sydney penchant for a
day out on the water. Even the ferry commuters often made a pleasure
of necessity; for many years a society called the Hot Potato Club,
formed by businessmen using the late-night ferry home to Mosman,
kept a supply of pies and potatoes warm near the ship's engines, and
washed them down each evening with a convivial drink. The Sunday
harbour picnic became an institution, too – Kipling called this 'a city
of picnics'. On especially picnickable days the path to Yurong Point,
in the Domain, was lined with stalls selling boiling water for tea-
making, and there are innumerable pictures of the populace spreading
its cloths on green swards, or hanging expectantly with wicker baskets
over the rails of steamers. Picnic dances were popular too, and came

to be known as Gypsy Teas; a favourite spot for them was Rodd
Island, the exotic-looking islet we glimpsed from the planned suburb
of Haberfield. All around the harbour there are reminders still of
those period delights, in little parks, and gazebos, and old landing-
stages. The memento I like best is the pavilion–café in Nielsen Park,
on the south shore; a nostalgic curio of cream, brown and stained
glass, decorated with potted ferns, it looks out over a bathing beach
where even on the windiest day elderly Victorian-looking gentlemen
are quite likely to be stimulating their circulations with heavy breast-
strokes, or paddling like dogs along the sand.[1]

The harbour remains the greatest Sydney consolation. The week-
end sight of it, with its thousands of yachts, is a very epitome of
pleasure; the start of the Sydney-to-Hobart Race, and the spectacular
passage of its yachts through the Heads, is one of the prime occasions
of the Sydney year; the Australia Day ferry-boat race, direct successor
to that original race of the watermen in 1827, must be one of the most
entertaining of all sporting events – such a chuffing and foaming and
lurching, as the tough little ships strain themselves along the brief
course from Pinchgut to the Bridge![2] For many Sydney people a boat
on the harbour is still the best of possessions, even if it is only for
lazing about on, drinking beer, in the shelter of some placid cove.[3]
The harbour picnic may not be quite what it was, the Gypsy Teas are
over, but Kipling would certainly recognize the spirit of a Sunday
lunchtime at Watson's Bay – crowded white-clothed tables of restaurants, old ladies on benches eating seafood off plastic trays, families

[1] Yearning for the old days may be moderated, all the same, by reading a list of the
objects hauled out of the harbour by scavenger boats in the single year 1914. They
included the corpses of some 3,500 rats, 2,000 dogs, 1,500 hens and chickens, 1,000
cats, 200 rabbits, 29 pigs, 20 sheep, 13 calves, 9 goats, 8 lambs, 8 wallabies, 7 hares
and a monkey.

[2] And such embarrassment, too, when in 1984 the forty-eight-year-old ferry-boat
Karrabee, having done its best in the race, returned to its pier at Circular Quay and
sank.

[3] 'Wanted' (says a perhaps apocryphal small advertisement in a Sydney shop window),
'woman to cook, clean fish, dig for worms and make love. Must own boat and
outboard motor. Send photo of boat.'

strolling beneath the palms of the little park, bright umbrellas every-where, scavenging gulls, launches foaming in, yachts and tourist coaches, and away in the distance the flags on top of the Harbour Bridge just showing over Bradley's Head.

Excursion boat-trips are still perhaps the most popular of all Sydney outings. Sometimes they can be rowdy disco charters – 'hose-down trips', they are called, because the boats so often need a good wash the morning after, and there were some disreputable cruises during the Vietnam War, when American servicemen interpreted Rest and Recreation as a synonym for sex afloat. Mostly, though, the excursion boats are as innocuous today as they were a hundred years ago, and one of my own sweetest memories of the harbour is of a wedding reception which came floating past my balcony one fine day in March. In the cabin of the boat I could just see the bride, a shimmer of satin happiness among a shirt-sleeved, summer-dressed crowd, and in the prow one of the bridesmaids stood alone and contemplative like a figurehead, her long pale dress fluttering, one hand holding the jack-staff, the other a glass of champagne.

For years the harbour was enough. The ocean beaches came later. In 1857 Henry Gilbert Smith, a rich emigrant from Sussex, Eng-land, decided to turn the fishing hamlet of Manly, which straddled a spit between the harbour and the open sea, into an ocean resort for the city. Perhaps he was remembering Brighton, after which he originally intended to name it. Certainly he made of it an em-blematic pleasure place, still a kind of blueprint of your ideal seaside town. From the ferry station on the harbour shore (which has its own small beach, fun-fair and shopping plaza) you walk down a wide pedestrian street, called romantically the Corso, until there opens out before you the wide surf-ranged crescent of the ocean beach, lined with now raggety Norfolk Pines planted by Smith him-self. There is an aquarium and a museum, there are innumerable ice-cream shops and pizza parlours and fish-and-chip places. Manly calls itself a village, a rare usage in a country where every huddle of shacks is a township; and what with the homely satisfaction of it all, and the green headlands, and the level sweep of sand beneath the pines, and the terrific surf pounding the beach, it remains everything that a Victorian entrepreneur could want of a populist watering-place. High above it, as a kind of logo, stands a large sandstone kangaroo, placed there by Smith in 1856, and surveying the whole lively scene from its plinth on Kangaroo Road.[1]

It was at Manly, in Edwardian times, that Sydney consummated its affair with the outdoors. Bathing had not always been a universal pastime here. In the earliest of days genteel people thought it a practice only for convicts, who bathed to get clean, and in 1838 it was forbidden between six in the morning and eight in the evening 'near or within view of any public wharf, quay, bridge, street, road or other place of public resort'. People swam in the early hours, or after dark, or on secluded beaches, and there were inspectors to enforce the law – at Manly a man with a big dinner-bell came around each morning to signal the end of bathing-time. On 2 October 1902, the proprietor and editor of the *Manly and North Sydney News*, William Henry Gocher, put this preposterous law to the test by openly, and with full publicity, donning his neck-to-knee swimming costume and entering the Manly surf at midday.[2] The police declined to prosecute, the case aroused much hilarity, and finally the law was ridiculed out of existence. Sydney's obsession with sand, surf and sea, later to be dignified as the Beach Culture, began with Mr Gocher's act of defiance, and five

---

[1] Most people like Manly, but one disappointed visitor was Sir Arthur Conan Doyle (who came to Sydney to lecture about spiritualism). Having heard about the wonders of its rolling surfs, its beach crowds and its pines, he took the ferry there to see it for himself, but supposing that the tame little harbour beach around the ferry station was itself the resort, did not bother to disembark and returned to Sydney without seeing the ocean front at all.

[2] At least this is how Gocher himself remembered the occasion: according to Alan Ross (*Australia '55*, London 1955), a policeman on duty at the time said the editor had gone into the water wearing a frock-coat, striped trousers and a hard hat, with an umbrella under his left arm. 'I can see it all quite clearly,' said the cop.

years later he was presented with a gold watch and a purse of fifty sovereigns as an expression of public gratitude.[1]

The beach culture almost instantly exploded, in a splurge of new tram and ferry services to take the populace to the sea beaches, and Sydney appropriated it as peculiarly its own. The side-stroke, hitherto used by all the fastest swimmers, gave way to the Sydney speciality called the Australian crawl. The great Duke Kahanamoku from Honolulu introduced the city to the art of surfing. Life-saving teams, stylizing their techniques into a strutting kind of pageantry, succeeded the old Volunteer Fire Companies as expressions of local pride, and as vehicles of working-class comradeship. The world came to think of Sydney people as beach people, and they themselves propagated the notion in posters, brochures, jokes and slang. The name of Bondi in particular, the most popular of all surfing beaches, went into the vernacular in many contexts. To go like a Bondi tram means to go as fast as the trams which, urged on by enthusiastic customers, used to rocket across town to the Bondi beaches; and when in 1973 Ruth Park, writing the *Companion Guide to Sydney*, searched for an idiom to describe the fizzily eclectic architecture of Sydney Town Hall, she called it Bondi Renaissance.

Needing a lavatory one day, importunately I entered the premises of the Bondi Surf-Bathers Life-Saving Club, a very ark of the beach culture. The cavernous club-house was entirely empty in the middle of the afternoon, but from its walls there looked down upon me a grand gallery of old members, ranked there arms folded in their swimsuits – or rather, I suppose, their Bathing Costumes. They were an older Sydney *in excelsis*, bronzed, resolute, Dinky-di Aussies every one. Attended by triumphal trophies, secure in their tradition, they looked down at me, I felt, as they might have looked down upon an effete non-swimming Pom of long ago, or declined to salute some weedy officer. The beach culture is often collated with philistinism, and of

---

[1] But then as the *Manly News* pointed out when he died in 1912, his action had 'added pounds to every foot of land in value'.

course it is true that there is nothing very cerebral to Sydney's week-end rush to the ocean. It is an instinctive escape to an environment where several Australian ideals can be fulfilled – perfect social equality, perfect freedom, perfect chances to display yourself, perfect idleness combined with strenuous physical exercise if you want it. They are homely ideals really. I am told that the sands after dark have conven-tionally been the places for young love's first experiences, but compared with beaches elsewhere in the world the more decadent pleasures are rarely apparent at Manly and its peers along the Sydney coast. The few nudist beaches are said to be remarkably chaste. The declared ideals of the life-savers are almost unctuously altruistic. The competitions of the Iron Men, stupendously demanding contests in swimming, run-ning, rowing and jumping, are karate-like in their asceticism.[1]

The beach culture has slipped a little lately. The Bondi Life-Saving Club, where son traditionally followed father into the rituals, finds fewer competitive members these days. Family loyalties are weaker now, people have more and easier distractions, the object of young ambition is not so often to parade high-stepping along the sands holding a flag at a life-savers' carnival, or to be immortalized upon a clubhouse wall. Fears of skin cancer and pollution have reduced the magnetic pull of the beaches. Nevertheless on a fine weekend afternoon Sydney's ocean shore is still joyously crowded from the mouth of the Hawkesbury in the north to Botany Bay in the south – one of the world's supreme hedonistic spectacles. I suppose there is no other great city with quite such a gift: the beaches of Los Angeles or Rio de Janeiro have none of the domestic appeal of these Sydney ocean fronts, which are like sand-and-surf extensions of the family suburbs behind them.

*

[1] It was a 6 foot 6 inch champion of Bondi, indeed, who was chosen to play the invincible extra-terrestrial hero in the Japanese TV series *Ultra-Man*. The Iron Man cult began in California, but the first Sydney people to be called Iron Men were convicts who could withstand without a murmur the torture of the lash. In 1990 first place in the Narrabeen Iron Man Triathlon was won by the three pastry-cooks of the Paris Cake Shop, Bondi.

A passion for sport is part of Sydney's escapist talent – just look at the space devoted to it in the papers. They say the city has never been so sports-crazy as Melbourne, where crowds at fixtures are far greater: but Sydneysiders suggest this is because in Melbourne there is nothing else to do, and certainly by any other standards Sydney's devotion to racing, cricket, football and tennis would be hard to beat. It is a non-sectarian, extra-class devotion, shared by nearly everyone.

The Sydney racecourses have their posh enclaves, in club stand and champagne bar – the Randwick course, in the southern suburbs, is the headquarters of the Australian Jockey Club – but the races are as popular as family jaunts as they are as social events or financial speculations. Horses became a Sydney preoccupation very early in the city's history. In the National Trust's Ervin Art Gallery, on Obser-vatory Hill above the Rocks, there is displayed the pedigree of a famous local racehorse, Merriwee: it was drawn up in 1896, but traces the animal's descent through eight named generations back to Hap-hazard, in 1797. The first horses were mostly imported from South Africa, the first racecourse was laid out at the north-west corner of Hyde Park in 1810 and the first race meeting was attended by all the civic swells and celebrities, Lachlan Macquarie to Simeon Lord.[1]

By the 1880s racing enthusiasms were so infectious that hansom cabs bringing punters home from Randwick used themselves to race each other hilariously back to the city. By 1990, however, when I went racing one afternoon at Canterbury, another of Sydney's four courses, it seemed to me an unexpectedly relaxing experience. Perhaps I stumbled upon an especially quiet afternoon, but I was struck by a general lack of excitement. The stands were not overcrowded. Chil-dren hopped about the green playing ball and eating ice-cream. Grandmothers had spread newspapers on the ground for picnics. The red-coated stewards rode around the track in a languid and easy way, as though they had all the time in the world, before scooting non-chalantly back in front of the field when a race began. The bookmakers,

[1] Ignoring the water-down-the-bath-plug analogy, the horses ran clockwise, as in England, and in New South Wales they still do: elsewhere in Australia (except in Queensland) they go the other way round.

in the yard behind, seemed possessed by no urgency. Even the races themselves appeared to arouse little emotion, and though of course there was the usual gallimaufry of threadbare gamblers haggardly studying race cards, considering odds, and greeting the finish with shouts and bitter oaths, half the people there seemed to take no notice of the horses at all.

It is another matter, I know, at Sydney rugby matches, and it is certainly another matter with cricket. 'Leave our bloody flies alone, Jardine,' a Sydney cricket-goer shouted when, in 1932, the unpopular English captain D. R. Jardine slapped an insect on his cheek in the field. In Sydney cricket has traditionally been fiercely played, rudely watched and spectacularly fulfilled, and the Sydney Cricket Ground is one of the historic sites of the game. It was here in 1929 that Don Bradman of New South Wales made 452 not out, the greatest score in first-class cricket, here in 1932 that England's bodyline bowling tactics almost split the British Empire, here in 1940 that another of the Sydney Morrises, A. R., made his unique debut in first-class cricket by hitting a century in each innings.[1] The ground is also home to The Hill, the most famous barracking stand anywhere, whence an entire anthology of insults has at one time or another been shouted across the pitch, so I assumed that if I went to a match there at least I would not be bored.

Nor was I. I chose a match of floodlit cricket, Sydney's own particular contribution to the contemporary game, and it was terrific. It was the old charm of cricket with all the young thrill of football. Australia were playing New Zealand, and as evening fell upon Sydney feelings ran very high. The stadium glowed and throbbed in the dark. Bright beneath the floodlights the players themselves, colourfully dressed and using a white ball, were as much like performers on a stage as sportsmen on a pitch, and the mostly young audience behaved much as they would at a rock concert. Sometimes a vast tide of cheers, orchestrated by some invisible conductor, swept from one end

[1] Fortunately it was not the scene of another memorable event in New South Wales cricket history, the game in which (at Melbourne in 1926) Victoria made 1,107 in two days, beating NSW by an innings and 656 runs.

of the stadium to the other, to break like a wave and return again as an ebb of boos. Sometimes, as a bowler began his run, he would be accompanied by a vast crescendo of banging feet. If a wicket fell, or a catch was missed, the crowd burst into instant and magnificent displays of emotion, throwing hats, paper cups and balloons into the air, banging the barricades, shouting, whistling, clapping, booing and cheering. Much beer and Coke was drunk, many chips were eaten, and as the match approached its last climax I felt a tremendous sense of restless and perhaps slightly menacing excitement – rather as one might feel it, I thought, in the hours before a revolution.

Nothing very terrible happened, of course (Australia won), but at one period of the evening I chanced to look over the balcony into an open space outside the stadium, and there I saw a succession of young men being hauled in handcuffed by plain-clothes policemen – briskly questioned, photographed there and then with Polaroids and shoved into a windowless van from whose interior emerged muffled thumps of protest. I don't know what they were to be charged with, but I did notice that a few yards away, within sight of the police but on the safe side of a high wire-mesh fence, three small boys were getting their own kicks by sniffing aerosol cans . . .

But it would be wrong to end a chapter of consolations with scenes of squalor. Let me end instead with a Saturday afternoon I once enjoyed, doing nothing in particular, in the park at Parramatta, the wide expanse of rolling green, intersected by the river, that was originally the demesne of Government House. A fair was happening just outside the park, so that everything was permeated by thumping music and the smell of hot-dogs, and for the most part the goings-on were thoroughly traditional. There were people playing bowls, riding bikes, knocking golf balls about. There were the inevitable Sydney picnickers. There were jolly volunteers working on the Parramatta Steam Tram, an ancient prodigy which itself sometimes came snorting along its track beneath the trees. Small boys scrambled down the steep bank to the muddy Parramatta at the bottom. On one sward the Pike and

Musket Society of New South Wales was practising its tactics, march-
ing and counter-marching with gleaming breastplates, while in a
glade nearby its ladies rehearsed a pavane dressed in becoming com-
binations of farthingales and cut-down jeans.

In a little gazebo, built in 1823 as a bathhouse for the Governor
and his guests, I came across another of those Sydney school reunions.
Summer frocked and gleamingly dentured, young Ockers and Sheilas
of long ago sat in a circle inside the building, finishing off a buffet.
They all seemed very fond of each other. 'Didn't you have any enemies
at school?' I asked one beaming lady, as she pressed me to a cup of
tea. 'How could anyone be an enemy to someone like *him*?' she replied
– and she pointed to a benignly gap-toothed, red-faced old codger
nearby, who sat on a chair with his knees apart and gave me a wink.

PURPOSES

1. Function

SOMETIMES, UNDER THE INFLUENCE OF DRINK OR TOO MANY oysters, I feel a sense of amiable unreality to Sydney. It is after all a most unlikely place. Born a concentration-camp thousands of miles from the next town, maturing so improbably on the underside of the world, more than most cities it seems artificial of purpose. It really need not exist at all. No ancient crossroads or trading routes make sense of its location, it is not the centre of anything, its indigenes did not demand it and its annihilation tomorrow would not deprive the world of anything essential to the well-being or the heritage of mankind. It is in short, say I to myself as I order another half-dozen, a self-indulgent place, created solely to be itself. Sometimes I even find it possible to fancy that it has never happened at all, and that I am resident in an agreeable hallucination; for as the writer Colin Wills once observed, on a Sydney evening one can sometimes feel 'a sympathy for the strangest experiences of the spirit'.

Two centuries ago this great city was nothing but an idea in a few London heads – a wild intent, to establish a settlement upon an unsurveyed shore, visited only once by Europeans, and that only for a stay of a few days. No reconnaissance party preceded the First Fleet. Sydney was an *ad hoc* kind of place from the beginning, and for me it retains a sense of permanent improvisation, making itself up as it goes along, and edging as I say, when the mood and the circumstances dictate it, headily towards illusion.

The city's first seal, struck in 1790, succinctly expressed its official purposes. It showed Industry sitting on a bale of goods receiving the convicts to their tasks, and is all too reminiscent of the slogan above the gates of Auschwitz – Work Shall Make You Free. Almost at the same time, however, Josiah Wedgwood of Derby, England, struck a commemorative medallion, modelled in Sydney clay sent to him by Governor Phillip. He based its design upon a poem by Erasmus Darwin – Charles Darwin's grandfather – which was called 'The Voyage of Hope to Sydney Cove', and was itself vatically inspired by the reports that came home from the penal colony:

> There shall broad streets their stately malls extend,
> The circus widen, and the crescent bend;
> There, ray'd from cities o'er the cultured land,
> Shall bright canals, and solid roads expand.
> There the proud arch, colossus-like, bestride
> Yon glittering streams, and bound the chasing tide;
> Embellished villas crown the landscape-scene,
> Farms wave with gold, and orchards blush between.
> There shall tall spires, and dome-capped towers ascend,
> And piers and quays their massy structures blend;
> While with each breeze approaching vessels glide,
> And northern treasures dance on every tide!

Fired by this prescient verse, Wedgwood produced a medal far more

cheerful than the official seal. Hope presided over it, and bestowed
her blessings upon Peace, Art and an unshackled Labour; and sure
enough Sydney's original purpose was very soon overtaken by all the
opportunities of a free society. Before long, in one of the more blessed
of historical ironies, no city on earth less deserved images of restraint
upon its escutcheon.

Just to be seen behind Hope's skirts, in the Wedgwood medallion,
were the blades of an anchor, and very proper too, for Sydney's most
obvious function is the function of a sea-port.[1] At the very beginning,
before the Blue Mountains were crossed by Europeans, the sea offered
its settlers not only the one way into Sydney, but the one way out.
Even when its hinterland was opened, the city remained primarily an
outpost of a maritime Empire, looking to the ocean for its commerce
and profits. Seals and whales, sandalwood and Tahitian pork – these
were some of the first of the Sydney commodities, and for years this
was one of the archetypal Conradian schooner ports of the south
Pacific, where every captain came some time or other to sell his cargo,
to look for charters, to repair or victual his ship, to replenish his
crew.[2] In 1841 a newcomer counted 140 ships in the harbour – deep-
sea sailing ships, coastal brigs and schooners, paddle-steamers serving
the Hunter River settlements, colliers from Newcastle, grain lighters
down from the Hawkesbury River. It was to Sydney that the wool
clippers came, in the epic days of sail. Sometimes eight or nine were
in port at the same time, and for seven consecutive years in the 1880s
and 1890s the most famous of them all, the *Cutty Sark* and the *Ther-
mopylae*, sailed together through the Heads in a pageantry of canvas at
the start of their long races home to Britain.[3] The passage of such
beautiful ships through the harbour was a glory of the place; one of
Sydney's worst tragedies was the midnight wreck of the clipper *Dunbar*

[1] It is revealing that the piers of Circular Quay are numbered from the seaward side –
seen from the land they run backwards, Pier 1 to the right, Pier 7 to the left.
[2] Conrad himself came several times, though never as a captain, and wrote about
Sydney in *The Union of the Sea*, 1906.
[3] Won without exception by the *Cutty Sark*, whose fastest journey took seventy
days.

at South Head in 1857, when 121 people were drowned, and only one man was found alive next morning, huddled in a crevice of the cliff.[1]

Even in the early twentieth century the maritime association was inescapable. A much larger proportion of the population then lived close to the harbour, and almost everything in Sydney proper still looked down to the ocean, the wharfs, the Customs House and the warehouses. Whole families lived as seamen, dockers, ferry-men, fishermen or pilots. The wharfie, the Sydney docker, dominated labour affairs; suburbs like Balmain or Pyrmont depended upon the jobs of the quays and shipyards. The P. and O. liner service from London was one of the municipal institutions, giving rise indeed to a variety of local architecture called the P. and O. Style, and at the end of every shearing season dozens of wool steamers, lumpish successors to the windjammers, loaded their bales at the Pyrmont wool wharfs. In those days the central waterfront was a clutter of berths, ships docking all around Sydney Cove, round the point in Darling Harbour, and up the innumerable straits and inlets of the Parramatta's mouth. Every old photograph shows the inner harbour gloriously crowded with riggings, and there were many Sydney houses whose gardens were overhung by the prows of ocean-going vessels. Even when international air travel began, before the Second World War, it was to Sydney as a seaport that the first flights came; the flying-boats of Qantas and Imperial Airways used a base at Rose Bay, on the south shore of the harbour.[2]

The old sense of jostled maritime intensity is lost now. For one thing only a few cruise ships dock at Sydney Cove's Ocean Terminal, the rest of the quays being given over to ferry-piers, while Darling Harbour is dedicated to tourism. Most of the big container ships dock at a terminal in Botany Bay, and from Captain Cook's original landing-place, marked by an obelisk and sundry plaques, their superstructures can be seen towering over the melancholy waters. In Sydney as everywhere the picturesque old finger-piers have mostly been de-

[1] The ship's anchor stands beside the track up South Head upon which we met, in an earlier chapter, those well-disciplined schoolgirls.
[2] Where that dashing pilot of page 124 still lands and loads her seaplane.

molished, or survive in rickety hazard, and the last of the regular P. and O. liners sailed for what was then still called Home in the 1970s.[1]

Nevertheless this remains one of the best of places to watch the ships go by, and when I walk out to my balcony at McMahon's Point there are almost sure to be vessels passing. Sometimes they are nosing upstream to the oil berths and coal docks still tucked away in un-suspected coves west of the bridge. Sometimes they are negotiating the bends into the Pyrmont wharfs, where for the next couple of days I shall see their masts and upperworks protruding above the buildings. Often trim white Japanese fishery depot boats come by, and sometimes I am just in time to catch some gaudy cruise ship being nudged into the Ocean Terminal. A couple of tugs swing down the harbour to meet an incoming freighter. The pilot launch hurries towards Balmain to pick up a pilot for duty. Rusty Chinese container ships moor at Millers Point, opposite my window, gigantic vessels full of cars some-times wake me with their sirens in the morning, and I was amused one day to observe that the crew of the Soviet freighter *Byelo-Russia* did not for a moment pause in their game of basketball as their ship steamed below the grand arch of the bridge, past the benedictory Opera House, past all the shine of Sydney to the sea.

Hardly had Sydney been founded than a watchpost was established at the South Head, to communicate by flag or beacon with the Observatory above Sydney Cove, and from there to Parramatta. From that day to this, on the very same site, the port has maintained a signal station, now communicating by radio with a concrete control tower at Millers Point which is still, as it happens, in line of sight across the city. If you climb up its narrow nineteenth-century stairs you will find the duty man watchful as ever at his charts and radar screens, monitoring the movement of each ship in and out of the harbour (and sometimes exchanging signal light banter with passing

[1] The P. and O. cruise ship *Fairstar* still sails out of Sydney Cove, but it is registered – *O tempora, O mores!* – in Monrovia.

warships, for he is almost sure to be an ex-Navy man himself). There has been a navigational light next door, too, since 1794, when they first hung an iron fire-basket from a tripod up there. In 1818 Greenway designed a lighthouse for the site (he was given his pardon on the strength of it), and when the present building replaced his in 1919 it was built more or less to the same pattern: for a time the two of them stood side by side, like a pair of queer white twins.

The pilot station is not far away. It stands on Watson's Bay, which is named for one of the first pilots – Robert Watson, harbourmaster too until he was sacked for theft in 1815. For years the pilots were taken out to ships in whale-boats and small schooners, but their first steam-cutters became the pride of the harbour. Named one after the other after Captain Cook, they were lovely rakish ships with tall funnels and bowsprits, like rich men's yachts, and their scrubbed decks and varnished wood, their deck-crews swanky in wide straw hats and braided collars, would perfectly have satisfied a J. P. Morgan or an Edward VII. It was the last of them, *Captain Cook III*, that welcomed Charles Causley's aircraft-carrier on the crystal morning of his poem. She survived until 1959, and until then the pilots were still transferred from cutter to ship in rowing-boats. Today they go out in diesel launches, boarding their charges directly from them four miles out at sea; but when I once paid a visit to their base at Watson's Bay, and found the duty pilot eating his lunch over the *Sydney Morning Herald*, I thought he might easily have been waiting for one of the old steam-cutters, or even for a whale-boat rowed by Maoris, so timelessly seaman-like did he seem in the all-but-lost British kind.

From the start the harbour was tightly organized, like all British imperial harbours. The waters of Woolloomooloo Cove were always a naval preserve, and various inlets of the northern shore were reserved for particular purposes. In Sirius Cove warships were overhauled, it being sufficiently remote, it was thought, to keep idle seamen out of trouble. In Neutral Bay foreign merchantmen were obliged to drop anchor; in the days when it took months for news to arrive from Europe, nobody could be quite sure whether a foreign flag was friendly or hostile. And when a whaling industry was started it was confined to what is now Mosman Bay, where the atrocious smells of the processing plant could not offend the citizenry.

Mosman Bay is surrounded by houses now, of course, and Mosman is one of the most desirable of all the harbour suburbs. Yet the ferry from Sydney Cove still noses its way around the bay's crooked entrance as into a lonely fjord somewhere. The bustle of the harbour is left behind, and there is a sense of old seclusion. The city noises are extinguished – no road runs around the bay. The banks are steep, so that the wind dies down as you enter. The inlet is heavily wooded, and at its end there is a thick green park, giving it to this day a bushland feel. On the eastern shore, half hidden by trees, a solitary sandstone building, now belonging to the Boy Scout movement, is a last relic of Archibald Mosman's old whaling station, and powerfully suggests to me still the steaming and the bubbling and the hacking, the grease and the stink, the clatter of chains and the shouting of foremen, the dark hulks of the whales on their slipways beneath the bush, that I would have found here 150 years ago.

Eldorado was ever the goal of Empire, and in Sydney from the start men dreamed of gold and other treasures of the earth. If the Blue Mountains beckoned some as a hint of liberty, they enticed many others as possible mining country. In the very first year of the settlement, in the very first of Sydney's celebrated frauds, a convict named James Daley (seven years for theft) momentarily galvanized everyone by producing a lump of gold he claimed to have dug up: he had made it by melting down a guinea and a brass buckle, and got 100 lashes for the deceit.[1] They really did find coal in Sydney, and it was briefly mined at Balmain, but in the end the city turned out to be Eldorado by proxy, as it were. For a time it was vastly enriched by the Bathurst goldfields, for which it provided not only so many of the speculators, but also the financial services, the supplies and the exchange. More

[1] Besides being ordered to wear a canvas smock with the letter R for rogue sewn on it. How many Rs would we see on the streets of Sydney now, if such penalties were still enforceable?

permanently, it has prospered by the woolly gold of the sheep herds, grazing in their countless thousands beyond the hills. Sydney's first great magnates made their money in the sheep business, the huge wool warehouses of the nineteenth century were proclamations of the civic function, and to this day the bush (as Australians indiscriminately call both farm country and wilderness) plays its important part in the Sydney consciousness.

'Sydney or the bush', used to be a Sydney catch-phrase, meaning all or nothing. Most Sydneysiders prefer to live, nevertheless, in the suburban no-man's-land between town and country, and I often fancy in their city collective yearnings for more rural, more organic arrangements. There is, for instance, the preoccupation with gardens. Almost everyone in Sydney has a garden, or wants one, and one of the city's seminal sites is the green expanse of the Royal Botanic Gardens in the Domain, which was the first of them all. Gently inclining in a scatter of palms and gums down to the water's edge, rich in lush or spiky foliage and haunted by esoteric birds, it forms an exhibition at once of nature cultivated, of nature wild and of nature mutated – for it is also full of the trees and shrubs imported from England, South America and South Africa to vary the impact of the indigenous flora, and in 1991 a colony of 600 fruit bats settled in its palm grove. It occurs to me too that Sydney has more than the usual quotient of memorials to animals. Behind Circular Quay a fountain commemorating the old Tank Stream is decorated with sculptured lizards, snakes, crabs, a spiny anteater and a turtle, recalling, a plaque says, 'mankind's past dependence on this flowing stream and our links with life around the region'. A memorial to Matthew Flinders the navigator has beside it a smaller memorial to his cat Trim, with Flinders' own epitaph to the animal: 'To the memory of Trim, The best and most illustrious of his race, The most affectionate of friends, Faithful of servants, And Best of creatures'. In 1950 they erected a memorial to the horses killed with the Desert Mounted Corps in the Middle East more than thirty years before – 'They did not come home,' says the text. 'We will not forget them.'

Perhaps all this animism is folk-memory. By the nature of things

Sydney, though a place chiefly of townsmen from the start, was born countrified. Cows, pigs, sheep, goats, horses and poultry were fellow-migrants with the convicts, and Phillip, who had farmed himself during periods of half-pay in England, did his best to make an agricultural go of things. His original Government garden is preserved as a kind of shrine within the Botanic Gardens, planted with the same cabbages, carrots and beetroots: it was not much of a success in 1788, and the cabbages still look pretty mouldy to me. Most of the original cattle soon ran away into the bush, but were discovered years later generated into flourishing wild herds. Lesser farm stock infested the streets of early Sydney; hens were all over the place, goats were a pest, pigs roamed the town as licensed scavengers. The surrounding countryside was a disappointment at first, and dreams faded of a plantation colony, reclining among palms and bananas in the West Indian kind. Soon enough, nevertheless, the first agriculturalists were flourishing, some of them military men and officials farming on the side, some free settlers and ex-convicts.

The first of them all, and the first man to receive a land grant in the colony, was a convict from Cornwall named James Ruse (seven years for breaking and entering). He was one of the few farmers on the First Fleet, and Phillip gave him thirty acres at Parramatta. This was the beginning of Experiment Farm, whose house is now one of the two oldest houses in Australia, and whose acres are represented by a small rubbish-strewn park adjacent. It was also the real beginning of Australian agriculture. Ruse failed in the end, and became someone else's farm overseer, but he was evidently conscious of his status as the Father of the Australian Farm, because he wrote in his epitaph, carved on his tombstone at Campbelltown:

> My mother reread me tenderly
> With me she took much paines
> And when I arrived in this Coloney
> I sowd the forst Grain
> And Now With my Heavenly Father I hope
> For ever To Remain.

*

By the early 1800s farm settlements were spreading far into the bush. Although the free farmers and emancipees had convicts to work for them, still they were true pioneers, in the kind that were later to become emblematic of the imperial and American frontiers, and the whole tradition of the Australian outback, its squatters, its pastoralists, its homesteaders, its stockmen, its shepherds and its swagmen, was really born in Sydney town.

There were two kinds of agriculturists. The grazier, dealing chiefly in sheep, was the smart kind, the country gentleman, putatively evolving into the landed magnate. The cocky was the simpler sort, and was roughly sub-classified as a cow cocky, a scrub cocky or a fruit cocky. The grazier's ambition was achieved when he found himself master of a couple of thousand square miles with a few hundred thousand merino sheep upon it. The fulfilment of the cocky's hopes was surely symbolized by the moment when, one day in the 1860s, Maria Ann Smith of Eastwood, near Parramatta, threw the remains of some Tasmanian apples out of the back door, and found them apotheosized into the Granny Smith. Both kinds of farmer looked to the city of Sydney for their markets and their urban needs. The driving of the herds into the Sydney slaughterhouses was part of Sydney life; many an inn along the Parramatta Road depended for its trade upon the cockies coming to market; shearers and farm labourers were familiars of the Rocks taverns; the more fashionable of the graziers would travel a couple of hundred miles rather than miss a Sydney ball.

The wealthy New South Wales grazier is still a potent figure of the Sydney social scene. He lives on his wide acres somewhere, in his ample station, but he perhaps has an apartment in Sydney, he probably has a club there, he sends his children to Sydney boarding-schools and he shows up aristocratically at grand functions now and then. Together with the cocky, he comes most visibly into his own on the occasion of the annual Sydney Royal Show, the Easter junketing of the Royal Agricultural Society, which is one of the great events of the civic calendar. Then, for ten days, the country comes back to Sydney. The show-ground is part fun-fair, part exhibition, part show-ring, part shopping mall, and to Go to the Show has been part of the

Sydney family tradition for a century. There are judgings of horses, sheep, cattle and farm produce. There are competitions of steer-riding, show-jumping, wood-chopping. There are displays of cats, needle-work, jams or tractors. There are bands and roller-coasters and big dippers. There is the old Sydney custom of the show-bag: shops and companies put together small samples of their goods and sell them in plastic bags – the Bertie Beatle Show-bag, for instance, contained in 1990 four Bertie Beatles, one Violet Crumble, one Smartie and one Hooly Dooly. There is a monumental display of country produce, laid out in intricate patterns of apples, honey-pots, oranges, pumpkins, corn-cobs, reaching from floor to ceiling in meticulous design – even onions occupy their pickle-jars ornamentally. Everywhere are the farmers, unmistakable rurals, with rubicund bulldog faces, with sticks as often as not, preferably wearing moleskin trousers and a wide-brimmed kind of hat called an Akubra, and stumping around the place with an agricultural gait. They seem to me like people from an earlier Sydney altogether, a Sydney without an Opera House or a single Vietnamese bistro, and indeed when I once told my acquaint-ances that I had been to the Show, some of them sneered a little, and said it was no longer relevant.

I would not have missed for anything, though, its greatest spectacle, the Grand Parade of exhibitors around the big oval show-ground. This is likely to be attended by the Governor of New South Wales, who arrives in a coach and four, and by nearly everyone who is anyone in the Sydney Establishment, but it is dominated by people from the bush. In the background the fun-fair proceeds, a big dipper rises and falls and an aerial cable-car comes and goes. In the fore-ground the countryside presents itself in an astonishing crescendo of pageantry. The exhibitors parade in concentric circles. Dashing rodeo players on their ponies, tent-peggers with lances, impeccable dressage competitors, lolloping cattle led by sturdy men in boots, immense Shire horses, sheep trundled round on the backs of trucks – all revolve at a steady pace which, as the arena becomes increasingly crowded, and the circles tighten, and the excitement rises, and the dust billows, begins to look more and more like the movement of some beleaguered caravan – a huge ceaseless swirl of men, women and animals. On its perimeter, giving the scene a final thrilling touch of laager, scores of spanking pony-traps whizz round and round, much faster than anything else, constantly outlapping the assorted livestock and driven by stern-faced, tight-lipped Australian gentlefolk, tweedy and bowler-hatted, who time and again race unsmiling past as though they are circling for the kill.

Heavy industry has never dominated Sydney, and is not much apparent in the central city now. A poet celebrating the International Exhibition of 1879 could suggest, as New South Wales' own contribution to the grand display of produce, only minerals, gold, wine, lusty herds and merry maidens, and it would be more or less true if Sydney were mounting an exhibition today. Cars were assembled here for a time, but the factories closed. Ships used to be, but are not so often now. Reference books mention textiles, machines and transport equipment, but you would not know it. Although the statistics say that more than 300,000 Sydney citizens work in manufacturing industries, when I asked several informants what all these people made, nobody could suggest anything in particular.

The native Sydney industry is the industry of the entrepreneur, the middle-man, and he came into his own with a vengeance during the boom years of the 1980s. All the service industries gave a new vigour to Sydney then, the dealers in futures and options, the real-estate people of course, the publicity and marketing people, the computer kids, the brokers, the bankers, the art dealers, the lawyers, the auctioneers – and when boom turned to bust 'new links were forged', as a Sotheby's spokesman smoothly put it, 'between auction houses and the liquidation industry'. Here as everywhere tourism, the ultimately unproductive industry, burgeoned, preened and was given its own Sydney manner. The facts and figures of Sydney tourism are happy-go-lucky, if not actually impromptu, and so is the manner. 'Shoot me in the head if I know the answer,' I heard one tour-guide answer without a moment's hesitation when asked a question, and I was not surprised to read that two of the Opera House guides had lost their jobs after 'psychological testing'; it seemed to me that the trade as a whole might perform oddly in a Rorschach test.[1]

More than in most cities, I think, in Sydney the state of the economy has a direct and immediate effect upon the citizenry. In good times almost everyone prospers, there and then; in bad times people go bankrupt all over the place, firms sack employees by the hundred, TV stars find their salaries devastatingly cut and suddenly Sydney realizes that it, like any other city, has its fair share of the homeless, the unemployed and the unhappy. This is nothing new. Australia's economy depends to a dangerous degree upon world commodity prices, and throughout its history Sydney has been a place of capitalist ups and downs – in this respect if in no other, it has been said, the city was 'born modern'. Its blue-collar workers have to fight hard for security, its money-manipulating classes live on the edge of their nerves. GREED IS GOOD, said an advertisement I cut out from a paper one day, RESULTS ARE BETTER – not a very relaxing philosophy. At night in downtown skyscraper windows you may see the young merchant bankers at their work; it used to be only the flower-pinafored cleaners, scarves over their heads, now it is young men sprawling shirtsleeved in their revolving chairs, drinking out of plastic mugs and keeping an eye on the constant green flicker of the computer screens – when it is midnight in Sydney it is three in the afternoon in Frankfurt, and the markets are just opening in New York.

I imagine that, *mutatis mutandis*, similar young men have been similarly preoccupied in all Sydney's periods of economic thrust, only to slow down rather, or invite Sotheby's in for a valuation, when recession sets in. Easy come, easy go. In Sydney 'riches have wings', as a reporter for the *South Asian Register* reported in 1828, observing a former banker selling mutton pies in the street, and proper to the ambience, I think, is the text on the grave of Joseph Potts, infant son of an early bank manager of this city, who died in 1838 and is buried beside Botany Bay:

[1] Not that the tourists seem to mind. Later I overheard the guide who gave the suicidal answer being thanked for the tour by a Japanese: 'A little interesting. See you again.'

> Let us not murmur at thy
> Dispensations
> Oh Heavenly Father. They were but
> Loans.

Anyway, in an environment so naturally nonchalant and benign as Sydney's, the more impersonal kind of money-making can seem comically anomalous. One lovely gusty day in May, when the very spirit of libertarian hedonism was in the air, and I was on my way to some of those waterside oysters, I picked up a paper that came merrily blowing down the street towards me. This is what it said, word for word: 'X doesn't appear to offer the refined main DB-based market allocation we want. They only have generic drop down into Decision Support module.'

It used to be thought that in functions of the mind Sydney was a backwater even by Australian standards. Melbourne was the place for culture and intellect. Sydney was all brassy show. Perhaps it was true. The possession of a piano may have given George Worgan a special status in the Sydney of the 1780s, but for 150 years or so Sydney society does seem to have been terribly philistine. Times changed very gradually, and at first according to strict English precedents. When Sydney University was founded in 1852 it was inevitably equipped with a medieval-style Oxbridge quadrangle, and at its inauguration one of the learned founders, Dr John Woolley, prophesied that before long 'the quiet bays of our beautiful harbour will mirror in their crystal depths many a reverend chapel and pictured hall and solemn cloister and pleasant garden like those which gem the margin of the Isis and the Cam'.[1] Fitfully, though, a more Australian intelligentsia came into being, the arts became more generally welcomed, until at last, with the opening of the Opera House, with the presentation of

---

[1] He never lived to see it, if only because fourteen years later he was drowned in a shipwreck in the Bay of Biscay.

the Nobel Prize for Literature to the Sydney novelist Patrick White, with the intercontinental fame of the Sydney opera singer Joan Sutherland ('La Stupenda'), with the distribution across the world of Sydney writers, film-makers, painters and actors, in our own time culture became a civic function.

The press began the process. Some of the cleverest Sydney people had always been connected with newspapers, if only as mouthpieces for their own political ambitions, and had brought elements of public wit and debate to the mostly unlettered city. For the more educated young immigrant journalism offered the nearest thing to an intellectual occupation, so that here as in New York the newspapers were nurseries of good writing and mental activism. The pyrotechnical young editor Edward Smith Hall, for example, who arrived in 1811, was a leader in the campaign for democratic system in New South Wales, and he maintained it with a torrent of editorials so fierce that he lived a life of lawsuits and imprisonments – he once characterized the Governor of the day Ralph Darling, as a tyrant outranked only by the Great Moghul, the Tsar and the Emperor of China. The *Sydney Morning Herald*, founded in 1831, became one of the best-known papers in the British Empire. The weekly *Bulletin*, founded in 1880, developed into one of the most outrageously brilliant magazines in the English language: its declared aims included a republican form of Government, the abolition of all private land ownership, a universal system of compulsory life insurance and an Australian entirely Australian – 'the cheap Chinaman, the cheap Nigger, and the cheap European pauper to be absolutely excluded'.

Then as now, it was a dangerous thing to cross the Sydney press. The *Empire* said of a politician in 1853 that his oratory was reminiscent of a dredger, 'slowly and laboriously jerking out deliberate buckets full of slush'. The *Bulletin* called the improvident Sir Henry Parkes, in 1887, 'a cold-blooded, ungrateful old vendor of mortgaged allotments'. *Truth* said of the generally idolized Melba, in 1903: 'Many a stage star has shot an erratic course, but none has done it with such vicious vulgarity, such bourgeois bumptiousness and such indiscriminate cruelty.' The art critic of the *Triad*, reviewing two nudes painted by

Tom Roberts in 1920, said of them that 'barring an occasional contour that would intrigue a cheese merchant, they were hardly worth undressing'. Patrick White was told in 1956 that he wrote 'pretentious and illiterate verbal sludge'. Sidney Nolan's paintings were described in 1958 as possessing 'a decadent, inbred, hilly-billy flavour of tenth-rate German expressionism'. An American film was described in the *Sydney Morning Herald* in 1990 as 'an egregious pile of mindlessly violent idiot fodder', and a restaurant was said to offer 'indifferent food, non-existent atmosphere, appalling noise levels and Keystone Cop service'. Libel actions have naturally been incessant, and in recent years even architectural and food critics have found themselves in court, having rashly maligned lobster salads or mocked housing developments.[1]

Artists flourished in early Sydney, when they were the indispensable memorialists of history. Later they were treated with less respect, and Sydney more rumbustiously than most cities has gone through the usual phases of artistic prejudice and reappraisal – now sneering at Impressionism, now deriding Cubism, now laughing at abstracts and finally realizing, late in the day but with a particular gusto, that there was money in them all. An indigenous Sydney school of painting did not really come about until 1886, when the Melbourne artist Julian Ashton came to the city and founded an art school. He was followed by many of the leading Australian painters of the day – Arthur Streeton, Tom Roberts, Norman Lindsay, Lloyd Rees, and for the first time Sydney and its harbour were interpreted not as reflections of European ideals, but as sources of beauty in their own right. It was the lure of the southern climate that attracted most of these artists, with its suggestions of mauve seductive twilights, Whistler-like nocturnes, languid dalliances in dappled gardens, bohemian liberties and classical echoes: as the poet J. A. R. McKellar put it in a poem about a ferry-trip through the harbour:

[1] Though my own favourite Sydney critique, in the *Sydney Morning Herald* recently, was nothing if not balanced. Writing about a concert of twelfth-century French hurdy-gurdy music, the reviewer observed that the players 'brought a style to this music which bears the intimation of authenticity, though other approaches can be imagined'.

> The lips of ocean murmur at delay,
> The lovely moon no longer will refuse,
> And from the arms of darkness slips away
> To tryst with young Ephesians on Vaucluse . . .

It was also relatively easy for an artist to earn a living in Sydney. This might be an uncultured place still, but it always had its eye on the main chance, and an alliance between art and commerce was presently arranged. The carriage-trade Sydney department stores established art galleries of their own, and eventually Sydney became one of the most calculatingly art-minded of all cities. Nowadays the names of fashionable local artists are household words, and there is a lively sub-culture of art dealers, inhabiting parts of inner suburbia generically known as 'the gallery belt'. Some galleries flourish perfectly frankly as centres of investment rather than aesthetics, some are focal points of social networking, some make great fortunes for their owners – when the most prominent of contemporary dealers retired from the scene, he bought the billionairess Barbara Hutton's former house in the Kasbah at Tangier. But there are highly civilized dealers too, and however mixed the motives, Sydney has become a city unusually concerned and familiar with art. Where else would one see advertised on the backs of taxis, as it might be a rock concert or a revival meeting, a forthcoming competition for a portrait prize?

A civic interest in literature is less apparent. A handful of internationally celebrated authors are resident in Sydney, but the great city hardly seems to realize their presence; and anyway with one or two very visible exceptions they spend much of their time either abroad or plunged in hermit-like withdrawal, periodically emerging into the local limelight to be tall-poppied by reviewers or obituarists. There is no shortage of good bookshops, and an astonishing variety of literary prizes appears to be available, as one can see from the curricula vitae of Sydney authors, almost all of whom seem to have won one or another (not to mention the two authors, at least, who have won the Booker Prize in London). Literary people of the academic kind evidently fare well enough, if I am to judge by social encounters, and

know all there is to know about structuralism, minimalism, con-
textualism, post-Marxist formalism or pluralistic imagery. Nevertheless this has often been stony ground for littérateurs. The balladeer
Barcroft Boake, in 1892, hanged himself with his own stock-whip in
the scrub at Cammeray, beside Middle Harbour. Henry Lawson,
slowly staggering down the ladder of alcoholism, died in the suburb of
Abbotsford sotted, impoverished and all alone in 1922, and wrote self-
pityingly of himself:

> In the land where sport is sacred, where the labourer is a god,
> You must pander to the people, make a hero of a clod.

Many another Sydney writer, from his day to our own, has felt the
need to run away abroad – it was the Sydney magazine *Truth*, after
all, which observed in 1906 that if Australia had not been propitious
to poets, it had to be remembered 'what a drivelling, drunken lot
most of them have been'.

As to the theatre in Sydney, it has been for the most part thoroughly
populist. The very first play ever put on was Farquhar's *The Recruiting
Officer*, presented by a cast of convicts before Governor Phillip in
1789. This seems to have been a great success: 'I am not ashamed to
confess,' wrote Tench about it, 'that the proper distribution of three
or four yards of stained paper, and a dozen farthing candle-sticks
stuck around the mud walls of a convict-hut, failed not to diffuse
general complacency.' Restoration comedy hardly proved the norm,
though. The Sydney taste was more for melodrama, farce and bur-
lesque, and in later years the theatrical trade obliged. Barnett Levey
gave the public just what it wanted, and the impresario who presently
came to control most of the downtown theatres, the American J. C.
Williamson, was above all a showman for the people – like the Harbour Bridge and the Manly ferry *South Steyne*, his firm proudly boasted
itself The Biggest in the British Empire.

Sydney was a music-hall town, an extension of the British vaudeville
circuit, and if ever a classical performer came, it had to be a star of
stars whom everyone knew. Jenny Lind came, for instance, the
Swedish Nightingale who seems to have been ready to play to any

audience anywhere. Lola Montez danced her celebrated Spider Dance, leaving behind her a reputation for heavy drinking and a cocktail called the Lola Montez – rum, ginger, lemon and hot water. Sarah Bernhardt came accompanied by two dogs, a bear, possums, parrots, a tortoise and 250 pairs of shoes. In earlier times the theatres themselves were full of democratic vigour, frequented alike by gentry and by workmen, with larrikins hanging around their doors looking for mischief to perform, and prostitutes roaming the stalls during intermissions.

There are three much-admired professional dramatic companies in Sydney, ranging in their work from the familiar classical to the incomprehensible avant-garde, but as a whole the theatre is still dominated by big musicals from New York or London, and more serious plays are generally confined to fringe houses outside the downtown quarter. It is a theatre, wrote the Melbourne playwright Jack Hibberd in 1986,[1] 'obsessed with colour and movement, voluptuous effects, whimsy, corn, and sybaritic romps' – or as one critic more recently put it, 'sweaty, sexy, fast and furious'. Television entertainment too is mostly razzmatazz, or what the local industry calls 'kid-led', but some distinguished films have been born here, enough of them to justify Sydneysiders talking about 'our film culture', and there is ballet to see, and opera of course, and live rock music is everywhere, and it is a pleasure of the city that one often comes across theatre people and theatrical events. In 1990 part of the Oscar Award ceremony was telecast direct to Hollywood from one of the restaurants of the Opera House in Sydney, and I went along to press my nose against the windows, joining a handful of fans or groupies there. Oh, the glamour of the showbiz scenes within! Through the windows on the other side of the restaurant I could see a fireboat spouting its hoses beneath the Harbour Bridge, and against this spectacular background the Sydney stardust glittered. Among the potted foliage were semi-familiar figures of TV or cinema, sweetly waving to friends at other tables, applauding lavishly when an Australian name cropped up in the ceremony,

[1] In his contribution to Jim Davidson's *The Sydney–Melbourne Book*.

smiling all the more adorably, chatting all the more vivaciously, whenever a camera swivelled their way. There were hats, and many bracelets, and a pair of orchid earrings as big as soup-plates. 'Oh my God,' cried one of the girls beside me, 'isn't that Craig McLachlan?' 'Oh my *God*,' I echoed, '*could* it be?'

Better still, walking around the little park at Blue's Point one day I came face to face with an actor pacing the path with a script in his hands, silently rehearsing his lines – an extremely actorial actor, too, with presence and a flashing eye.

Visitors (and Sydney expatriates) still sometimes profess to find Sydney philistine, and it certainly has its yobbo elements, but for myself I am astonished by the energy of its cultural appetite. It is rather like Chicago half a century ago, brilliantly striving to catch up. The five Sydney universities burst with eminent scholars. The Sydney publishing industry is fertile. The Sydney Symphony Orchestra is very polished. The Sydney Dance Company is indefatigable. The State Art Gallery is crowded out every weekend. The State Library is superb. The Powerhouse Museum of Applied Science, occupying the former power station of the Sydney trams at Darling Harbour, is really a museum of nearly everything, and is generally agreed to be one of the best of its kind in the world. In an average year the Opera House offers sixteen different operas, almost nightly in the winter season. Every year a thousand people apply for the twenty-five places at the National Institute of Dramatic Art.

In the Sydney pantheon, among the sportsmen, the millionaires, the crooks and the politicians, the hero-clods that Lawson so resented, people of intellect are readily recognized now. John Anderson, Professor of Philosophy at the University of Sydney from 1927 to 1958, crops up repeatedly in conversation as a kind of presiding guru of the Sydney Renaissance. Martin Place, the city's very hub, is embellished by that incongruous memorial to William Dobell. Patrick White the novelist, now that he is dead, is sure to be municipally canonized before long. Joan Sutherland the opera singer, though still alive, is

more or less sanctified already. And one of Sydney's honoured sons is
the city's most celebrated applied scientist, Lawrence Hargrave, who
died in 1915 and is not only indisputably the Father of Australian
Flight, but one of the world's great innovators of aviation.

We could do worse, in fact, than end our survey of Sydney functions
with a remembrance of this gifted citizen, for he was an inventor in
the classic mould, a draughtsman, an astronomer, an archaeologist
and a bit of a crank. Sometimes to be seen walking on the water of
Double Bay on inflatable shoes, he believed strongly that Spanish
seamen had landed at Sydney long before the British, and claimed to
have found rock inscriptions proving it. He was the inventor of the
box kite, an immediate precursor of the aeroplane. In 1894 he was
lifted sixteen feet off the ground by an assembly of four such kites, and
this success seems to have been a seminal influence upon the Wright
brothers when they came to make the first powered heavier-than-air
flight seven years later.

Hargrave never patented anything, freely publicized his ideas and
shared his conceptions with anyone who asked. He sounds the perfect
Sydney functionalist. He looks back at us now not only benignly
eccentric in the city's memory, walking the water, flying his kites or
arguing about those Spaniards, but with a visionary gleam from the
back of the $20 note.

2. System

This immensely sprawled and complicated metropolis, held together
physically by such elaborate means, must be the very devil to administer. It is hardly surprising that Sydney is heavy with bureaucracy.
From the Federal Government at one end, by way of the State
Government, the City Council, all the local administrations and
multitudinous boards, trusts and commissions to the Hunters Hill
Municipal Council at the other – from top to bottom the city festers
with governmental and political activity. Perhaps this helps to foster

Sydney's traditional contempt for the whole process. The general election of 1990 seemed to me to be followed in this city with the utmost cynicism; the graffito POLITITIONS ARE GANGSTERS appeared to express the public attitude very well.

The city's supreme political arena is the Parliament of the State of New South Wales, in its chambers on Macquarie Street, delightfully overlooking the Domain and lately fitted out with a roof-garden and a swimming-pool. Walking past Parliament House one carefree afternoon I decided on a whim to go inside and listen to the debate in the Legislative Assembly, the lower house. This was a shock to me. The chamber is small and intricate, and that afternoon it was jam-packed, both on the floor and in the galleries. Entering its confinement after the sunny liberty of Macquarie Street, I found that its sudden smallness, its artificial lighting and its feeling of intense privacy put me in mind of an eighteenth-century cockpit. There was a Rowlandson-like atmosphere in there. . forget the subject of debate, but it had certainly raised grotesque passions. Sometimes even the gallery joined in, with shouts and sarcastic laughs, and down on the floor insults, vicious badinage and reproach flew this way and that across the House – 'mongrels', 'long-haired gits', 'deeply deranged'. A Government supporter angrily alleged that members of the opposition were passing bags of sweets around. A Minister, complaining that somebody had stolen his notes, was told to get stuffed. Disconcertingly prominent among the combatants was a man I happened to know, and thought of as a civilized and benevolent fellow. He was transformed. He strode around down there like a mad prosecutor, he called his opponents madmen, cheats, scoundrels, he waved his papers like spells or menaces. His face was distorted with malignancy. He was a man possessed.

But when I later commented to a colleague upon this alarming metamorphosis, 'Oh,' was the reply, 'he didn't really mean it.' Sydney politics is like that. So many interests are chafing against each other, such layers of authority are there to clash, that an archaic formalization of virulence seems more or less expected, as a kind of safety-valve perhaps. In few other cities of the west would it be said, as was said in

Sydney in 1990, that voting for an opposing political party would be like a child knowingly accepting candies from a loony in a raincoat, or that an opposition candidate had as much charm as a used suppository. That debate in the Assembly was nothing special, and certainly nothing private. The chamber is open to everyone at all times, with a minimum of fuss, and it was really a family squabble, rather than a hole-in-corner sporting event, that I had wandered into so innocently.

The inflammatory urge in Sydney politics first arose, I suppose, when in 1808 the officers of the Rum Corps marched up to the Governor's House and arrested Bligh on the grounds of his authoritarian behaviour.[1] It has never again erupted into rebellion, but it has never been exorcized either. It has been institutionalized instead. Groans, laughs, hisses, hoots, boos, cheers, cries of 'Shame!' and sarcastic interventions have always punctuated reports of Parliamentary debates – Henry Parkes, in 1880, said of his fellow-Parliamentarians that they be-slimed the face of the earth with their unsightly and unclean carcasses. Visitors from Britain, inspecting the progress of this distant *alter ego*, were often quite taken aback. Not only were political proceedings in Sydney rowdy and unseemly, they also appeared to display an unstable tendency towards the radical and the democratic, not to mention the disloyal.[2]

In particular it was ironic to discover that in a colony founded upon such rigid principles of Authority, the voice of Labour was so disrespectful. Even in penal Sydney there was an element of labour power – convicts worked by task, rather than by time, and in their free hours they could sell their labour to anyone who would pay for it. The Masters and Servants Act of 1828 was severe indeed upon

[1] His daughter met them at the door with drawn parasol, but they found the Governor under his bed, hiding State documents according to his own account, hiding himself according to the rebels.
[2] Even the socialist Beatrice Webb found the political scene distasteful; after meeting Sydney civic leaders in 1898 she reported that the Lord Mayor was illiterate in speech, awkward in manner, extraordinarily muddled and 'heavily scented with whisky'.

employees (up to six months' gaol for negligence at work), but gave
the employee rights of complaint too, and by the 1880s the formidable
Mort, when he was building his dry dock, felt obliged to offer a
freehold allotment to every labourer who completed his contract. In
the 1930s the unions sometimes seemed all-powerful, and they still
play a more subtly influential part in Sydney civic affairs than in most
cities of the west: for example municipalities have lately been induced
to pay their employees for sick leave they do not take, and the
gravediggers' union has recently been campaigning for a monthly day
off.

The powers of the Lord Mayor of Sydney, in theory the supreme
civic official, have fluctuated down the years, because owing to incompetence or corruption his City Council has repeatedly been super-
seded by Commissions. In any case his writ has been circumscribed.
He is Lord Mayor only of the downtown area, containing 2 per cent
of Sydney residents, which was constituted a city in 1841 – and even
within that the Commonwealth and State Governments have enclaves
under their own control. All around his fief other administrations
hold sway in one degree or another, and attempts to create a Greater
Sydney Council, on the old London pattern, have always failed.
Greater Sydney makes up most of something called the County of
Cumberland, but within it there are thirty-six municipalities and six
shires, with territories ranging from just over a thousand square miles
to less than three square miles.

The suburban administrations are often prickly in their independence, and critics have always complained that Sydney has no civic
loyalty, only a multitude of separate local prides. One suburb at least
has declared itself a Nuclear-Free Zone. Time and again I have been
told I really must come to Lansvale, or Lindfield, or Engadine, if I
want to understand what Sydney is all about, and people in the outer
suburbs still talk about 'going to Sydney', as their forebears did in the
days when Bankstown was an unfrequented patch of bush, and Penrith
a rustic outpost. In the 1860s one municipality, Waverley, actually
came to blows with the city of Sydney, concerning rights of access to
the land that was later to become Centennial Park: led by a fiery

Welsh mayor, its people pulled down fences, burnt bushes, and finally, men and women alike, physically attacked the city representatives – and 'palsied', according to a contemporary newspaper, 'they fled'.

The general assumption is that Sydney people are endemically anarchic. Nowadays it does not often seem so, and the city gives the impression of being fussily over-governed. A little brief authority goes a long way in this town, and people clad in it are two a penny. Some of the women traffic wardens in particular – Grey Ghosts in the vernacular – have become almost caricatures of petty officialdom, as they strut pouter-chested along the pavements: when I was in Sydney last one notoriously bossy traffic warden was reported to have booked a police car for illegal parking, and scolded the driver of a postal van for stopping too long at a post-box. If you drive a car at random around the city you will constantly come across centres of Authority. The whole city has its symbolic headquarters downtown, of course, in the Town Hall. It is, however, *only* a Town Hall, not a City Hall, and is only one of many which supply similar intimations of pomp to the different quarters of the place.

Generally speaking the Sydney suburbs run indistinguishably into one another.[1] There often comes a moment, though, as one meanders through the unmemorable streets and innumerable traffic-lights, when the place opens out a little, a few trees or municipal flower-beds appear, and there stands the local town hall. It often has a tower; it sometimes has a court room attached; there may be a police station beside it, or a post office, a memorial of some kind, even a statue perhaps; it speaks of a long tradition of municipal dignity stretching back to the civic aspirations of Victorian Britain. The complicated tower of the North Sydney courthouse-cum-post-office-cum-police-station was for years the tallest structure on the north shore, looking across the harbour to Sydney Cove like a declaration of independence – and indeed, as Bradfield prophesied, the modest suburb it once commanded is now almost a twin city to downtown Sydney across the

[1] Though it is true that the shire of Hornsby declares itself in the best Sydney style: WELCOME TO HORNSBY SHIRE. WE ARE COMMITTED TO ENHANCING THE QUALITY OF OUR SHIRE BY PROVIDING COST EFFECTIVE SERVICE TO OUR CUSTOMERS.

bridge. The town hall of Balmain has survived successions of scandals and disenfranchisement to provide an elegant centrepiece still for its scrambled suburb. Even in the most formless districts the municipal buildings provide some promise of cohesion, and some probably specious promise of organization.

For despite this proliferation of mayors, aldermen and clerks across the vast metropolis, a strong sense of the slovenly pervades the Sydney system. 'No worries' – 'It'll do, mate' – these dear old Sydney mantras have all too often cast a spell upon the running of the place: the most unconvincing notice I know in Sydney is the one that says TOTAL PROJECT CONTROL above a door at the central railway station. Phillip's original Sydney was inevitably makeshift. Very few people in the First Fleet knew how to build a house or even plant a potato, and the most efficient officers of the Royal Navy were amateurs when it came to the business of organizing a colony. For the first thirty years there was no currency, and the economic system was based upon barter, debt, bills of exchange, military paymasters' notes, miscellaneous foreign coins and the Holey Dollar – a Spanish coin whose centre was punched out, the ring having one value, the centre another. Nearly everything had to be improvised, from the mortar (made from crushed clam shells) to the treatment for dysentery (using the leaves of the red gum tree) or the beer (brewed from the remains of the maize milled for the convicts' porridge, flavoured with gooseberry stalks). Government House leaked and stank. The first Sydney-made ship could hardly move.

This slipshod survives. 'Sorry, our computer's down' is one Sydney *cri-de-coeur*, and 'Lift out of order' is another. When I went to board the McMahon's Point ferry once they had forgotten to bring the gangplank, so that elderly passengers had to be manhandled aboard, and one constantly hears of more extreme examples. A cat falls through the ceiling of an operating theatre at the Prince Henry Hospital. A Vietnamese man rings the emergency number, 000, after four youths ransack his house and threaten his family with knives and a gun; he fails to make himself understood, so is told to fuck off. A lady, buying a bag of garden fertilizer, finds upon it a telephone number to call for advice about its use; she does so, and gets information about AIDS in the Macedonian language. When Sydney trains are running late, it is revealed, they are told just to ignore a scheduled stop or two, to make up time. Far more dreadfully, between 1963 and 1979 a private psychiatric hospital in the northern suburb of Chelmsford used a system called 'Deep Sleep', which put patients into a lengthy coma often without their knowledge: twenty-six people died, many more were permanently maimed, but although patients often had to be admitted to public hospitals for recovery, it was years before Authority took any action.[1]

The most famous example of bumbling tergiversation was the building of the Opera House. No city ever undertook a task more daring or more admirable – to create as its architectural centrepiece an opera house and concert hall, designed by a foreigner in a style almost unexampled and to techniques altogether unproved, on the most prominent of all city sites. An international competition had found the architect and the design, much of the money was raised by lottery, but from first to last nothing went right in the construction of this lovely thing. It took five years to discover how to build the flying roofs. The cost rose from an estimated A$7 million to a paid-out A$102 million. The interior design was drastically altered. The schoolboy son of one of the lottery winners was kidnapped for ransom, and suffocated in the boot of the kidnappers' car. The opera stage proved so inadequate that performers have been complaining about it ever since. There was no provision for car parking. The original begetter of the idea, Sir Eugene Goossens, conductor of the Sydney Symphony Orchestra, was caught with his pornography and left Sydney in disgrace.[2] The architect Jøern Utzon quarrelled with everybody and left too.[3] State Governments rose and fell around the issue of the Opera

---

[1] In 1988 a Royal Commission was appointed to inquire into the tragedy. By then the presiding doctor of the hospital had killed himself, like twenty-two of his patients.

[2] Although he was, as it improbably happened, a direct descendant of Captain Cook: his maternal grandfather was the operatic bass Aynsley Cook.

[3] BRING UTZON BACK, said a graffito of the time, but there was soon an addition to it: AND HANG HIM.

House, and when it was at last finished Utzon understandably refused to return for the opening, and has never been near Sydney since.

One might suppose that in this vibrant sparkling city all arrangements would be up-to-the-minute. On the contrary, in some respects the place has been astonishingly slow to move. Until the mid-1970s several suburbs had no sewerage, and in one, Leichhardt, horse-drays were used to sweep the streets. At Revesby in 1991 a milkman ('Milko') does his rounds with a cart-horse named Stumpy. Arthritic telephone poles totter anachronistically across town. As I write some of the signals on the suburban railway lines are still lit with kerosene lamps; their wicks are trimmed once a week.

Trimming the wicks is vital, for few cities of the world have to depend upon such extended and multifarious lines of inner communication. These offer a general impression of genial and fairly energetic chaos. Ferries were the original vehicle of public transport, and to the outsider they set the tone of it still (though far more people commute by bus or train – and even, it is claimed, by bicycle). Sydney's topography means that it is the second busiest ferry port in the world, outclassed only by Hong Kong, another metropolis divided by the waterway that is its *raison d'être*.

The very first Sydney ferry was a punt that took people extremely laboriously up the river to Parramatta, and it was followed by rowing-boat services across Darling Harbour to Balmain, and then by the Old Commodore's trans-harbour enterprise. The first Sydney-built boat was also used on the Parramatta run: she had oars and sails and was nicknamed The Lump, partly because that was what she looked like, and partly perhaps because she sometimes took a whole day to make the fifteen-mile journey. Sydney took a brave step towards mechanical water-transport with the Horse Boat *Experiment*, which was propelled by the energies of four horses and carried 100 passengers, but it was the arrival of steam that altered everything. Steam opened up hitherto inaccessible corners of the harbour, and allowed daily commuting from the more distant suburbs. Manly indeed was really the creation of the steam ferry: until the service opened in 1848 it could take days to get there from the city centre, and only twelve lonely families had settled there – even as late as 1928, when the first road bridge was built across the Middle Harbour, Manly's freight went from Sydney by sea.

The ferries became essential to Sydney's functions. They have been blamed for delaying the coming of the railways, but for generations they offered the only sensible way of travelling around the harbour – even along its southern shore, which was corrugated by many creeks and inlets. Pictures of the 1920s show the Milson's Point ferry wharf, the busiest on the harbour's northern side, looking very like one of the Manhattan piers in the heyday of the Hudson River ferries: a cavernous shed with a clock-tower, tall funnels belching smoke around it, hurrying crowds coming and going, and on the road behind a line of waiting trams. In the single year 1928 more than 46 million passenger journeys were made on the ferries, and D. H. Lawrence wrote of Sydney people 'slipping like fishes across the harbour', so accustomed were they to jumping on a ship somewhere. Most of the regular passengers were middle-class people, but there were busy workmen's services to and from Balmain, and there were always pleasure services too, so that the ferries were almost as busy at weekends as they were on working days.

Tales and images of the ferries went into the literature, the art and the folklore, and into the books and pamphlets of innumerable ferry buffs. Who had not heard of the bisection of the *Greycliffe* by the liner *Tahiti* in 1927, or the capsizing of the *Rodney* in 1938, or the time the *Baragoola* collided with the whale, or the farcical affair when the *Dee Why* went aground with 700 passengers on Christmas night, 1946? The tall-funnelled steam ferries of the nineteenth century – the big double-ended craft between the World Wars, which sometimes look to me like drawing-board mistakes – the rushing hydrofoils of today – all have become in their time municipal symbols, prominent in lithograph or colour printing wherever Sydney has been publicized.

The boldest and biggest of them have always been the boats to Manly. This service demands of its vessels an average daily sailing of about 100 miles, and entails crossing the unprotected water just inside the Heads. It can be a rough ride – there are photographs of waves, sweeping in from the open sea, towering high above the ferry decks – and the ships have always been potentially ocean-going vessels, some of them sailing out to Australia under their own steam from shipyards in Britain. In former times they were often heavily overloaded, too, and sometimes wallowed precariously into their piers with passengers clinging like limpets all over them, gunwale to superstructure. The long line of these ferries, starting in 1848, stood high in Sydney affections, and even their names could stir the susceptible exile – *Bingarra, Kuringai, Burrabra* . . .[1]

The ferries reached a majestic climax in the massive *South Steyne*, the last of the steam ferries and, as they said when she appeared in the harbour in 1938, The Biggest Ferry in the British Empire – 17 knots, propellers fore and aft, 1,780 passengers, 1,200 tons (nearly twice the size of the *Cutty Sark*)! Very heavy-looking, like a bulldog, or perhaps a London bus, with two squat bolt-upright funnels and bridge-houses at each end, the *South Steyne* was a sight to see: she flew flags at prow and stern, and she stormed through the harbour for thirty-six years with a characteristic Sydney air of mingled toughness and festivity. When she left the scene in 1974, leaving only diesel-engined ships and hydrofoils, many were the lyrical words written about the lost smell of the grease and the steam, the pounding of the pistons, the warmth emerging from engine bays on winter evenings and the clang of engine-room telegraphs. It was sad to think of such grand old ships scuttled, as several of them were, in the deep water off the northern beaches.

Still, their successors are bright and bustling, and the hydrofoils are always exciting to watch (though earlier ones, built in Italy, ran at a deficit, frequently broke down, and were sometimes to be seen forlornly progressing to their yards high out of the water on lighters, propelled by tugs fore and aft). The hustle of the ferries is part of the

---

[1] Though the spellings were varied and unreliable – *Bingarra* sometimes had two Ns in it, *Kuringai* sometimes had a hyphen, *Burrabra* was sometimes two words.

fun of Sydney, and Circular Quay has always been a place of recreation as well as transport; for a time one of its piers was actually an
amusement pier, and I can remember myself when deck musicians
travelled back and forth on the Manly boats. The ferries are nearly
all municipally-owned now, but a private company runs a service
between McMahon's Point and Circular Quay, including stops according to a complex timetable at two or three places along the way. This
is usually maintained by a venerable launch, blistered of paint, creaky
of woodwork and recognizably descended from the old river boats,
whose water-insect progress here and there, looking rather as though
it has lost its way, gives the scene a piquant touch of frailty. Sometimes
there hurtles across its prow a speedboat taxi, and I love to see the
contrast: the ferry so quaint and elderly, the taxi like a crazy glass
beetle scudding and bouncing over the water with an angry buzz of
engines, driven most probably by a cheerful youth in a singlet.

Besides, it is still the prerogative of your true Sydneysider uncon-
cernedly to jump the gap between ship and shore just before the
ferry docks.

In 1928 there were 46 million ferry passengers; in 1933 there were 23
million. But the opening of the Harbour Bridge in 1932 not only
shifted the pattern of function in Sydney, it changed the city's conception of itself – even its place in the world, for this was the largest of all
arch bridges, and thus the first world-class artefact ever built in
Sydney. The bridge was like an icon, an instantly recognizable symbol
of Sydney-ness, satisfying civic visions and fulfilling one at least of
Erasmus Darwin's prophecies. It was only proper that the poster
announcing its opening should be dominated by a triumphant life-
saver, in those days the city's talismanic figure, supported by yachtsmen and sunbathers.

The harbour was so fundamental to the nature, the activity and the
reputation of Sydney that throwing an arch across it was like bursting
through some great psychological barrier. They had been talking
about it for 150 years, generally imagining a crossing at the site where

the bridge was eventually built. Greenway was perhaps the first to
propose a bridge, claiming that it would 'bring magnificence, credit
and glory to the colony'. In 1840 there was a proposal for a floating
bridge, 45 feet wide, guided by fixed chains across the harbour and
propelled by steam – 'at incredible speed', claimed the proponent of
the idea. Drawings survive of a scheme devised by an engineer, Peter
Henderson, who had worked under the great bridge-builders Robert
Stephenson and Isambard Brunel in England. His spectacular construction would have been an unsupported flat span of cast-iron, supported
by towers at each end and lit by oil-lamps all the way across. Then
there were plans for a pontoon bridge, and a seven-span bridge,
and there was even a suggestion that the harbour might be filled
in between Milson's Point and Dawes Point. For years the matter of the bridge was a great public issue – 'O, who will stand
at my right hand,' was an election cry in the 1880s of the old ham
Henry Parkes, 'and build the Bridge with me?' There were counter-
proposals for a tunnel, too, but finally in 1922 the Sydney Harbour
Bridge Act authorized the building of a bridge. Its founding
father was John Job Crew Bradfield, an implacable modernist who
was the city's chief designing engineer, but Dorman Long of England won the tender for its construction, and the contract price was
£4,217,721 11s. 10d.

The bridge was built at the deepest point of the harbour; the height
of its road above the water about equals the depth of water below.
Many an old corner of the Rocks had to be demolished for its approach road, and many a humble terrace on the other shore. For
seven years, as the great shape reached out across the harbour, Sydney
waited with some scepticism for its completion –

> Our 'arbour which art in Sydney,
> Good-o be thy name.
> Thy bridge be done,
> If not in '30, then in '31 . . .

It was '32, in the event. The work was then declared complete, with
its 1,650 foot span, its dual road, its four rail and tram tracks and its

ornamental pylons in the Egyptian manner.[1] It was tested with a load of ninety-six steam locomotives and forty-eight coal tenders, buffer to buffer, and pronounced ready for its official opening.

This was to be the greatest public occasion ever known in Sydney. The city was fond of its bridge by then, if only because it had provided hundreds of jobs through the bleak depression years. It was more than just a bridge, said the *Australian Worker*, but represented 'oneness, unity, completion . . . symbolic of what shall yet become universal'. The opening ceremony was broadcast live throughout Australia, and in Britain and the United States. The Governor-General represented King George V. There were aerial displays by the Royal Australian Air Force, and a Venetian Carnival on the harbour. There were pageants, balls, a sailing regatta, a race meeting, a celebratory cricket match. There was a procession that included 'lady life-savers', Aborigines and surviving veterans of the Sudan War, 1885. For the first and last time the whole bridge was thrown open to pedestrians, to stroll over it as they would, and the first scheduled train crossed heavily crested and beflagged. A million people are said to have shared in the celebrations.

It was all very grand, all great fun in the Sydney tradition of festivity. The swells looked fine in their top hats and medals, the lady life-savers were stunners, the newsreel cameras satisfyingly whirred, the aeroplanes gave everyone a thrill. But the touch that was to be remembered best of all, from a day of great memories, occurred at the exact moment of the bridge's formal opening. This was to be performed by the Labour Premier of New South Wales, Jack Lang, 'the Big Fellah', after the reading of a message from the King himself, but the arrangement was not to everyone's taste. Lang was thought by many conservatives to be almost treasonably radical; the idea that he should perform the ceremony in conjunction, as it were, with His Imperial Majesty particularly stuck in the gullets of a right-wing

[1] Which are not actually connected to the bridge arch, though from a distance they look as though they are, and had no functional purpose until in 1990 the two northern towers were adapted as ventilators for the tunnel being built on the harbour-bed below.

paramilitary organization called the New Guard, who believed Lang and his Government to be no more than a pack of Communist puppets – 'we, a people of pure British stock, are under the domination of a band of imported agitators of low type . . .'

The moment came. The Premier, the Governor of New South Wales, the Mayor of Sydney in his ermine, J. J. C. Bradfield, various senior officers with their swords and busbies, approached the ribbon which had been stretched across the southern entry to the bridge. The cameras were ready. The radio commentators in their booths busily set the scene. The Governor-General's mounted bodyguard was drawn up behind. The crowd was hushed. And suddenly there erupted from behind the cavalry ranks a solitary wild horseman in Army uniform, brandishing a sword. Galloping up the roadway and through the astonished dignitaries, he slashed the ribbon with his sword and shouted that he had opened the bridge 'in the name of the decent citizens of New South Wales'.

He was pulled from his horse by the police, the ribbon was tied together again, and the ceremony proceeded.[1]

The Harbour Bridge did for Sydney what the Brooklyn Bridge had done for New York half a century before – Bradfield declared in fact that the suburbs of the northern shore would be a Brooklyn to Sydney's Manhattan.[2] He also foresaw that its existence would greatly

[1] The ebullient miscreant was an Irish member of the New Guard, Francis de Groot (1888–1969), the owner of a furniture factory who by this single act immortalized himself. He was taken to a psychiatric hospital but declared sane, and was later fined £5, with £4 costs, for offensive behaviour in a public place. Charges of damaging a ribbon to the extent of £2 were dismissed. De Groot found many admirers – some say the Governor-General's guard had lent him the horse – while within the year Jack Lang was dismissed from office by the Governor of New South Wales, Sir Philip Woolcott Game, CB, KCB, GBE, KCMG, GCVO, GCB, a future Commissioner of the London Metropolitan Police.

[2] In earlier, even more completely British years, the popular analogy would have been not Manhattan and Brooklyn, but Liverpool and Birkenhead. Anyway, there was a Sydney Brooklyn already, up on the Hawkesbury River; its name confusingly commemorated the Union Bridge Company of Brooklyn, New York, builders of the Brooklyn Bridge, whose engineers had constructed a nearby railway bridge in 1899.

intensify Sydney's centrifugal tendencies, encouraging people to live ever further from the city fulcrum. By now a vast web of roads has grown out of the original convict-hacked highway to Parramatta; parts of it have been given high-sounding names like the Great Western Highway or the Pacific Highway, which hold out some promise of clarity, but most of it remains a drab obfuscation. Suburban railways clatter in all directions, there are elaborately networked systems of buses and subways, hundreds of bridges cross creeks and inlets, there is a brief mono-rail track and there will soon be the harbour tunnel too, a few yards east of the great bridge, but built by Japanese.

The first forms of public land transport were the trams, horse-drawn at first, then steam and finally electric. I would like to have seen the city when the trams were still about. They operated in ramshackle partnership with the ferries, and must greatly have added to the city's flavour. Like streetcars everywhere, they were always objects of popular affection – a tombstone at Rookwood is decorated with a bas-relief of the No. 51 tram that ran over the deceased – and are now remembered with nostalgic regret. The horse trams sound striking enough, since they were painted bright yellow, were sometimes double-deckers, and were often pulled by teams of four or five horses. The steam trams were better still. The first of them were American, imported for the 1879 International Exhibition. Hauled by violently exhaling locomotives with Cyclopean headlights, they sometimes trundled around town in trains of five double-decker cars, leaning dramatically as they rounded curves.

By the end of the century, when the system was electrified, Sydney had one of the largest tram networks in the world. Trams went everywhere, it seems. They ran all the way round Circular Quay. They ran at Manly and at Parramatta. They were propelled by a fixed cable at Edgecliffe, like the San Francisco cable-cars. They were conveyed in specially-equipped punts across the Middle Harbour. Down many a harbourside slope they scraped their way to meet the ferries at the bottom. Through the eastern suburbs they plunged, displaying the white or red disc that warned they were on their way to Bondi, and on race days, bursting as they were with merry punters, they hardly needed the three green diamonds that stood for Canterbury. Three times at least, in the 1940s, trams fell into the harbour, sliding down the slushy hill to Athol Wharf on the northern shore, and hurling themselves uncontrollably through all obstructions; but at Balmain they were restrained on the steeper hills by a trailer called a dummy, upon which it was the delight of reckless urchins to ride.

The last Sydney tram ran in 1961, and the trains and buses are not so much fun, though I do find a certain shabby romance in the double-decker commuter trains which clank past my balcony, over the Harbour Bridge, and away through forty-nine stops to their terminus in the distant haze of the Blue Mountains. The fact that trains and city buses still converge upon the original landing place at Sydney Cove adds something to history's patina, and until a year or two ago there were places on the rail system which spoke most evocatively of an older Sydney – brass knobs, Bakelite switches, Instructions to Employees in copperplate script behind metal-framed glass, names on destination boards that seemed to me then as rhythmic and evocative as the English country-station names so beloved of romantic poesy: Warrimoo, Bullabarra, Blaxland, Falconbridge or Emu Plains.

The Darling Harbour mono-rail is entertaining to ride, sliding as it does high above the city streets, so close to the corners of office blocks that you feel sure it is going to hit them. But the most enviable land journey in Sydney is one I have never tried: the slow haughty journey of the Inclinator, the opulent device that takes fortunate residents of the harbour front smoothly down their steep bluffs, past their hillside palms and lawns, to the pools and yachts awaiting them at the bottom – like a divine progress, it looks from the outside.

A potent element in the Sydney system is corruption. It always has been. Mayhem was rampant in the penal days, and not only among convicts: the officers of the Rum Corps were crooked to the core, the doctors at the hospital sold its drugs at huge profits to their private patients, and I cannot help suspecting a whiff of nepotism in the result of the competition instituted by Governor Darling for a Government House design in 1827 – it was won by his wife. In later years innumerable developments were accompanied by hints of jobbery: insider trading in land, for instance, where a railway was likely to be built, or untendered contracts for public works, or dubious complicity between architects and contractors. A surprising number of estate agents stood for municipal office, where they would get inside knowledge of planning decisions. When the Premier Sir Robert Askin died in 1981, it was alleged in his obituary that illegal casino owners had been paying him A$700,000 a year hush money.[1] More recently a famous scam surrounded the taking of driving tests, which were conducted by a system of organized bribery: seven faults was the official failure rate, but one woman, sufficient money having passed under the gear lever, was given her licence after committing seventy-two. A private investigator, the Independent Commission Against Corruption was told in 1990, sent the following bill to an insurance company:

To attend to your attorney's instruction to conduct certain inquiries in this matter, including the corruption of several members of the Police Force and obtaining printouts relating to the man's criminal form, then drinking with them for long periods, and reporting as attached: Hours, many, but say four at A$25 = A$100

Most contemporary scandals have concerned the police. In Sydney they speak cynically of 'the police culture', implying a general rottenness of morality. We are told standards have improved, but when an eminent villain was recently asked about the prevalence of organized crime in the city, he mentioned six conspiratorial groups – two Australian brotherhoods, one Lebanese, two Chinese Triads and the New South Wales police. Certainly in the 1920s the police were blatantly in cahoots with the crime syndicates, and even in 1950, when the Superintendent of the Metropolitan Police retired he was

---

[1] Askin, a Grand Commander of the Order of St Michael and St George, was also well-remembered for the order he gave his driver when, in 1966, hostile demonstrators threatened to block President Lyndon Johnson's motorcade through Sydney: 'Run over the bastards.'

given a banquet by 300 underworld leaders, together with a generous cheque.

I have seldom been in this city when a Royal Commission of Inquiry has not been investigating some rort or other. The very first such inquisition was mounted by Commissioner John Bigge, who was sent out from England in 1819 to investigate the alleged extravagances of Governor Macquarie, and who by a combination of nitpicking and cheeseparing succeeded in squashing Macquarie's plans for the shape of Sydney.[1] Since then Royal Commissions have inquired into every sub-species of public misdemeanour, and during my research for this book one was looking into the matter of Harry the Hat, a senior police officer accused by his own force, with maximum publicity, of having raped eight women over a twenty-five-year period of his career. The charges were later dropped. The inquiry into this odd affair was quite odd enough itself. Processions of poker-faced policemen appeared one after the other in the witness box, dressed for the occasion in high tight collars and business suits; the presiding judge looked remarkably sceptical through-out; a number of fearfully expensive barristers cross-examined; and in the front of the court, accompanied by his wife and sometimes putting his feet up for comfort on a chair in front of him, sat bespectacled and balding the man at the centre of the case, so recently accused by his own colleagues of having been a sexual monster. He was exonerated absolutely, and his character was agreed to be so irreproachable that according to the Sydney wags it made Mother Teresa look like a sex-maniac. On the other hand the police operation against him was characterized as incompetent, gross, slipshod and deceitful.

But then twenty years before, as a Deputy Police Commissioner blandly deposed, looking on the bright side I suppose, Harry the Hat, secure within the closed ranks of the police culture, would not have been charged if he *had* been a rapist.

*

[1] Of a pretty Gothick toll-gate the Governor had commissioned this disagreeable inspector wrote that 'while it must excite the derision of everyone acquainted with style in architecture it must also raise in responsible breasts a strong emotion of regret at the vast disbursement on this inelegant and fugacious toy'.

It is only to be expected that Sydney should be especially interested in matters of crime and punishment. They dominate whole pages of the newspapers, they crop up frequently in conversation, and their monuments are intrusive. One of the best-known buildings in Sydney is the old George Street police station, scene of many an ancient misery, which is now a café but is still surmounted by a lion holding a policeman's truncheon in its jaws. The National Art School is housed in the former Darlinghurst gaol, upon whose façade the very same lion is holding a key; classes are held where the cells once were, and the gallows yard houses a toilet block. The best-known of the modern Sydney prisons, Long Bay, is as familiar in idiom, in joke, in simile and in allusion as it is in grim silhouette on the road to La Perouse, if only because a surprisingly large number of Sydneysiders have had some family connection with it: as the art historian Joan Kerr wrote dryly in 1986, it is 'the architectural monument most commonly identified as the ultimate destination after reaching Sydney's social pinnacles'.[1] Here, as in Britain, imprisonment is still a favoured punishment for misdemeanours of all kinds; as I write one New South Wales citizen in every 1,500 is in gaol, and they are busily building 1,500 more cells, and planning several new prisons to cope with future demand.

For most of Sydney's original citizens, of course, crime was a natural way of life. The Newgate pickpockets of the 1780s did not lose their cunning when they came to Australia, but enthusiastically stole from their comrades, from their gaolers and from the Aborigines. Ralph Clark, having started a vegetable garden on his eponymous island in the harbour, found that no sooner did his vegetables start to grow than somebody stole them. Brick houses were conveniently easy to break and enter – householders of early Sydney often awoke to find a hole picked in the wall during the night – and when Governor Gipps moved into his new Government House in 1845 some of his silver was nicked on the way. Dead-end streets became so uncomfortably

---

[1] It is commonly known as The Bay – just what penal Sydney used to be called among the English criminal classes.

connected in the Sydney mind with thievery that well into the twentieth century town planners were reluctant to sanction them.

For years the city's natural instincts, like my own, were with the
criminal rather than the gaoler. Sydney's first public heroes were the
bushrangers, convicts or adventurers gone feral and living by their
wits as highwaymen. They had bold names – 'Captain Thunderbolt',
'Bold Jack', 'Mad-Dog Morgan' – and robbers and murderers though
they were, and often anything but romantic, they were seen as popular
champions of liberty, expressing in their lives many a pent-up grudge,
and many a yearning for wider horizons. It would be hard for any
poor convict of spirit, permanently ill-treated by destiny, to resist the
appeal of the bushranger ballads:

> Some dark night when everything is silent in the town,
> I'll kill the tyrants one and all, and shoot the floggers down.
> I'll give the Law a little shock; remember what I say –
> They'll yet regret they sent Jim Jones in chains to Botany Bay.

or:

> Come, all my hearties, we'll roam the mountains high,
> Together we'll plunder, together we'll die.
> We'll wander over valleys, and gallop over plains,
> And we'll scorn to live in slavery, bound down with iron chains.

The most celebrated of all the bushrangers was the Irishman Jack
Donaghoe, transported for life in 1825, who was sentenced to hang in
Sydney for robbery but escaped between the courtroom and the con-
demned cell. For eighteen months he ranged the countryside west of
the city, sometimes, so local legend said, appearing bold as brass in
the city itself, suave in a blue coat and laced boots. Donaghoe appealed
to many atavistic Sydney instincts, not just as a dashing defier of
Authority, but as an Irishman cocking a snook at the English, and he
was to live in the folklore long after he was caught and shot. He was
the real hero of the ballad which has perhaps affected the Australian
psyche more than any other:

He was scarcely sixteen years of age when he left his father's home,
And through Australia's sunny clime bushranging he did roam.
He robbed the wealthy squatters, their stock he did destroy,
A terror to Australia was the Wild Colonial Boy!

The Wild Colonial Boy – still perhaps, somewhere deep in the civic unconscious, a Sydney cynosure!

After the bushrangers came the Pushes, gangs of young hooligans, mostly based in the Rocks, who infested the whole downtown area and at once fascinated and appalled respectable citizens. Some of these were just groups of thugs, and their style was captured by a poem, attributed to Henry Lawson, in which one of their captains anathematizes an enemy:

May pangs of windy spasms throughout your bowels dart;
May you shit your fucking trousers every time you try to fart;
May itching piles torment you, and corns grow on your feet,
And crabs as big as spiders attack your balls a treat;
And when you're down and outed, a dismal bloody wreck,
May you slip back through your arsehole and break your fucking neck.

Other gangs aspired to dandyism. They wore pearl-button jackets and cocky narrow-brimmed hats, and their high-heeled boots were sometimes inlaid with mirrors, reflecting the finery above. Most Victorian memoirs have something about the goings-on of these tiresome but distinctive youths – knocking people's hats over their eyes outside the theatre, indulging in noisy internecine fights, hitching rides on the backs of carriages or making curses of themselves at pleasure-places of the harbour – 'He put a rock in the heel of a sock / And went down the bay to Chowder'. In them the bushrangers' heritage was transmuted into the urban tradition of the larrikin, and if little else about them was very engaging, their disrespect for the established system perhaps still touched Sydney hearts. The word Push, which the gangs invented for themselves, went into the language not entirely pejoratively: in later years various social cliques liked to call themselves Pushes, and when in the 1980s a group of historians published a

journal concerning the origins of Australia, *Push from the Bush* is what
they called it.

The more outrageous of Sydney's crooks and racketeers, the assorted
Mr Bigs of organized crime, the Colourful Racing Identities, the con
men and the fraudsters, to some degree inherited the mantle of John
Donaghoe. They were villains, but they were heroes of a sort too, wild
colonial boys, and the tales that were told about them acquired the
vitality of myth. My own favourite concerns the Tichborne Claimant.
The mystery of the Tichborne inheritance was well-known in Victorian Australia. Roger Tichborne, heir to a great estate in England, was
generally supposed to have drowned in a South American shipwreck
in 1854, but his mother Lady Tichborne, the family matriarch, was
convinced that her son was still alive somewhere in the world. In 1866
Arthur Orton, son of a London butcher, having arrived in Sydney
after a scallywag career at sea, in Tasmania and in up-country New
South Wales, boldly took up this challenge, and declared himself to
be the missing aristocrat. He was semi-literate, fat and very vulgar,
while Tichborne was an excellent linguist and a former officer in the
6th Dragoon Guards, but he was so successful in his act that Sydney
society was fulsomely deceived. He was invited to grand houses, he
was allowed to run up enormous debts, and an ancient pensioner of
the Tichborne family, by then himself retired to Sydney, swore that
he remembered the rascal well. Off Orton went to London, where
he inexplicably convinced poor Lady Tichborne too, squeezing a
handsome annual allowance out of her: but the rest of the family
contemptuously rebuffed him, and after eleven years in English gaols
for perjury the Tichborne Claimant came clean at last, and published a full confession of his enterprise. As an irresponsible rogue, a
deceiver of toffs and an enthusiastic gambler, he was a man after
Sydney's heart.

Later the swaggering kings of the syndicates were stars of a kind,
and lived filmic lives. When the hoodlum Phil Jeffs died in 1945 the
tabloid *Truth* began its obituary: 'Phil the Jew, Sydney racketeer,
gangster, drug peddler, procurer, sly grogger, alleged phizz gig for
some detectives, gunman, wealthy friend of some politicians and many

police, died on Tuesday.'[1] Richard Reilly, who was himself murdered by the syndicates, began his career as a dance-hall bouncer, became a wartime racketeer, ran a roadhouse called Oyster Lil's, drove a Maserati sports car, lived in a mansion and was known as the King of Baccarat. The gambler Chicka Barnes, murdered in 1957, was found to have four bullet-scars in his abdomen, one finger shot from his left hand, two stab-scars on his chest, a knife-scar on his throat, bicycle-chain-scars on forehead and shoulders, various scars on his chin and lips and the bullet-hole in his back that killed him. When Colourful Racing Identity George Freeman died in 1990, the *Sydney Morning Herald* called him Big Crime's Artful Dodger. He was Mr Big Enough for twenty-five years, the paper said, and it added that during all that time the best the police could manage against him was a couple of fines for illegal betting, though he certainly had contacts with the Chicago underworld and the Chinese Triads, was generally assumed to fix horse races and run illegal casinos, was strongly suspected of heroin smuggling and had been refused entry to England as an undesirable. 'His word was his bond,' an old friend was quoted as saying, and many devoted Colourful Identities were photographed at his funeral.

I kept random notes of crime and misbehaviour over a few months in Sydney, and the profusion was astonishing. Here for instance is a man on his seventy-ninth charge of having refused to pay restaurants for meals he has eaten: this time he has dined on soup, oysters, fillet steak, dessert wine, cognac and Campari. Here another Racing Identity, convicted of stabbing a man to death in a street fracas, finds himself in the same gaol as his twenty-one-year-old son, who has recently assaulted a Chinese cab-driver.[2] A gang of Fijians, Tahitians and Samoans clashes with a gang of bikies in the western suburbs. A

[1] A phizz gig was a police informer, a curious Sydney derivation from an old word which (so the Oxford Dictionary tells me) can also mean a frivolous woman, a kind of top, a harpoon or a silly notion.
[2] He suffered from Parkinson's disease, and was described by a colleague as being as shaky as a dog shitting razor-blades.

senior railway official is accused of fiddling an expense account for an apple and a Devon sandwich.[1] A solicitor is found guilty of keeping a brothel. The Maritime Services Board says that during the past eighteen months people with chain-saws have stolen 200 solar-powered panels from navigation lights. Illegal hot-dog vendors, says a report, are battling with each other to preserve their territories.

What's this now? A visiting Commonwealth MP is bitten on the wrist by a female drug-addict. Seven schoolboys, aged eleven to fifteen, are charged with breaking 300 train windows in two months. A surgeon is accused of deceiving patients; he pretends to operate on them for Ménière's disease, but a skull is presented as evidence to show that he never drills deep enough. A report says that the Philippines have become a second home for leaders of the Sydney underworld, who arrange many of their drug deals there, and control much of the prostitution. The Corrective Services Minister, sentenced to seven and a half years for taking bribes to arrange the early release of prisoners, appeals and has his sentence increased to ten years. Here is a complete newspaper story which was printed on 21 March 1990, but which had, I thought, something particularly timeless to it:

GIRL ROBBED

Four boys walked off laughing, after robbing a 19-year-old girl of $150 outside Campbelltown public library yesterday. One threw her empty wallet back and shouted 'You stupid bitch'.

It sounds appalling. In fact I have never once felt frightened in Sydney. There are few places in this city where one cannot walk with safety, even after dark, and in recent years Sydney's murder rate has been considerably lower than London's, and something like one-fifteenth of Los Angeles'. As to petty crime, it is probably no more

[1] Devon is a processed food containing meat, spices and cereals; its pink colour fades in bright light. I read somewhere that until the Second World War it used to be called Fritz, but a Pom-busting informant assures me that so bland a victual always did have an English name.

common here than anywhere else, but I sometimes feel it is regarded differently – more as a folk-custom perhaps. I remember well the goggle-eyed astonishment with which a young couple on holiday from Adelaide listened to a ferry deckhand, the very image of a Sydney larrikin or hoon, telling all and sundry how he habitually got home after night duty – he took a cab to a nearby address, asked it to wait for a moment and disappeared. And it was on a ferry too that a kindly woman warned me one day to be especially careful about pickpockets on public transport in Sydney. I thanked her for her advice, and when we parted she returned to me my purse, which she had extracted from my handbag in the course of the conversation.

Yet despite it all, despite all the energies of this rich and vigorous place, despite the restless undercurrents and procrastinations, still I often irrationally feel that Sydney exists simply to be – and to present itself. This it does with infinite panache. Everything looks so easy here, at first sight, that the stranger can hardly imagine the cauldron of complexities bubbling behind the scenes, while Sydneysiders as a whole bear themselves as though possessing citizenship of this city were purpose enough in itself.

Sydney is born to show itself off. Like Venice, it is its own advertising slogan, for ever blazoning its own merits. Elsewhere, as the poet Vincent Buckley once remarked, the play may be the thing: in Sydney it's the première. Perhaps it all began with the flash of criminals long ago. Certainly visitors to Sydney down the generations have commented on the swagger of things, the showy techniques of horse-tram drivers, the flaunting gear of larrikins, the confidence amounting almost to exhibitionism of working-men. Showmanship of a kind is everywhere here. It may be just the crazy driving of a cab-driver, skidding zigzag through the traffic on the New South Head Road. It may be an aerobics class glimpsed through a North Sydney window, prancing like so many blonde demons to the beat of rock and the whirring of ceiling fans. There is a street group called the Aussie

Small-Change Brass Band which might well represent the city at ceremonial functions, so alive is it with the authentic Sydney mixture of fun, fizz and chutzpah: its players are three very small boys in very large hats, with two trumpets, a tuba and extremely powerful amplifiers, and I can tell you they play 'Puttin' on the Ritz' like nobody else. Virtuoso infant trumpeters – dress-up silks in the middle of the morning – scud of seaplanes off Rose Bay into the sun – chess-players in Hyde Park concluding their games with majestic scowls, as though they have torn up a treaty – GORGE at the ice-rink – Harry the Hat with his feet up before the Royal Commission – curly-wigged strutting barristers at the Supreme Court, bemedalled worthies at royal rituals, bowler-hatted trap-drivers at the Easter Show – all these characters and glimpses, and thousands more, together with the Grand Guignol of awful memory, and the flourish of true achievement, add up to the histrionic purpose that is Sydney.

CONNECTIONS

Aᴌᴡᴀʏs, sᴏᴍᴇᴡʜᴇʀᴇ ɪɴ Sʏᴅɴᴇʏ's ᴡᴀᴛᴇʀs, ɢʀᴇʏ ᴡᴀʀsʜɪᴘs can be seen: lying in dock, steaming out to sea, or standing morosely month after month in Atholl Bight, between Cremorne Point and Bradley's Head, waiting to be scrapped.[1] A pictorial album of Sydney is like a naval register, as the little *Sirius* of 1788 gives way to the bulky three-masters of the Victorian prime, to the prim-looking men-o'-war of *fin-de-siècle*, to the rakish three-funnelled County-class cruisers that gave a particular touch of elegance to the Sydney of the 1930s, to the bold carriers of the Second World War and the destroyers of today enmeshed in electronics. Sydney is the main base of the Royal Australian Navy, which hived off from its parent the British Royal Navy in 1911, but which still honours some of the old British traditions, and the naval presence is symbolical. The British Empire was a maritime dominion, built upon sea-power, and of all the cities it

[1] Old Sydney riddle: Why did Cremorne Point? Because it saw Atholl Bight off Bradley's Head.

nurtured from scratch around the world, Sydney is the most auth-
entically imperial.

For the first decades of its existence it was entirely an Empire town
– a Navy town, in fact, since its first Governors were all naval men.
Some scholars believe that its original purposes were more ambiguously imperial than London was ever to admit, and it was certainly
not envisaged only as a penal colony. The first proponent of a settlement seems to have been the American-born James Matra, who had
sailed to Australia as a midshipman with Cook, and who saw it, after
the American Revolution, as a possible new home for dispossessed
American loyalists. They should be accompanied, he suggested, by
poor English emigrants, and supplemented by Chinese labourers, and
in no time the new colony would be supplying timber and flax for the
Navy, produce of all sorts for the markets of the east. Phillip, as we
have seen, always foresaw Sydney as a free British city of the future,
and is justly surrounded, in the Victorian statue of him that stands in
the Botanic Gardens, by figures of Navigation, Commerce, Mining
and Agriculture.

One thesis argues that a fundamental object of the New South
Wales enterprise was strategic. For myself I still have to consult the
globe to grasp the historical significance of Sydney's geographical
position – Mercador's projection grossly misrepresents it. The city lies
about equidistant from South Africa, one of the key staging-posts of
British imperial trade routes, India, the centrepiece of the whole
imperial structure, and both the east and the west coasts of South
America – Argentina going one way, Chile the other. One can see
that it could indeed have been yet another stronghold to reinforce
British control of the oceans. From Port Jackson, strategists argued at
the time, Britain might conveniently threaten all the rival empires of
the Pacific: the Spanish possessions of South America, the Dutch
colonies in the East Indies, even Russian or American outposts on the
coasts of North America. When Alessandro Malaspina brought his
ships to Sydney in 1793, ostensibly on a voyage of scientific discovery,
he was really spying for the Spanish Government, and he went away

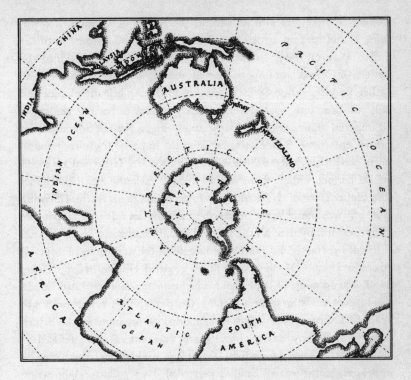

convinced that perfidious Albion was establishing there a base for the extension of British power throughout the southern seas, from which armies of horrible convicts would be conveyed by the Royal Navy to fall in looting and rapine upon the colonies of the Spanish Main.[1]

In hindsight he seems to have misread the signs of the settlement, just as one feels sure that his artist Juan Ravanet must have been blinded by the sheer Britishness of the Sydney officials, who all look in his pictures supernaturally tall, slender and gentlemanly. If a military

---

[1] Malaspina was treated with courtesy by the not terribly warlike British officers, who were delighted to have visitors, and was obliged to admit in one of his dispatches to Madrid that they had been very nice to him – 'We shall remain for the rest of our lives eternally grateful for the gracious hospitality for which we have been obliged to the colony.'

role for Sydney was plotted behind the scenes in London, it never came about, and no armed expedition set sail from Sydney until the Sudan War of 1885. In fact Sydney never did fit easily into the pattern of Victorian imperial expansion. It belonged really to an earlier Empire. When Sydney was settled the American colonies had only just been lost, while India, which was later to become central to all imperial affairs, was still hardly more than a field of adventure for private enterprise. Sydney was far from the imperial trade-routes, and in its early years offered little economic promise. It carried no evangelical banner, either: there was no urge to raise the local Aborigines to a higher state of civilization, or to reconcile them to the Christian God – it was many years before the missionaries advanced upon the indigenes, and by then all the Ioras of Sydney had gone.

Sydney certainly did not figure largely in the ambitions of imperial administrators – 'My language fails!' groaned Hilaire Belloc's Duke, finally abandoning all hope that his lachrymose grandson Lord Lundy would ever make a success of life. 'Go out and govern New South Wales!'[1] For many years Sydney remained synonymous in the British mind with Botany Bay. Sidney Smith, 'the wit of wits', refused to believe that a colony founded as 'a sink of wickedness' could ever be improved, and it was an English journalist, Henry Carter, who wrote the most famously contemptuous lines about the convict pioneers:

> From distant climes o'er wide-spread seas we come,
> Though not with much eclat or beat of drum,
> True patriots all; for be it understood,
> We left our country for our country's good;
> No private views disgrac'd our generous zeal,
> What urg'd our travels was our country's weal,
> And none will doubt but that our emigration
> Has proved most useful to the British nation.[2]

---

[1] '. . . and gracious! how Lord Lundy cried!'
[2] For many years, though, the lines were supposed to have been written by an anonymous convict as a prelude to the performance of *The Recruiting Officer* which we attended on page 176 – legend said it had been declaimed by George Barrington, a celebrated pickpocket known as The Prince of Thieves.

But as the imperial pride swelled, the possession of Australia did become a rather hazy source of satisfaction to the British – it was so particularly far-flung. To Dickens' Mr Micawber it was a place not of exile but of possibility; and by the end of the century a representation of Captain Cook, implanting the flag for the very first time on the shores of New South Wales, was a favourite illustration in children's books about the glory of Empire. Kipling, in his 'Song of the Cities', had Sydney singing about a birth-stain 'turned to good'. 'Farewell Australia,' wrote Lawrence, remembering his departure from Sydney Harbour in 1922, 'farewell Britain and the great Empire. Farewell! Farewell!'

In return many Sydney citizens cherished a revived pride in the Mother Country – not just a snobbish nostalgia, but a sense of comradeship in a great enterprise. The Imperial Factor, which had brought the city into being, powerfully affected its affairs for many generations, and is still apparent now.

The oldest surviving European graffiti in Sydney are on Garden Island, the main naval headquarters – HMAS *Kuttabul* in service usage. This is not in fact an island any longer, but in 1788 it was still separated from the shore by a couple of hundred yards, and seemed a good place to establish a vegetable garden. Seamen were assigned to do the gardening, and it was presumably three of them who scratched their initials on a rock on the highest point of the islet, together with the date 1788 – FM, IB and WB, now protected by glass pyramids like garden cloches. I was taken out to see them one morning by a retired civilian employee of the base, who had spent most of his working life there, who knew every inch of the place, and who had for years been puzzling out the identities of FM, IB and WB.[1] I shall always remember this delightful man's comical consternation when I

[1] One of whom seems to have been fairly certainly established as Frederick Meredith, steward to the captain of the transport *Scarborough*; he has many descendants in Sydney still, and when a celebratory party was thrown on Garden Island in 1988, forty of them turned up.

happened to see another set of initials – FP – on a nearby rock; through all those years of infatuated study, through hundreds of visits to the spot, he had never noticed them before!

Actually we came to the conclusion that they were a recent vandalistic addition (Sydney graffiti remain vandalism for a century or two, before they are protected with glass pyramids).[1] I think my companion's original dismay, though, concerned the defiance of tradition – that there should have been four pairs of initials, instead of the long-attested and Admiralty-approved three. Garden Island is soaked in the imperial tradition. For generations it was the Royal Navy's principal base in the South Pacific, and some of Sydney's most handsome buildings stand around the dockyard. Fine workmanlike structures in the Georgian tradition, they are the southernmost examples of the British dockyard architecture that dignified naval ports around the world – Simonstown and Bermuda, Bombay and Portsmouth itself. A succession of twelve British admirals presided over the fortunes of Garden Island, from their enviable Admiralty House at Kirribilli across the water,[2] and it was men of the Royal Marines who, in the 1880s, laid out its tennis-courts above the sea.

Between the two World Wars it was decided that the imperial navies must be provided with a dry dock for their largest warships at the southern end of the Pacific, supplementing the vast installations at Singapore in the north – a first confirmation, it might be said, of Malaspina's instincts. The Captain Cook Dock, which finally linked Garden Island with the mainland, was completed too late for the Second World War, but even so Sydney became one of the great naval ports of the conflict. Hundreds of allied warships frequented it, hundreds of thousands of troops passed through it. Fabulous liners like the *Queen Mary*, the *Queen Elizabeth* and the *Aquitania* appeared as troopships camouflaged in its harbour.[3] For men all over the world

[1] Unless they are Aboriginal, in which case they are never graffiti at all, but rock art.
[2] Which had a speaking-tube connecting one floor with another.
[3] The *Aquitania* had last been seen by many Sydneysiders standing offshore at Gallipoli a quarter of a century before.

Sydney was to provide a lasting memory of romance, gaiety and hospitality – as Charles Causley remembered of his visit with the *Glory*:

> O like maidens preparing for the court ball
> We pressed our number-one suits,
> Borrowing electric irons and starching prime white collars,
> And stepped forth into the golden light
> With Australian pound-notes in our pockets.[1]

Today much of the Australian fleet can be seen there at Garden Island any day – destroyers, frigates, repair ships, towered over by an immense cantilever crane which is one of Sydney's best-known shapes.[2] The grey mass of it all, cluttered about with masts and superstructures beyond the Botanic Gardens, gives central Sydney a clout that I rather relish.[3]

All around the harbour, too, the Navy presence is familiar. There are repair yards at Cockatoo Island, and various depots and training places are dotted on headlands, and an enchanting little naval chapel, high above South Head, is one of the very first buildings to welcome vessels of the fleet back home. Minesweepers lie upstream, moored in a blaze of lights at Berry Island, and most compelling of all is the sight that awaits you at Neutral Bay, in one of the most thickly populated parts of the harbour's northern shore. A small park stands at the head of this cove, with shady trees and a cricket pitch. Pleasant houses stand around, and there is a yacht club. If you stroll down from the main road through the green you will probably find children playing, yachtsmen preparing to sail, pensioners eating sandwiches on benches, and even (I swear to you) an occasional lady in hat, coat

---

[1] Mr Causley tells me, by the way, that he was suspected of hyperbole because he wrote of the aircraft-carrier as being 'prefaced by plunging dolphins' when she passed through the Heads – but on that summer day of 1945 prefaced by dolphins HMS *Glory* was.

[2] It was built to the same plans as the master-crane at the Singapore dockyard, erected in 1939 but blown up in 1941 before the Japanese could get it.

[3] But which many local residents could do without – not least those who, living in the nearby suburb of Woolloomooloo, claim that the Navy's testing of its radar equipment interferes with their television reception, sets car alarms off and makes them feel ill.

and skirt practising her croquet shots. And down at the water's edge, there in the heart of the great amiable city, a pair of black submarines is almost certain to be lying alongside a pier at their flotilla head-quarters – sinister predatory boats, but by now almost disregarded features of a saunter round the bay.

There are fortifications all over Sydney, but contrary to Malaspina's suspicions they have been motivated more by fear than by aggressive instinct. Until 1870 this was an imperial garrison town. The New South Wales Corps, mustered in 1790 and nicknamed the Botany Bay Rangers, was ignominiously abolished in 1810, to be replaced by a battalion of Highlanders. Thereafter battalions of fourteen British regiments came out in rotation to the Sydney station. Their main barracks were on George Street, and are said to have been the Empire's biggest: m̀ imposing buildings, if we are to go by the old pictures, standing around a wide parade ground, with an officers' mess said to be as comfortable as any the British Army possessed, and their own military windmill on the high ground above. They were demolished in 1848, but two fine examples of Victorian military archi-tecture survive: Victoria Barracks at Paddington, which looks like a toy fortress, and has sentries stumping up and down outside it, and the Lancers' Barracks at Parramatta, an elegant affair of sandstone and ironwork which has been in continual use since 1820, and is thus the oldest military establishment in Australia. The Sydney garrison church was Holy Trinity Church, in Argyle Place, and this pleasant and beloved building is rich still in military mementoes, flags, crests, pamphlets and miscellaneous ephemera that form, accumulated as they have been generation by generation, a kind of imperial palimp-sest.[1]

In the beginning the convicts were the enemy. The original fort, on Observatory Hill, was built under Phillip as a refuge for the officials if

[1] One item is the flag of the Australian 7th Infantry Battalion. In 1940, during the Second World War, this was taken from the battalion guard-room in Egypt by

a convict rising occurred, and all that remains of it now is a small uninteresting segment of a wall, outside the observatory garden. Vanished too is the pretty castellated fortress which Greenway designed for Lachlan Macquarie on Bennelong Point, which was partly a protection for Sydney Cove, and partly an architectural folly, but chiefly a watchpost to prevent convicts escaping by sea. Later defence works had the Empire's foreign enemies more in mind. It is said that Napoleon himself conceived the idea of seizing Sydney, and a French squadron which turned up in 1802 is thought to have been making a preliminary reconnaissance – certainly its cartographer mapped the settlement with exquisite care. Sydney's vulnerable isolation, however, does not seem to have worried the colonists much until one morning in 1830 the city woke up to the news that during the night four American frigates had sailed through the Heads, up the harbour and into Sydney Cove without anyone noticing. 'Had war existed,' helpfully observed their commander, Captain Charles Wilkes, 'we might, after firing the shipping, and reducing the greater part of the town to ashes, have effected a retreat before daylight in perfect safety.' Later Governor Sir William Denison imagined such an event even more graphically – a few frigates might come in at night 'and the first notice I should have of their arrival would be a 32-pound shot crashing through the walls of my house'.

A fever of military activities ensued. Sydney was several thousand miles from the next British naval station and, in a world where almost every nation was a potential enemy of the British Empire, had nobody to save it but itself. The Americans were one possible threat, the Spaniards were another, the French a third, the Crimean War brought the Russian bogy even into these distant seas and in later years there was always the Yellow Peril. There was a rumour once that ferocious Irish Fenians were on their way from California, and during the

Private T. Flannery, who sold it to Private Brian Fitzgerald-Fogarty, who passed it to Corporal T. M. Fennessy. In these various hands it was carried all through the Libyan, Cretan and Greek campaigns, and after the war it came back once more to Fitzgerald-Fogarty, who gave it to the regimental association, which laid it up at last, in 1976, peacefully in Holy Trinity Church.

American Civil War it was thought that Yankee privateers, in what would surely have been one of the most exciting of all skulduggeries, might raid the city for the gold stored in its coffers. Successive administrations, backed by the imperial authorities in London, accordingly turned Sydney into a fortified base. 'I had no idea,' wrote Anthony Trollope after viewing the works in 1871, 'that the people of New South Wales were either so suspicious of enemies, or so pugnacious in their nature': and to this day on almost every headland or islet there are militant remains.

The centre of the defence system was Pinchgut Island, which we first saw as a wooded mount with a gallows on its summit. This had been cut down to water level and converted into a citadel. Renamed Fort Denison, after that apprehensive Governor, it was equipped with a Martello tower, one of the last such fortifications to be built anywhere – a plan to erect another on the reef called the Sow and Pigs, just inside the Heads, was unfortunately abandoned. For years the island–fort was armed with muzzle-loaded 8-pounder guns, during the Second World War it housed two anti-aircraft guns, and now it is one of the prime tourist sights of Sydney, looking very much like a surfaced submarine, or perhaps a monitor of the American Civil War, a few hundred yards from the Opera House. The daily one o'clock gun is fired from Pinchgut, the tide records are kept there, and since it is occupied as I write by a caretaker with a large family, it is equipped on its north side with a large rotary washing line, well-hung with the morning laundry.

Until the Second World War, when Australia took up arms against Japan, nobody cared to test these works. By then the headland batteries had been reinforced by a boom across the harbour mouth, from Watson's Bay to the Sow and Pigs and across to the northern shore. This had to be removed to allow the passage of any vessel, and a launch would hurry out to lift it whenever necessary – very frequently, during the daylight hours, if only for the Manly ferries.

In May 1942 an attack group of five large Japanese submarines arrived at a point some thirty-five miles out at sea, two of them equipped with aircraft, three with 46-ton midget submarines. On 31 May one of the aircraft was sent on a reconnaissance of the harbour, no doubt spotting the boom, and also noticing the presence of several warships, including the 9,000-ton American cruiser *Chicago*. That night the three midgets, each with a two-man crew, were launched from their mother ships and crept through the Heads into the harbour. One got tangled in the boom and blew itself up. One disappeared for ever. The third, I–22, sailed past Bradley's Head into the inner harbour and, finding the *Chicago* in its sights, let loose two torpedoes, missing the cruiser but hitting the shore of Garden Island. One torpedo failed to explode, the other wrecked an old ferry-boat, the *Kuttabul*, which was moored alongside a quay as a floating barracks; nineteen sailors were killed – the only people ever killed by enemy action in Sydney, unless you count those who died in skirmishes between whites and blacks in the early days of the settlement.[1]

Once Sydney realized what was happening, chaos erupted. Guns were fired all over the place, small craft buzzed around the harbour dropping depth charges, the night was alive with flashes and tracer bullets. The *Chicago*, firing one of its 5-inch guns, chipped a small piece off the corner of the Pinchgut tower. Passengers on a ferry-boat, reported the *Sydney Morning Herald* later, 'had the thrilling experience of seeing large-calibre guns blazing seemingly directly at them'. The artist Donald Friend, watching the racket from his flat above Elizabeth Bay, decided there and then to spend all his money and enlist. I–22 lay low, but in the small hours was sighted by three patrol boats in Taylor's Bay, beside Bradley's Head, and sunk with depth charges.[2]

*

[1] The *Kuttabul* dead included one touching representative of the Mother Country: Boy D. Trist, Royal Navy.

[2] The Japanese did destroy the *Chicago* in the end, off the Solomon Islands in 1943. In 1979 the officers of a later American cruiser of the same name presented a picture of their ship to be hung on Pinchgut Island, with the inscription: 'The later missile cruiser USS *Chicago* made this presentation to atone for the bad gunnery of its predecessor.'

The Japanese claimed to have sunk two merchantmen and an American cruiser, but one takes it that the action was conceived chiefly as an attack upon morale, and six nights later another submarine, standing offshore in the darkness, lobbed ten shells out of the ocean towards Rose Bay, wounding two civilians. It appears to have worked. The morning after the submarine raid King's Cross was full of removal wagons, taking nervous householders to suburbs further from the front line, and though most of these refugees soon returned the city seems to have remained jittery throughout the war. The firing of the midday gun was suspended, in case it alarmed the citizenry. Towers and belfries were removed from many buildings. Some (notably the Post Office Tower) were taken down because it was thought they would act as markers for Japanese bomber pilots, presumably unable to recognize the Harbour Bridge, others (the dome of Balmain Town Hall, for instance) because it was feared that in an air raid they might fall off and hurt somebody. The worst never happened, though. There was never another naval attack on Sydney, and the nearest air raids were at Darwin, 1,500 miles away. One by one, when the war was over, most of the towers and spires went up again; for years the Post Office Tower looked a slightly different colour from the rest of the building, because they had taken the opportunity to clean it while it was down.

The wars of the British Empire, nevertheless, have left their sad mark upon this city. The first to involve Sydney soldiers was the Maori War of the 1860s, when several hundred Australian volunteers fought with the imperial armies, but the first proper Australian expeditionary force sailed away from Sydney in 1885, and is commemorated by a bronze plaque (paid for by a bequest from one of its soldiers) on the sandstone bluff behind the Opera House.[1] The 750 men of the force, which was raised by the New South Wales Government, had

---

[1] All that remains of the sandstone ridge which ran out to Bennelong Point, before it was quarried away. It was nicknamed the Tarpeian Rock by one of the more cultivated officers of the First Fleet – or perhaps one of the more cultivated convicts – after the rock on the Capitoline Hill in Rome over which murderers and traitors were thrown.

volunteered to fight in one of the most passionate of the imperial crusades, the campaign to reconquer the Sudan after the death of General Gordon at Khartoum. The expedition got off to an ignominious start, one of its troopships colliding with the cruiser *Nemesis* before it had even left the harbour, and its return was rather bathetic too, for it had reached Africa too late to see anything but a few skirmishes.[1] It had established a fateful precedent, though, and for the next century there was scarcely an imperial war in which men from Sydney did not fight and die.

This is a city of war memorials, so large a contribution have these conflicts made to the community's character and self-knowledge. There is a memorial to the volunteers of the Boer War, up on Observatory Hill. There is a memorial inside the Queen Victoria Building to holders of the Victoria Cross. There is a memorial in the porch o the Great Synagogue to the 113 Jewish servicemen who died in the First World War. In the naval chapel on Garden Island (which has a pulpit like a ship's prow) there is a touching series of stained-glass windows commemorating ships and classes of ship which have sailed from this port into battle – all the Second World War *Bathurst* corvettes, for instance, and all the First World War submarines. The Cenotaph in Martin Place commemorates the dead of both World Wars, and each Thursday at eleven sees a small ceremony there, with a band, a couple of platoons of soldiers and officers with swords. The whirling circular fountain at King's Cross remembers the victory of El Alamein in 1941. In Parramatta, opposite a service station on the Cumberland Highway, the symbols K13, standing in gigantic concrete in a scummy ornamental pool, were erected in 1961 as a memorial to submariners of both World Wars, by a local survivor of the submarine K13, lost in 1917.[2]

When I first came here the greatest of these monuments, the Anzac

[1] The British had decided to withdraw from the Sudan after all, and it was another thirteen years before Lord Kitchener took the flag back to Khartoum without benefit of Aussies.

[2] The twenty-two British K-boats were steam-propelled, and formed the most unsuccessful class of submarines ever built – eight of them accidentally sank, K13 on her acceptance trials.

Memorial in Hyde Park, seemed to me central to the city's conceptions of pride, manhood and mateship. It was one of the keys, I
thought then, to the Sydney character. It honoured all the dead of
the First World War, but was associated in everyone's minds with
the tragedy of Gallipoli, which had changed Australians' conception
of their place among the nations. Never again would the leaders of
the British Empire, far away in London, be regarded as infallible
or omnipotent, and I interpreted the memorial as a permanent re-
kindling not merely of sadness, pride and resolution, but of bitter
disillusion too.

I still consider it one of the most moving of war memorials, and one
of the most under-estimated, being often dismissed by Sydney people
as pompous, romantic or just embarrassing. The Sydney architect C.
Bruce Dellitt designed it, but its glory is a series of sculptures by
Rayner Hoff, a young Sydney artist who had himself served in the
trenches. A squat flat-topped monolith of reinforced concrete, faced
with granite outside and marble within, it is like a truncated pyramid
on a shallow plinth. Around its summit sit a number of solemn thoughtful figures, not heroic at all, but infinitely sad. They sit there almost
crouching, looking into the distance – here a sapper, there a gunner,
an infantryman on one corner, a sailor on another. Inside the building
120,000 stars shine down from the ceiling, representing every man who
went to the Great War from New South Wales; far below a pitiful
bronze ensemble of Sacrifice, three women and a child mourning a
dead soldier on a shield, stands in the place one might expect to find a
gilded catafalque. There is no false triumph about this noble cenotaph.
Gallipoli in particular, the memory of which lies at the heart of its
message, was nothing but terrible failure, and there is no pretending
otherwise.

A Sydney generation has grown up now that hardly knows where
Gallipoli was, and long ago I came to feel that the Anzac Memorial
had lost its awful charge, and stood there in the park like a spent
reactor. However some time during any evening at a Returned
Services Club a dimming of the lights is likely to interrupt the cheek-
to-cheek dancing, the laughter at the bar, the slamming and tinkling

of the poker machines. A hush falls upon the club, as the members one and all stand and turn in the same direction – towards Gallipoli? Towards Flanders? Towards the remote half-imaginary imperial country Sydney used to call Home? Many of them are Italians or Greek nowadays, but they all stand silent as a sepulchral voice declaims over loudspeakers the great mourning dirge of Laurence Binyon – 'They shall not grow old, as we that are left grow old ... at the going down of the sun and in the morning we will remember them.' 'We will remember them,' mumble the revellers respectfully. Up go the lights, the band resumes the foxtrot, the poker machines crash back into action.

For many years nobody thought of Sydney as anything but a British port and settlement, part of the vast imperial network. Convicts were sent to the penal colony not only from Britain and Ireland, but from Canada and South Africa, and officials came to Sydney as a posting in the course of worldwide imperial careers. Watkin Tench had served in the American colonies, Lachlan Macquarie in India, William Dawes went on to West Africa, Barron Field to Gibraltar. William Balcombe, appointed Colonial Treasurer in 1823, had served on St Helena during Napoleon's exile there, and William Broughton the first Bishop of Sydney had started life as an East India Company clerk. In later years Governors came from other colonies and admirals proceeded to command other stations of the imperial seas, while the early Anglican clergymen of Sydney owed their duties to the diocese of Calcutta.[1]

These peripatetic Empire-builders brought with them from other possessions many an imperial prejudice, method, style and even protégé – Governor Macquarie was accompanied everywhere by his Indian servant George, acquired as a child for 85 rupees, and Governor Darling imported from Mauritius his friends the Dumaresq

---

[1] The most famous of whose bishops, Reginald Heber, gave his name to the suburb of Hebersham.

brothers, destined to be great colonial swells. Anglo-India was the chief exemplar, of course. The Sydney style of architecture, with its emphasis on the veranda and the wide eave, was recognizably descended from Anglo-Indian precedents. The bungalow, the very ark of the Australian suburban faith, was a form out of India; Sydney's military structures were obviously derived from those of the cantonments; the Queen Victoria Building is alleged to be in an American Romanesque style, but it looks to me, with its domelets and Hindustyle *chattris*, at least as directly influenced by the hybrid Anglo-Indian architecture of the time. There is a supposed likeness between the ground plan of downtown Sydney and that of Calcutta, the Domain of the one city being the Maidan of the other. Certainly in early years the relationship between the two New South Wales Government Houses, at Sydney itself and at Parramatta, was very like that between the Viceroy's twin palaces at Calcutta and Barrackpore, even down to the gubernatorial barges which conveyed Their Excellencies from one to the other – serenaded sometimes, in Australia as in Bengal, by water-borne bands.

Imperialism often rode high in Sydney, in the heyday of the creed. Bishop Broughton said that while there was certainly 'an eternal purpose' to the existence of the place, there was also a historical purpose: 'the exaltation of the English nation, and its gradual extension of power to the limits of the habitable world'. Charles Wentworth thought that one day Sydney might actually replace London as the centre of British dominion. The memorials in St James's Church would perfectly satisfy any vicar in Poona or Leatherhead, recording as they do so many officers, barristers, clergymen and other figures of the imperial Establishment, dying after esteemed careers in the public service, going down with their ships, killed fighting Germans, Turks, Blacks or 'Natives in the valley of the Horokiwi'. Loyalty to the Mother Country could sometimes be fulsome and sometimes ridiculous. One had to be fairly obsessed to name a slab of Sydney bush Chipping Norton, to build a Mortlake and a Putney on the banks of the Parramatta River, to cause the postmen in this brand-new country to be dressed up in the white pith helmets, scarlet jackets and striped trousers of British livery, or to equip St Andrew's Cathedral with bits of stone not only from Westminster Abbey and St Paul's Cathedral, but also the Houses of Lords and Commons.[1]

An imperial occasion in Sydney could be imperial indeed. In 1868 the young Duke of Edinburgh became the first royal personage ever to visit the city, and a Citizens' Ball was held in his honour. For this Sydney erected, in Hyde Park, one of the largest wooden structures in the world. It had a ballroom 250 feet long, a supper room almost as big, and its fountains spouted varying colonial perfumes, courtesy of E. H. O'Neill's, Druggists, King Street.[2]

But then the city had grown rich by virtue of the imperial connection. Once the East India Company had relinquished its monopoly of British trade with the east, Sydney soon became a lively participant in the Empire's oriental trades; and when the imperial economic system reached its Victorian climax, and for a time the British Empire seemed likely to become a permanently self-supporting unity, the one part of it providing raw materials, the other manufactured products – then for a few brief decades Sydney appeared to have a secure and rational function, part of a system, part of a generative process.

Out through the port went the wools and the gold, in came the machinery, the clothes, the books and the spectacle-cases. Sydney's currency was the pound sterling; its ultimate exchange was the City of London; its carrier was the British merchant fleet; its ultimate legal sanctions came from the English courts. Its economic partners were

[1] Though when, in 1863, Sydneysiders wished to honour the future King Edward VII's new wife by naming a suburb for her, they spelt it wrong, and it has been Alexandria ever since.

[2] The Duke was followed to Sydney by a well-known prostitute he had got to know in Melbourne, but not invited to the ball was the family of William Augustus Miles, a former Sydney Chief of Police, who was an illegitimate son of William IV. Miles is buried in Camperdown Cemetery, and his epitaph there says pointedly that though his beating heart sank into death unmourned, it *might* have been Blessed by Thousands – he might, in short, have been William V.

London and all the dependent cities of the Empire, with whom it was linked first in the fraternity of Free Trade, later in the device of Imperial Preference: the emblematic devices on the Customs House represented the West Indies, South Africa, Canada, Calcutta, Singapore, Cape Town, Quebec, Hong Kong, Durban, Rangoon and Vancouver, as if nowhere outside the Empire really mattered. British money sustained the growth of Sydney, and more often than not British settlers wishing to move to Sydney, as part of the natural imperial process, could often rely upon a Government subsidy to help them – it was well after the Second World War that the last of the £10 immigrants dubiously filed down the gangplank (for by then the whingeing Pom was in full flower) to the transit camps of this city.[1]

All this meant that for generations the imperial factor was inescapable in Sydney. Other Australians often thought the city excessively loyal, and the writer Francis Adams, looking at it in 1886, could only marvel at 'the appalling strength of the British civilization', so powerful were the influences of Empire. The rich shamelessly aped the British, in the noonday of British prestige, and if they could not actually send their children to England to be educated, saw to it that their schools in Sydney were impeccably British in style. Most of the ships that lay at the Sydney wharfs flew the Red Ensign; when the flying-boats came to land in Rose Bay they were, if not those of Queensland and Northern Territory Aerial Service (QANTAS for short), those of Imperial Airways. What a thrill when, in 1930, telephonic voice contact was first made with London, the Mother City! How moving to hear, every Christmas courtesy of the British Broadcasting Company's Empire Service, the crackling voice of the monarch himself, sending his message of paternal goodwill to his subjects wherever the flag flew! As late as the 1950s the directors of the *Sydney Morning Herald* were claiming their newspaper to have 'the largest circulation in the colonial empire', and in 1958 Frank

---

[1] How well I remember their pale images, still dressed as I recall them in suits, cardigans and trilby hats, lining the rails of their ships, and sometimes patriotically waving, as they passed through the British-held Suez Canal!

Hurley's book *Sydney* still felt itself to be describing the Empire's 'second white city'.

Even now imperial vestiges survive. The Governor of New South Wales, up there in his castellated mansion above Sydney Cove, still wears on ceremonial occasions the plumed hat and striped trousers of the British colonial administrator, and strives through presentation and garden party to cherish the imperial strain of gracious ceremonial. It is true that his powers are limited to 'assenting in the Queen's name to bills passed by the Parliament of the State', and that all too often the Court Circular in the morning paper records only his opening of a new primary school, or his reception of a delegation from the New South Wales Cheese-Making Society. Nevertheless it seemed very proper when one recent incumbent was Sir Arthur Roden Cutler, VC, who had only one leg and looked indeed like a hero of the frontiers. The Governor's superior the Governor-General of Australia also lives in sovereign spaciousness, when he comes to Sydney. His official house at Kirribilli is full of fine portraits, ancient silver and mementoes, and when His Excellency arrives there from Canberra, to look out over the harbour from the spacious bedroom of the Admirals, he must feel that he is indeed surrogate to the Queen of Australia herself.[1] Titles, though abandoned in New South Wales now, are still much in use here – in 1990 there was a knighted minister of the United Church in Sydney, and a knighted Cardinal too – and there are plenty of people in this city to whom the imperial conventions are important. When British royal persons come here, as they are rather fond of doing,[2] part of the populace greets them with indifference or derision, but another part reverently puts on its tail-coats and flowered hats, prepares its curtseys and perhaps reminds itself of its own family links with the English nobility – enough to send a shudder down a Welsh republican spine.

[1] The Prime Minister of Australia has an almost equally enviable official house, just around the corner, but of course he is just a Politition.

[2] Though Elizabeth II is the only reigning monarch to have set foot in the city.

In some ways Sydney is still much like a British city. Most of its people are of British stock – in 1986 220,000 of them had actually been born in Britain – so that even now I often find it difficult to determine whether a stranger is an indigene or a Pom. The line between the two is hazed, too, by practice and relationship: thousands of Sydneysiders spend parts of their lives in Britain, thousands of Britons are always at large in Sydney. Sydney motorists still drive on the left, Sydney lawyers still wear wigs, Sydney schoolchildren are still dressed in flannel shorts and blazers, Sydney letters sometimes get posted in a letter-box with a crown on it. Television here is still partly British-inspired – they even call the ABC 'Aunty', which is what the British call the BBC – and the *Daily Express* in London actually publishes a special Sydney edition, for suitable expatriates living here. British investment is still enormous. Sydney rabbis go to London for their training. Until the connection was ended in 1986 the New South Wales bar resorted to the Judicial Committee of the Privy Council in London, the old Empire's supreme tribunal, more frequently than any other overseas bar, except Hong Kong's. Everything most horribly English is stoked by the young women who come here from London to work as Personal Assistants to friends of Daddy's, or public-relations persons in Sydney branch offices, whose supercilious manners and nasal distortions of the English language they themselves seem to suppose evidence of superiority.

But sometimes I am touched by reminders of the imperial past. The Strand Arcade, an antipodean version of London's Burlington Arcade, can give me a momentary *frisson* of homesickness, with its faintly Dickensian suggestion of bright lights shining comfortably on damp winter evenings, and its stately uniformed beadle perfectly equipped to say 'Morning, m'Lord' to familiars walking through to Albany.[1] Some of the more venerable apartment houses of the Older Money suburbs can be evocative too: dark wood, polished brass, ornate and sluggish Edwardian elevators, name-plates by the door announcing

[1] Though once when I inquired after him I was told I would probably find him taking refreshment at Mrs Sippy's Coffee House.

the residence of Professor This, His Honour Judge That or Sir Manly Parramatta QC. What could be more essentially British than the Frank Cash Memorial Prize, awarded annually at Shore School to a boy who (1) is a regular chapel attendant, (2) achieves steady progress in school work throughout the year, though *not* achieving a top mark, (3) is neat and tidy in the care of his clothes, (4) is a willing hand at chores and (5) is 'a likeable fellow with his mates, respectful and thoughtful to others'?

I poked my nose one morning through the doors of the fire station at the downtown corner of Castlereagh and Bathurst Streets, designed by James Barnet in 1887. The inevitable icon of Queen Victoria guarded the establishment, flanked by sculpted fire-helmets and axes, and attended rather inappropriately, I thought, by a flaming torch. Inside there was no sign of life, but impeccably hung upon a line of hooks were the firemen's uniforms, their helmets shining, the brass buttons on their heavy serge jackets superbly polished and aligned. How tellingly they spoke of a grand old heritage – the pride, the diligence, the comradeship, the dutifulness which, together with many less commendable abstractions, Queen Victoria's Empire distributed around the world![1]

KEEP AUSTRALIA BEAUTIFUL: SHOOT A POM. By the historical nature of things, not everyone in Sydney regards the British connection with affection, or is sentimentally stirred by brass-buttonry. The penal origins of the city, the prevalence of Irishmen, the growth of republican sentiment, the unfortunate habits of visiting English people have all helped to make Sydney's Anglophilia less than unanimous. 'The Old Dart', an old Sydney pejorative for England, implies scheming and hypocrisy; many Sydneysiders thought it proper that when in the bicentennial year a memorial was erected at Circular Quay to commemorate the imperial connection, it should contain parts of a

[1] The qualities survive, I am sure, among the men of the Castlereagh and Bathurst fire station, but shortly after I paid my visit the fire service decided to give up brass buttons.

gigantic sculpted chain – bonds of friendship in one interpretation, but links of a shackle in another.

I suppose the first Bloody Pom was Governor Bligh, who so antagonized the local Establishment with his stiff-necked English regard for the proprieties, but republicanism certainly existed in Sydney from the beginning, when many of the convicts must have pined for the new liberties of the United States, and countless Irishmen detested the very notion of the Crown. That ardent Presbyterian Dr John Durmore Lang argued fervently for an Australian Republic, and hardly had the young Duke of Edinburgh been fêted at the Citizens' Ball than an Irishman tried to kill him at a picnic.[1] By the end of the nineteenth century, in the scurrilous heyday of Sydney political journalism, there was probably nowhere in the British world where Monarchy was more enthusiastically reviled. The *Bulletin* did not hesitate to call Edward VII 'a little fat dismal person with pig-eyes', while *Truth* thought him a turf-swindling, card-sharping, wife-debauching boozer. Even Queen Victoria herself, the ultimate Briton, was far from sacrosanct. In the celebratory year of her Golden Jubilee, observed with sickly sycophancy almost everywhere else in the Empire, a public meeting at Sydney Town Hall turned down a proposal for a Sunday-school fête on the grounds that 'to impress upon the children of the colony the value of the Jubilee years of a Sovereign is unwise and calculated to injure the democratic spirit of this colony'. Sydney cartoonists delighted in lampooning the Queen–Empress's dumpy figure and jowled features, and the *Bulletin* once definitively dismissed her as a fat old hunk of sauerkraut.

The antipathy has faded. The colonial chip on the shoulder is almost gone, and I get the impression that in general Sydney's attitudes towards its progenitors have matured into indifference. English people may still find themselves teased and patronized, but they are unlikely to be abused simply for being English. The imperial factor is an irrelevance now, and most people do not appear to care much whether Australia is monarchist or republican. The old trust in British

[1] The Irishman it was that died – on the gallows.

power, at once debilitating and inspiring, was terribly weakened by the catastrophe of Singapore in 1941, and was symbolically dismissed in 1951 when the Anzus Defence Treaty was signed, linking Australia not with Great Britain, as in effect the protecting Power, but with the United States. Since then American warships have been more familiar visitors to the harbour than the ships of the Royal Navy, and when the Royal Australian Navy celebrated its seventy-fifth anniversary the Americans marked the occasion by sending the immense battleship *Missouri*, more powerful than any warship the British ever built, to tie up at Garden Island opposite Admiralty House.

The constitutional connection with Britain is now remote indeed, having been weakened in stages down the decades. Once governed directly from London, Sydney became first the capital of a self-governing colony, then the capital of a State within an independent Australian federation, so that there are now no direct administrative links between this city and the old imperial centre. An Agent-General of New South Wales is stationed in London, but is hardly more than a trade representative; the British maintain a consulate-general in an office block overlooking Sydney Cove, like any other foreign Power. Britons need visas to come to Sydney now. 'My first feeling,' wrote Charles Darwin of his introduction to Sydney, as so many British travellers wrote then about so many imperial stations, 'was to congratulate myself that I was born an Englishman.' Now not one visitor in ten thousand, I would hazard a guess, thinks of this city as British at all. In 1990 Sydney's 1st East Miranda Scout Group, born by loyalty out of Empire, was the last in Australia to wear the kilt; but it could muster only four scouts and two cubs.

It was inevitable. Sydney was always on the far perimeter of the British Empire, and was bound to break away in the end. Founded in English contempt, and inhabited by people often genetically Anglophobe, it was remarkable that the place remained so British so long.

The first foreign intervention in the affairs of this city occurred before the city even existed. Six days after the First Fleet arrived in Botany Bay, the day before the move through the Heads, Phillip's men were astonished to see the masts and upperworks of two strange ships approaching from the sea. 'At first I only laughed,' Tench recorded, so improbable was the event. They turned out to be the French frigates *La Boussole* and *L'Astrolabe*, commanded by Jean-François de la Pérouse, on a voyage of discovery through the southern hemisphere. Taken aback by their arrival, the British embarrassingly managed to collide four of their own vessels as they beat their way out of Botany Bay, but put a brave face on the presence of their old enemy as they set about establishing the settlement at Sydney Cove. 'All Europeans are countrymen so far from home,' La Pérouse declared, and he and Phillip became quite friendly. Some of the convicts, having been disembarked at Sydney Cove, very soon found their way overland back to Botany Bay, hoping for asylum with the French (or at least sympathy from La Pérouse's lieutenant on *La Boussole*, the Irishman Sutton de Clonard); but they were rejected, it seems, and perhaps they were lucky, for when La Pérouse sailed away six weeks later he, his ships and all his men vanished into the Pacific for ever – wrecked, it was discovered long afterwards, in the New Hebrides.[1]

It was manifest then that Sydney could never be insulated against the world and its effects, and the bizarre arrival of La Pérouse in the first week of Sydney's history has never been forgotten. The suburb that is named for him, with its Aboriginal settlement, stands at the place on Botany Bay where his ships anchored, and a little enclave down there commemorates his stay. There is a memorial obelisk, a museum tells the sad tale of the expedition, and a French chaplain who died while they were in the bay lies in his tomb nearby – just down the road from the Snake Man. The crews of many French warships have paid their respects at this melancholy spot. It is not

[1] La Pérouse was well-known to the Empire. He had spent two years as a prisoner of the British after the battle of Quiberon Bay in 1759, and during the American wars he had destroyed two British forts on Hudson's Bay in Canada, courteously leaving some supplies behind for the use of their scattered garrisons.

true, as legend suggests, that it is actually French soil; but until 1983, when French nuclear tests in the Pacific soured relations with Australia, it was customary for the La Perouse Aborigines to celebrate Bastille Day, and the children would scramble for sweets showered among them by the French Consul-General.

Very soon Dutch, Spanish, Danish and American ships were coming to Sydney, and as the nineteenth century progressed foreign vessels of every nationality took to using Sydney as a port of call or repair. It may not have seemed so at the time, but it was really a prophetic moment when, in 1908, Theodore Roosevelt's Great White Fleet arrived in the harbour. This spectacular squadron, of sixteen battleships and four auxiliaries, was circumnavigating the world allegedly in the cause of peace, really in pursuit of American prestige, and it was by far the largest foreign force ever to be seen at Sydney, easily out-dazzling the elderly British cruisers which then represented the South Pacific squadron. Sydney adored the Great White Fleet, its spanking (if varyingly effective) warships, its good-natured matelots. It was true that after a reception for civic leaders on the battleship *Connecticut* some of the silver was found to be missing, but in general the Americans were given an extremely warm welcome. The city was plastered with American flags, eagles and portraits of George Washington; innumerable speeches of cousinly goodwill were exchanged; a five-storey replica of the Statue of Liberty was erected; the American admiral got hundreds of fan letters. During the week's visit a million passengers were taken by the Sydney Ferry Company to view the fleet, and thirty American sailors jumped ship for good. It was, though, more than a mere social triumph. America was displaying itself as a common enemy of the Yellow Peril, by then seen as the main threat to Australian well-being. As the correspondent of the New York *Sun* reported, in their effusive welcome to the fleet the Sydney-siders were 'telling something extremely important to Great Britain'; and perhaps the Great White Fleet did impress upon the civic mind the realization that there were other Powers but Great Britain in the world, and other ideals but Empire.

Nowadays I am constantly struck by Sydney's breadth of foreign

interests and connections. Ships from unknown ports frequent the
harbour, the *Sydney Morning Herald* regularly carries weather forecasts
from the South Pole, and while I was working on this book there
arrived at Sydney airport the world's largest freighter aircraft, loaded
with a cargo of 1.6 million nappies from Kiev. Tourists from everywhere come to this city nowadays: a young man I once saw clumping
up the steps of the Opera House in roller-skates turned out to be a
Frenchman who had skated across half the world to this, the object of
his pilgrimage. Some people claim to find Sydney Americanized, and
call it a little Manhattan. I feel no sense of cultural annexation,
though. The city feels to me no more Americanized than it did when I
first knew it – no more Americanized than London.[1] It is not the
impact of America that impresses me, every time I return to Sydney,
but the ever-growing impact of Asia.

Nobody talks of the Yellow Peril now, and every year Sydney is
more enmeshed with Asia. Sydney soldiers have fought in two post-
imperial conflicts, independently of the British, and they were both in
Asia – in Korea and in Vietnam, in each case a war to prevent hostile
Asians extending their power further to the south. Asian power gets
closer anyway. Japan has long replaced Britain as the main customer
for the commodities which pass through Sydney's port and, here as
everywhere in the Pacific world, is now a mighty investor too. Asians
from Vietnam and Hong Kong have flooded into Sydney, and a
Chinese community which used to be thought of as a coterie of
unhygienic restaurateurs, gamblers and opium-smokers is fast becoming a formidable economic force. Every time I go to Sydney Asian
faces are more common in the streets, the papers carry more references
to Asian affairs, and the ships that sail beneath the Harbour Bridge
are more likely to be flying Asian flags. When I was there recently
one of them flew not the innocuous moon ensign of the Japanese
merchant fleet, but the blood-red rising sun of the Japanese Defence
Force, successor to the Imperial Japanese Navy. I thought this re-

[1] But then I am of the opinion that most 'Americanization' is simply modernization,
and that the Big Mac springs directly from the human heart.

minder of old enmities might arouse disagreeable emotions in Sydney, since it was probably the first time the flag had flown anywhere near the place since the submarine attacks in 1942. In fact nobody took the slightest notice.[1]

Perhaps the truth is that this city has accepted its geographical destiny. The British Empire is dead and gone, the very concept of Australasia is tenuous, and the world is really divided into three or four enormous geopolitical units. Seen in these terms, Australia is the southernmost island of the Indonesian archipelago, reaching down from south Asia, China and Japan, and Sydney is no more than a regional port of the Pacific – its peers, partners and rivals now are not Liverpool, Bombay or Baltimore, but Singapore, Osaka, Hong Kong. Sydneysiders are perfectly conscious of these inexorable developments. Sometimes they respond with racist expostulation, sometimes they seem unnerved by the cleverness and diligence of their new Asian fellow citizens, but generally they appear to look forward fatalistically into a world very different from the comforting constructions of the lost Empire. Easy come, easy go! One evening I sat in a café at King's Cross, its television flickering all-but-disregarded above the counter, contemplating the cheerful scene around me. The noise level was high, the customers were young and fun. Thinking how prosperous the place seemed, how sure of itself, and how high-spirited, I caught out of the corner of my eye a very different scene on the television screen. It showed a boat-load of refugees from Cambodia arriving half-starved, destitute and wide-eyed somewhere on the Australian coast, I missed where. They were clinging all over their rickety vessel, hanging over the gunwales, draped over the wheelhouse.

It reminded me of old pictures of those overloaded Manly ferries, and just for a moment I thought it really might be one of the Sydney ferry-boats that the refugees had commandeered. The Australians on the screen stood aghast to see them come, and remonstrated for a while, but in the end they had to let them land – as it were on Sydney Cove just down the road, or at Balmoral beside the bandstand. What else could they do?

[1] And when the ship sailed out again beneath the bridge I saw four of its officers on the helicopter deck pursuing an amiable ritual of contemporary Japan: taking each other's photographs.

RETROSPECT

W HAT A FINE AND INTERESTING CITY, ALL IN ALL! WHAT AN
attractive people! Yet I find I cannot end this book about
Sydney without that streak of wistfulness returning. I used to think it was
because beyond the Blue Mountains, just out of sight from Circular
Quay, there extended an empty wilderness inhabited only by inexplicable
primitives. I used to quote the poet A. D. Hope's indictment of Australia:

> The river of her immense stupidity
> Floods her monotonous tribes from Cairns to Perth.

Now the Australian outback feels empty no longer, we think of the
land itself in a more comradely way, and we understand a little better
the arcane ideas of the Aborigines, but still Sydney feels on the edge
of some more metaphysical blank. Most of the world's great cities
have something inevitable about them, as though God decreed them
come what may. In Sydney, even now, I catch myself feeling sometimes that the place never need have come into being in the first place.

*

It ought to be a simple city to write about. Started from scratch in modern times, developed according to elemental economic principles, well-documented throughout its history and almost untouched by war, Sydney should offer its chroniclers a straightforward task. It does not seem an introspective place. It is frank about most matters. Its icons are there for all to see, and it has never been over-burdened with spirituality. Sydney, one might suppose, is Sydney is Sydney.

Yet the effect of this city upon its visitors is far from simple, and strangely fluctuates. Sydney is about the same age and size as San Francisco, but it inspires a far wider range of reactions. Hardly anybody hates San Francisco, but plenty of people hate Sydney. Once you have evolved a view on San Francisco you are likely to stick with it, but in my own experience one's responses to Sydney shift from decade to decade, day to day, even moment to moment. The citizens of Sydney are themselves ambivalent about it, and combine pride with doubt, assertion with apology. The only constant of all Sydney opinion, the one leitmotiv of writing about this city since the very beginning of its history, is the beauty of the harbour. It is as though Sydneysiders feel the harbour to be their one unassailable satisfaction. Every single Sydney man and every single Sydney woman, Trollope reported in 1873, asked him if he did not find the harbour 'rather pretty', and in a cartoon of half-a-century later Sydney is stuck all over with posters screaming 'You Should See Our Harbour', 'Have You Seen Our Harbour?', 'How Do You Like Our Harbour?', 'What Do You Think Of Our Harbour?', 'Have You Ever Seen Anything Finer Than Our Harbour?' It is extraordinary still how often Sydney people comment upon their harbour's beauty: and perhaps by now it is a matter of self-protective convention, like the British conversational obsession with the weather.

For I dare say a latent uncertainty gives this often boisterous city its oddly dappled character. The civic motto is a gnomic one – 'I Take but I Surrender' – and the destiny of the city is equally unclear. Dazzling though Sydney can be, it has always stood on the fringes of

history – repeatedly spurned by history, I sometimes think. There was
a time when it possessed real power, at least in theory. Its early
Governors were granted, by their royal commissions, hypothetical
authority over more than half of what is now Australia, and 'all the
Isles adjacent'.[1] It was from Sydney that Norfolk Island and Tasmania
were originally governed, that the first European expansionists burst
into the Australian interior, that Matthew Flinders sailed to circum-
navigate the continent, that the colony of Port Essington was established on the Cobourg Peninsula at the other end of Australia.[2] Then
for years Sydney was the capital of an imperial province, subject only
to London; New South Wales was virtually a nation, with its own
armed forces, fiscal policies, postage stamps and currency. Even Melbourne was subject to Sydney until 1851, and when the Commonwealth of Australia was brought into being in 1901, it was in
Sydney that the delegates from the six colonies sealed the agreement –
a memorial in Centennial Park remembers the event.

  Little by little this consequence was reduced, and the vast authority
of the early Governors shrivelled. Tasmania and Norfolk Island went
first. Port Essington was transferred to the new colony of South Australia. Melbourne was lost when Victoria was separated from New
South Wales. It was Melbourne, not Sydney, that became the first
capital of the Australian Commonwealth, and Canberra that was
eventually chosen to be its permanent seat of Government. Sydney
has been left feeling rather high and dry, like a metropolis of its own
disbanded Empire.

  Indeed it stands to its remaining dependency, the State of New
South Wales, much as Vienna stands to Austria. It is too big for itself.

---

[1] Australia was never annexed as an imperial entity, but when in 1840 a French
official asked the Colonial Secretary, Lord John Russell, how much of it was British,
'I answered him "the whole", and with that answer he went away.'
[2] An unsuccessful settlement whose forlorn ruins poignantly suggest to me how Sydney
might look, if Phillip had not seen it through its first cruel years: deserted stands the
little Government House on its eminence above the sea, the quay below is crumbled,
tangled foliage covers brickworks, sawmills, sergeants' mess and all, and one of the
tombstones in the cemetery says simply: SACREAD TO THE MEMOERY OF THE DR OF
THE SETTLEMENT.

It frequently lives beyond its means, and especially in the flashier things of life, aspires beyond its station. Perhaps this too contributes to Sydney's feeling of diffidence, anomalous in so brave a city. On the one hand when most people think of Australia, they think first of Sydney and its images, and many of Australia's national institutions are based here, from the Arts Council to the secret service. On the other hand Sydney is really nothing but a provincial capital, the equal of Perth, Adelaide, Hobart or Brisbane. The city looks out tentatively to the world at large, as though it is not sure of its status. Where does it stand in the order of things? Is it *really* world-class? Better perhaps to content itself with easier comparisons – livelier than Melbourne, brighter than Adelaide, the richest in the southern hemi-sphere, or even, as statistics sometimes solemnly suggest, the biggest in New South Wales. Better still to content itself with itself. There is remarkably little news about the rest of Australia in Sydney's news-papers, the Commonwealth flag flies rarely here, and even the old competition with Melbourne, which used to be real and vicious, seems to have subsided now into a kind of half-humorous convention, like the rivalry between Harvard and Yale, or calling the House of Lords 'the other place'.[1]

But what mere provincial capital ever aroused such passions and speculations? The vast momentum of the world proceeds far away from Sydney. Ideologies triumph or are discredited. The balance of the continents shifts. Yet it is still possible to wonder if it is here that a New Man may emerge. The peculiarity of the place, its originality of style and history, the fact that the new moon lies the wrong way round in the old moon's arms, as it rises pale over Barrenjoey – all these help to place Sydney beyond the usual category of cities. Its glittery image, propagated so jubilantly, does not do justice to the place. It is an image far too explicit. Tower Bridge may emblemize

[1] My favourite sally in this battle of badinage was made by James Fitzpatrick, who once said that Melbourne was a work of art, like the two-minutes' silence. But then somebody once said 'In the midst of life we are in Perth.'

London, the Eiffel Tower says the right things about Paris, but the
Opera House and the Harbour Bridge do not begin to epitomize the
true sensations of Sydney, which seem to me tantalizingly ambivalent.

We think of it as a young city, but it is not so young really. Many a
great city is younger – Toronto, Chicago, Hong Kong, Singapore,
Washington, Johannesburg. Sydney, though, *feels* young: if not young
physically, young in an abstract way, as though the generations succeeded each other extra quickly here. There is something fugitive to
the fascination of the place. Charles Causley, who responded with
such affection to the natural generosity of Sydney, felt this elusive
quality too, beginning and ending his poem, not so many years after
his visit with HMS *Glory*, with a gentle hint of it:

> Now it seems an old forgotten fable:
> The snow-goose descending on the still lagoon,
> The trees of summer flowering ice and fire
> And the sun coming up on the Blue Mountains.

An old forgotten fable – not the metaphor one expects of so splendid
and apparently confident a city. 'Sydney,' I wrote myself when I was
young, 'is not one of your absolute cities.' I was looking perhaps for
the black-and-white, sharp-edged resolution that usually characterizes
showy young towns of ambition, and all I found instead, I thought,
was aloofness and introspection.

Sydney is still not your absolute city, but what seemed to me so
long ago an affront to my sensibilities now seems a seduction – a kind
of divine opacity, making me feel that perhaps the city was God-given
after all.

I began this book with a harbour prospect on a sunny Sunday afternoon. Let me end with an evening stroll after the opera. Violetta,
being a particularly robust specimen of local talent, has not unexpectedly recovered from her decline in time to take several rousing
curtain calls. The lady in the next seat has remarked to nobody in
particular well, thank goodness it could never happen in this day and

age. We leave the great building euphorically, entranced into the Sydney evening.

There is something phosphorescent about Sydney Opera House. It glows almost merrily in the daytime, with the sun on its flying wings, and it glows refulgently at night. Walking now out of its foyer on to the wide terrace is like emerging into a holograph, so that we feel we are being absorbed into the light itself. Beyond this lustre there is a panoply of lesser lights – moving lights of ships, towering lights of waterfront skyscrapers, beacon lights, lights of oyster bars, coffee shops, restaurants, fairy lights glittering all over a tree at the foot of the Domain. High above is the hump of the Coathanger, with its stream of cars hurrying over it, and on the highest point of its arch the two jaunty flags are floodlit in the breeze – surely the proudest flags in the world.

But we will find ourselves some secluded harbour spot, above a little-used pier perhaps, where all those bright lights are far away, the rumble of the traffic is almost silent, the great city around us seems astonishingly remote, and a more ambiguous magic settles on the scene. The evening is warm, with a scent of night-flowers somewhere. Very likely there is a flash of torchlight from the jetty. A couple of men are fishing with lines down there, and we hear snatches of an unidentifiable language – Indonesian, perhaps, or Thai. When the torch goes out only the ember of a cigarette remains, looking rather like a wavering firefly, and in the voluptuousness of the moment we may be surprised to find ourselves feeling a little sad. Why, I wonder? The harbour is all at peace, the city is one of the world's happiest, those fishermen are delighted to be there, the recession is officially said to be past its worst, the bridge is strong, the Opera House is lovely, the flags are fine, Violetta is even now enjoying a hearty turf-'n'-surf with Alfredo. Yet at such moments as this, in the velvet sensual darkness on the harbour shore in Sydney, I sometimes feel myself haunted by a sense of loss, as though time is passing too fast, and frail black people are watching me out of the night somewhere, leaning on their spears.

*

THANKS

Countless kind Sydney people helped me to write this book about their city, and I thank them one and all. I am especially grateful to a number of friends and colleagues who honoured me by reading the book in typescript, in part or even most generously in whole, saving me from many errors and offering me many new perspectives: they include Rowena Danziger, James Hall, Ian Hicks and Anthony McGrath, and I hope they will not think this final version has let them down.

I have acknowledged in my footnotes the books I am chiefly indebted to, but I must mention here two famous essays about Sydney that I especially admire: the final chapter of J. D. Pringle's *Australian Accent*, London 1958, and Gavin Souter's *Sydney Observed*, Sydney 1968 – both illustrated, as it happens, by my oldest friend in the city, George Molnar.

Finally, my warm thanks to Charles Causley, whose poem *HMS Glory at Sydney* has provided a melodic line for my book.

Trefan Morys, 1991

INDEX